Parent Power!

Parent Power!

A Common-Sense Approach
to Raising Your Children
in the Eighties

by
John K. Rosemond

The East Woods Press

Library of Congress Cataloging in Publication Data

Rosemond, John K., 1947-
    Parent Power.

    Includes index.
    1. Parenting. 2. Child development.
I. Title.
HQ755.8. R67   649'.1   81-9716
ISBN 0-914788-42-6 AACR2

Illustration by Doug Dailer
Typography by Raven Type
Printed in the United States of America

An East Woods Press Book
Fast & McMillan Publishers, Inc.
820 East Boulevard
Charlotte, N.C. 28203

For Willie, Eric and Amy
with love

Contents

Acknowledgements

My heartfelt thanks to . . .

Anda Cochran

Beth Resler

Cathy Culpepper Wilder

Janet Johnston, Ed.D., for her suggestions on the manuscript and especially for her invaluable assistance on Part Two.

Anita Miller, for typing the manuscript and many constructive comments.

Susie Anthony, for proofreading and many helpful suggestions.

Everyone at at the Charlotte Observer, for their support and encouragement over the past few years, including Lew Powell (for the tip), Dannye Romine, Stuart Dim, Bob Ashley, Tom Jones, Joel Blackwell, Polly Paddock, Ken Friedline, Jerry Bledsoe, Pat Borden, Rich Oppel, Dot Jackson and Cynthia Struby.

The folks at East Woods Press: Sally Hill McMillan, Barbara Campbell and especially Linda Benefield, for her commitment and patient thoroughness in editing the manuscript.

And to Willie, for typing, proofreading, criticism, love, support and soul food.

Introduction

This book had its beginning on the morning of January 22, 1969. As the first light of the sun cracked the winter sky, my first-born announced his arrival.

I was 21, going on 17. My wife, Willie, was a much older and wiser woman of 19 (going on 20). We named our son Eric Brian because it conveyed a bold, authoritative feeling. He was, we were certain, destined for greatness. A name like Eric Brian was the least we could do to help him on his way.

At the time, I was midway through my senior year of undergraduate study and had been accepted by a graduate program in psychology. Yes, Eric Brian's daddy was going to become a psychologist. You know — predict the future, read minds and know the question to every answer.

Raising Eric was going to be a snap. After all, my intentions were pure ("I will always give him the very best I have to give"), my ideals were lofty ("I will never treat him the way my parents treated me") and besides, I was soon to know everything there was to know about human beings, birth to death, inside and out.

And then, there was Willie. She had grown up with five younger brothers and sisters and so knew all there was to know about the practical side of raising a child — feeding, changing, burping, bathing, and so on.

The Perfect Mother! The Perfect Father! Therefore, the Perfect, Problem-free Child!

Eric soon let us know how unimpressed he was with our perfection. For a few weeks, Willie breast fed him (The Perfect Mother). Eric showed his disdain for her selfless generosity by screaming before and after every feeding. Willie concluded she didn't have enough milk (The Less-Than-Perfect Mother?), so she (now we) switched to bottle feeding. But Eric continued to scream.

Eric screamed if we put him down. So we rarely put him down. If he was awake, which was most of the time, one of us was holding him ... vertically. Horizontally would not do. Soon, even that wasn't enough. He required us to sit and bounce up and down with him before he would cease his howling. Not a gentle bounce, mind you, but a rather high-flying one. In no time the springs in both pieces of upholstered furniture were shot.

It wasn't long before Eric the Bold and Authoritative started screaming for us to walk around the house with him while constantly flexing up and down at the knees. Of course, we complied.

Sometimes he would sleep. But only during the day. At night, he screamed. Willie and I took turns pretending to be asleep. After several months of this we called the doctor.

"Eric screams an awful lot," we said. He told us to relax.

Several days later, we called him again. "Eric screams when we try to relax," we told him. He said it was only a stage.

"Do things get better?" we asked.

"In time," he assured us.

We held one or more of these existential conversations with the doctor every week. Nothing changed.

By the time Eric was 15 months old, he was talking. His screams became intelligible. Well, almost. A master at exposing our imperfections, he would scream for a cup of milk ("Mok! Mok!"). We'd bring him the mok. He'd take one look at it, knock it to the floor and scream for orange juice ("Ahn-doosh!"). We'd bring him ahn-doosh. He'd knock it to the floor and scream because it was in the wrong cup. The *mok* cup was the right cup. We were slow learners.

He ran everywhere and got into everything. Willie and I ran after him, putting things out of his reach. He learned to climb.

Looking back on those first few chaotic years, I realize that for the most part my education did not make parenthood any easier. In fact it was a handicap. Instead of helping me understand the difficulties we experienced as first-time parents, my graduate training contributed to my confusion. It taught me to think too much about too little.

Most parents, I think, are afflicted with this tendency to think too much. It is our undoing. We speculate about what we should do or should have done. We agonize over what we already did or didn't do. We worry about the elusive "What-willhappenif?" We search for some hidden meaning in our children's behavior. Think, think, think. The Perfect Parent is a Perfect Thinker, trying so hard to redo the past and see into the future that he loses touch with the all-important, all-there-is present.

Parents who contract this peculiar malady become so preoccupied with their children that they lose touch with themselves—so entangled with their children that it becomes virtually impossible to tell who's who. They think so much they forget how to act. Their spontaneity drowns in an overflow of worry and guilt. Eventually and inevitably, all trust in themselves — in their own feelings and in their common sense about what is and isn't right for them and for them alone — has vanished.

For the past four years I have written a weekly newspaper column of comment and advice for parents (and anyone else with an interest in children and families). The column makes its first run in the *Charlotte Observer* and is distributed nationally by the Knight-Ridder News Wire. This book evolved from those writings (1978-81).

I want to change the way you think about your children and yourself in relation to them; I want to expand your options, to change the way you respond to your children; I want to pass along a practical understanding of childhood; I want to provoke you into reconsidering some of the ideas you may have taken for granted as absolute.

But more than anything, I want to help you improve the overall quality of your living with children.

The text begins with a tale, "Of Wizards And Kings And Living Things" — a children's story and an allegorical fantasy for adults. "Wizards" is the heart of this book.

What follows has been divided into four parts. Part One (Discipline: A Family Affair) focuses on broad issues involved in raising children. My aim here is to help you put your responsibilities into better perspective. I want you to realize that your child's success as a person, and your success with him, rests not on how many sacrifices you make, but on how well the overall needs of your family, particularly your marriage, are met.

In Part Two (It's Only A Stage) the theme is growth. These chapters describe some of the ways a child's growth is expressed during the first 13 years of life. This section will help you understand these developmental challenges and support your child through them.

Why (you may be asking) does Rosemond stop at age 13? Quite simple. I've not yet lived with a teenager, and as Bobo says, "Man who wisely keep mouth shut will never find foot there." (Editor's Note: Bobo is one of the author's many aliases.)

Part Three (Toilets, Tantrums and Other Unmentionables), tackles common and not-so-common problems parents may encounter in raising a child, with specific advice on untangling little snarls before they become big ones.

Part Four (Sounding Off) examines a number of controversial issues. Be forewarned! To read this section is to risk having some of your sacred cows defiled.

It doesn't matter if you read the chapters out of sequence. I do suggest that you read "Of Wizards and Kings and Living Things" first. If you are looking for something specific, go straight to the Index. If you don't find it there, write me a letter.

Before we go any further together, a word of caution is in order: You cannot simply imitate my ideas and become a successful parent. If you follow only the *letter* of my advice, you may find that it flops as grandly for you as it has succeeded for me.

Instead, use my ideas as models for designing your *own* solutions and developing your *own* child-rearing style. To risk failure is also to risk success — *real* success. If you merely clone my approach, you risk nothing. And, ultimately, you will have gained nothing.

Ready to risk success? Turn the page.

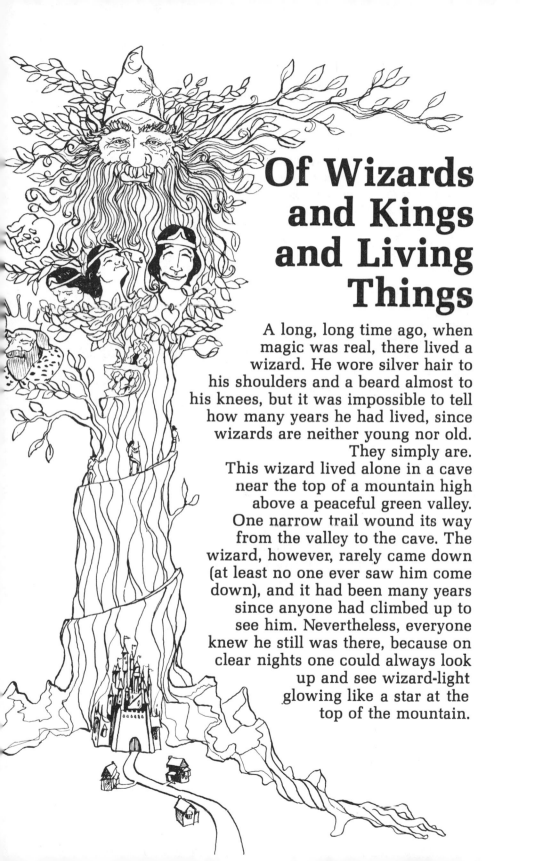

Of Wizards and Kings and Living Things

A long, long time ago, when magic was real, there lived a wizard. He wore silver hair to his shoulders and a beard almost to his knees, but it was impossible to tell how many years he had lived, since wizards are neither young nor old. They simply are.

This wizard lived alone in a cave near the top of a mountain high above a peaceful green valley. One narrow trail wound its way from the valley to the cave. The wizard, however, rarely came down (at least no one ever saw him come down), and it had been many years since anyone had climbed up to see him. Nevertheless, everyone knew he still was there, because on clear nights one could always look up and see wizard-light glowing like a star at the top of the mountain.

In the valley at the foot of the mountain lay a small kingdom ruled by a kind and gentle king who was loved and respected by all the valley people. The king was married to a beautiful queen, and they had three sons.

One day, the king called his sons before him and spoke: "Someday, one of you will take my place. Your mother and I have shared our love equally among you, but a kingdom cannot be shared. When I am gone, only one of you can sit on this throne, and he must be the one best suited to the task. I have given this much thought, but cannot choose between you. Therefore, I have asked the wizard for his help. The three of you must climb to his cave and do as he commands. Go at once, for it is impolite to keep a wizard waiting."

So the king's three sons climbed the narrow trail to the wizard's cave. When they reached the mountain top, they found the wizard sitting cross-legged on a small rock ledge at the cave opening. From there he could look down upon the whole valley kingdom and out to where the land dipped below the sea.

As he turned toward the three young princes, his eyes twinkled and he smiled at the proud and graceful manner in which they stood before him. Then he held out his hand, saying, "Here are three seeds. Each one, when planted, will become a tree. This is your task. Go at once, for it is impolite to keep a tree waiting." Each son took a seed from the wizard's hand, and together they walked in silence down the mountain.

The oldest son planted his seed on top of a small round hill. Every day he brought it clear water from a nearby stream. In the winter, he laid straw around its base to keep the roots warm. When the spring storms came, he fashioned a shelter to protect it from the powerful winds. As the years passed, the tree grew so large and thick that no sunlight could pass through its many branches. The grass on the hill underneath began to wither and turn brown. All through the warmer months, the oldest son worked carrying bucket after bucket of spring water to the tree, for it refused to drink any other. During the fall, he toiled from sunrise to sunset every day raking and hauling off the many thousands of leaves that fell from its branches.

The middle son planted his seed on another hill, not far away. To him, the shape of the tree was more important than its size. As it grew, he took great care to prune its branches, so they would not grow too thick. Using rope, he tied the trunk to wooden poles, making certain it would grow perfectly straight. He wired the branches so they would curve gracefully toward the sky. He inspected each twig and leaf and cut back those that did not please his eye. He spent nearly all of his time pruning, trimming, tying and inspecting.

The youngest son planted his seed on yet a third hill, very near the other two. When his tree was a young sapling, he tied the main stalk to poles so that it would not bend and break in the wind. But as time passed, he removed the poles and let it stand on its own. He would bring his young tree water only when the weather was very hot and there had been no rain. He trimmed just enough to let the sunlight filter through. In the fall, he raked the leaves away so they would not smother the grass below. In the winter, he kept *himself* warm.

One night, after many years, the old king died in his sleep. The next day, a great storm blew down off the wizard's mountain. A mighty wind pushed sheets of rain across the valley. Streams became raging rivers, and ponds became lakes. Black clouds boiled across the sky. The storm raged on through the next two days and nights.

On the third morning after the king's death, the rain stopped and the skies cleared. As the valley people emerged from their homes into the morning sunlight, they looked toward the three hills.

The hill upon which the eldest son had planted his tree had been nearly washed away. The roots lay exposed, and it was leaning heavily to one side.

No tree stood upon the second hill. It had been uprooted in the storm and flung into a nearby field. Broken branches were everywhere.

The youngest son's tree was still standing, its wet leaves glistening in the sun. During the storm, it had swayed in the wind and trembled in the roaring thunder, but its branches had not broken.

That afternoon, the three brothers made their way once again up the mountain trail to the wizard's cave. He was sitting on the same rock ledge, his eyes fixed on the horizon. After a long moment, he turned his gaze to the eldest brother and began to speak: "You gave your tree love, but no guidance. It became selfish and demanding. It would not share the sun with the grass below, and so the grass died. Because the hill had no cover, it melted in the storm. You are not well-suited to be king, but your ability to love other things will not be wasted. To that, I add the gifts of knowledge and authority. You will become a great teacher, and the valley people will respect and honor you." The oldest son felt the wizard's touch upon his shoulder, and his eyes filled with tears of happiness.

To the middle son, the wizard then turned and said, "You gave your tree guidance, but showed it no affection. It had a fine and beautiful shape, but its roots were not deep and strong enough to hold it in the storm. You cannot take your father's place, but neither have you labored in vain. To you, I give the gift of love. You will go forth among your people as a great healer, and they will hold you in much reverence." The middle son felt the wizard's gentle touch, and his heart swelled with joy.

Then the wizard turned to the youngest son and said, "You have learned much in your few years and have earned your father's crown. You gave your tree the right proportions of love and guidance. Such is the way all living things must be cared for. Always remember that just as every living thing is a kingdom unto itself, so is every kingdom a living thing."

Then the wizard stood and spoke to all three of them, saying, "Go at once, for there is important work to be done, and it will not be finished in your lifetime." With that, he turned and walked back into his cave.

The three sons returned to the valley and went about the work assigned them by the wizard. The oldest son did become a great teacher, and before he died the valley people built a great university in his name. Just as the wizard had prophesied, the middle son became a great doctor, and he lived to see the valley people build a hospital in which to continue his work. During the time that the youngest son was king, he accomplished many great things, and ever since that time, the little valley kingdom has enjoyed peace and prosperity.

The wizard was never seen again, but to this day it is said that on a clear night one can sometimes still see wizard-light glowing like a star near the top of his mountain.

PART ONE

Discipline:
a Family Affair

The Benevolent Dictatorship

I can still remember listening, as a graduate student, to one of my professors — he was teaching a course in marriage and family relations — lecture on the difference between "democratic" and "autocratic" families.

In the democratic family, he said, everyone was regarded as an equal. Therefore, obedience (from the children) was not mandatory, and disagreements were resolved through discussion, negotiation and compromise. Cooperation and harmony were the hallmarks of a democratic family. "How marvelous!" I thought, reflecting upon the way my parents had limited my freedom, kept me in a state of virtual servitude and said things like, "Because I say so."

In contrast, the autocratic family was a hierarchy, with parents at the top. Children were punished if they disobeyed and were not allowed to make decisions for themselves. Compromise between parent and child was possible only on the parents' terms. Obedience, rather than joyous cooperation, was the bill of fare for children of autocratic parents.

"How nasty!" I said to myself, "just like when I was a child (with emphasis on the past tense.)" I solemnly swore that when the time came, I would be a "democratic daddy."

Thirteen years and two children have put layers of dust on that promise. I tried my best, really I did. For the first three or four years after Eric was born, I regarded him as my equal. If he didn't like decisions I made, he rolled on the floor and I reconsidered. I thought it unfair to *make* him obey, so he didn't. The result of this exercise in democracy, however, was *not* harmony. The result was anarchy.

One night in a dream a wise-looking elderly gentleman appeared, calling himself the "Spirit of Rosemond's Future." In his hands he held a clear crystal orb, and while I gazed within, there appeared a vision of a slightly older Rosemond family, all of us trussed up nicely in stainless-steel straitjackets.

I woke up screaming, bathed in sweat, and life with father has never been the same.

Today, our children obey us. We insist upon it. They don't enjoy the *right* to make any decisions for themselves. However, we allow them the *privilege* of making *many* decisions, reserving, as our *right*, the option of taking this privilege away whenever it is abused or the potential consequences are not to our liking.

Compromise is possible—at our discretion. In short, we have created a nasty old autocratic family, and Willie and I are dictators—"Benevolent Dictators," to be exact.

Benevolent Dictators are gentle authorities who understand that their power is the cornerstone of their children's sense of safety and security. Benevolent Dictators rule by virtue of natural authority. They know what's best for their children. They don't derive any pleasure out of bossing children around. They govern because they *must*. They prepare their children for the time when they must govern themselves and *their* children.

Benevolent Dictators do not need to instill fear in order to communicate their influence. They are authorities, but they are *not* authoritarian. They do not demand unquestioning obedience. They encourage questions, but make the final decisions. They restrict their children's freedom, but they are *not* tyrants. They restrict in order to protect and guide. They make rules which are fair and enforce them firmly. Life with a Benevolent Dictator is predictable and secure for children. That set of certainties guarantees more freedom than would be possible under any other circumstances.

Actually, whether they are willing to admit it or not, all parents are dictators of one sort or another. Some are more benevolent than others, and some are benevolent to a fault.

That may be somewhat difficult to accept, because we usually associate dictatorships with oppression and torture and people disappearing in the night. But a dictatorship is simply a system of government where one person is in control and is responsible for making decisions for a group of people who count on him or her to make good ones. And that's what parents do, isn't it? Like it or not, parents are dictators, preferably dictators of benevolent nature.

Some time back, I was speaking to a group of physicians, explaining my concept of the family as a "benevolent dictatorship." One of the group, looking disturbed, raised a challenge:

"I think you're throwing this idea out in too general a fashion. Your 'benevolent dictatorship' may work quite well when children are very young, but with teenagers especially, we must give them more freedom and more opportunities for making their own decisions."

"Yes!" I replied, "what you are saying is absolutely true and dovetails perfectly with my 'benevolent dictatorship.' "

"You see," I went on, "the key in what you said was your use of the word 'give.' And I agree! Parents must be willing to *give* their children greater freedom and more choices as they grow older—even the freedom at selected times to make mistakes. But we must always retain control of the decision to give. We must *never*, as long as our children are dependent on us, hand complete control of their lives over to them."

There is no possibility of a democratic relationship between parents and children as long as children live at home and rely upon parents for legal protection and economic support.

Until a child leaves home, there can only be *exercises* in democracy which are carefully orchestrated by the parents.

Yes, increasing degrees of independence *must* be given as the child matures, but *given* from a secure position of authority.

It is parents' *right* to give the privilege and, likewise, their *right* to take it away. Within that framework, children learn the value of independence, not as something to be taken for granted, but as something to be worked for—and therefore something worth taking care of.

You are the boss. For *their* sake.

Your Marriage Comes First

Several months ago, at the beginning of a workshop I was conducting for about 50 working mothers, I wrote, "IN MY FAMILY, MY CHILDREN COME FIRST" on the blackboard. I asked if this was an accurate statement of their priorities. More than half of them raised their hands to acknowledge that it was. Since then, I've put several audiences through the same exercise and gotten the same results.

It seems we are our own undoing. "My children come first" is a one-way ticket to the place where parents worry about children who whine and fuss and won't do what they're told to do by parents who finally lose their patience and scream and then plunge headlong into that dark hole called *guilt*. It's a place where husbands come home to wives who complain because being a mother takes so much energy they have none left to be wives. It's a place where people hurt, but hide the hurt behind "my children come first."

It's easy to understand how people get to this upside-down place. Most parents have been there—some to visit, some to stay.

From one perspective, our collective preoccupation with children and childhood is an offshoot of our infatuation with youthfulness in general. From another, it is an extension of the my-children-are-going-to-have-it-better-than-I-did thinking that was prevalent among parents of children born during the boom following World War II.

But whatever the roots of the problem, this fact emerges — we have created for our children a position of preeminence in the family. We have placed "The Child" on a pedestal and adopted a self-sacrificing reverence toward his "potential" and his "self-esteem." We have accepted into our vocabulary the phrases "child-centered family" and "democratic family," seeming not to realize that when a child is regarded as being central, or equal, to his parents' relationship, their relationship is in jeopardy.

There is but *one* proper place for children within a family — the back seat. Exclusive possession of the front seat belongs to the marriage.

The marriage is the bedrock upon which the family is built and *everyone* in the family depends. The marriage is "where it's at" and always will be. The marriage *preceeds* the children and was meant to *succeed* them. But if you put your children first, if you plan your life around their presence, if you think that the meaning of "family" is synonomous with their existence, then the fabric of your relationship may not be able to endure the wear and tear of a life together.

The marriage is the nucleus of the family. It creates, defines and sustains the family. It transcends the identities of the two people who created it, and yet a healthy marriage not only preserves those identities but also brings them to full flower.

To say that your commitment is to your marriage, rather than to your spouse, is to recognize that *you* are an equal partner. For the marriage to remain vital, you must take care of your *own* selves as well as you take care of each other — no more and no less.

But what about the children? Well . . . what about them?

Children's needs are met if the needs of the marriage are met. Children who experience their parents' relationship as an ever-present core of stability at the center of the family will feel as secure as they can possibly feel.

From their parents' example, they learn how to share, how to disagree in ways which don't compromise anyone's dignity, and they learn the human art of caring. They learn that their parents' relationship does not include them — and yet they eventually realize that they are protected and nurtured *because* of it.

Children discover who they are by first having it defined for them who *their parents* are, and who they *are not*. They discover their *own* place by first being told where it *cannot* be.

It is this clear sense of "separateness" that encourages the growth of autonomy and pushes children toward the fulfillment of their own promise.

There isn't a child on this earth who needs more than that.

Independent Parents

This chapter is about being single and raising children, but it is not for single parents only. It applies equally well to each of use, whether married or not, parent or not. It's about the traps we build for ourselves out of myths and pieces of broken fairy tales.

I'm thinking specifically about the myths that color our perceptions of the single parent (and the way single parents view themselves). There are many myths, but foremost among them is one that says raising a child (or children) is much more difficult if you are single than if you have a partner.

That is simply not the truth. Raising a child on your own is surely *different* from raising a child within an intact family, but it is only as *difficult* as the single parent thinks it is.

For every argument supporting the belief that raising children is a herculean task for one person, there is another, more optimistic interpretation of the evidence. Someone might point out, for instance, that single parents deserve sympathy because they are on the front lines all of the time, with no one to fall back on for emotional support. It can just as easily be said that single parenthood is relatively uncomplicated.

One single parent curses his isolation, saying, "I have to make *all* the decisions." Another rejoices at her independence, saying, "I get to make all the decisions." As with any other enterprise, there are, upon comparison, advantages and disadvantages. Select the perspective of your choice.

Whose point of view is right? Everybody's! If you believe that raising children on your own is an insurmountable hardship, it will be just that. If, on the other hand, you convince yourself that raising children independently is one of the greatest opportunities for creative living you've ever had, then you will use that positive force to create opportunity after opportunity for yourself and your children. Whatever we believe of ourselves we generally manage to prove right.

This attitude problem about single parenthood might not exist were it not for an even more insidious set of myths about marriage. These say, in essence, that marriage can do for us what we feel inadequate to do for ourselves — namely, it can make us complete, happy and fulfilled. That delusion not only destroys many marriages, but scatters disillusionment and despair in its wake. In real life, marriage does not make someone happy, and divorce does not foreclose on the loan. In real life, we make ourselves happy, and we make ourselves unhappy (or angry or bitter or resentful or whatever).

Children from divided homes are swept into the melodrama. The prevailing view is that they are damaged, that there is something missing from their lives which handicaps them forever and ever, amen.

The myth says children must have two parents. The fact is that children need two parents who care for each other. The fact is that one parent who cares for them is preferable to two who don't really care for each other.

Those who accept the myth that single parents are playing at a loser's game have chosen to defeat themselves. Their feelings of helplessness, anger, isolation and frustration are entirely self-imposed. For better or for worse, we are in control of ourselves.

If you are a single parent, you are as capable as any two parents of raising healthy, happy children. No, you can't be a mother and a father too, but you can be a whole, fulfilled person, with more than enough vitality to share with your children.

The job is never too big for one person, if the person is big enough for the job.

Do you want to believe it?

Respect Your Child: Another View

In the past 25 years or so, we have grown increasingly dependent upon experts to tell us how to raise our children. In the process, we have become more childlike in our unquestioning attitude toward their "expertness." Unfortunately, some of their advice has been more harmful than helpful.

The permissive school of child-raising experts advised us to "respect" our children. They have not been specific about what this involves, because we have not required specificity from them. They are, after all, the experts.

As they use the term, "respecting your child" implies that parents should treat their children democratically — as equals. Most of us agree that every human being is worthy of respect. Parents *should* respect their children — for what they are and are becoming, but *not* as equals.

Respect between parent and child is a two-way street, but the traffic going in each direction is different *in every way*.

Children respect their parents by obeying them. Parents, on the other hand, respect their children by insisting that they obey.

Parents who enforce obedience are caring for one of their children's most basic needs.

Unfortunately, many parents equate obedience with passivity. Not wanting to raise passive children, they find ways to avoid making them obey. These parents often fear that making their children obey will stifle the children's independence.

The opposite is true. Learning obedience *enhances* a child's independence.

Obedient children have parents who effectively describe and enforce limits. Within that clear framework, obedient children are free to be curious, to explore, to invent—in short, to be as independent as their maturity allows.

Contrast this type of respect with the "respect" demanded by the authoritarian parent, who usually equates respect with fear. Children who fear their parents don't obey—they submit. Children who are obedient are not fearful. They are self-confident and secure. They are even secure enough to indulge in a certain amount of rebellion.

Children who fear their parents often become deceptive—they learn to lie in order to escape their restrictions. Children who are obedient are more likely to be honest and forthright, because the have been treated honestly and in accord with what they *truly* need.

At the opposite extreme from authoritarian parents are those who require no respect. Children whose parents do not require obedience live in a world of constantly shifting limits. Now they see them, now they don't. Their parents' "agendas" are hidden, and the children are forced to search for them. Their searching is usually frantic and attracts disapproval. Consequently, they are called "disobedient." I maintain, however, that there are *no* disobedient children; there are only parents who fail to accept their responsibilities and children who are scapegoats.

Children who don't know their limits must depend on their parents to reward them whenever they discover part of their parents' secret. Obedience, however, is its own reward. To the extent that children accept and function responsibly within the limits their parents define, those limits should steadily expand. Eventually, the children no longer need someone else to define limits for them.

Obedience, then, paves the road to maturity.

Strictly Speaking

Few words in the parlance of "parenting" have been so generally misused and misunderstood as "strict." Not only has the term descended to the depths of disrepute, but its original meaning has been corrupted almost beyond recognition.

Nearly everyone today agrees that "strict" is synonomous with severe, authoritarian, inflexible, dictatorial, uncompromising, puritanical, dogmatic, heavy-handed, tyrannical.

Strict! It even *sounds* harsh, like the crack of a whip.

In this do-your-own-thing age, the strict parent is seen as a virtual Simon Legree, keeping one jaundiced eye open to what his children are doing (or even *thinking* of doing) wrong, and the other eye closed to what they are doing right. But none of this is true. Strict parents have been labeled and slandered by permissivists who would confuse our lives as easily as they confuse language.

To begin redeeming this much maligned adjective, let me point out that not too many years ago (before it became stylish to worship children and let them walk all over us), "strictness" in child-rearing was considered a virtue. Way back when children were children and parents were the people in charge, to be strict meant defining rules clearly and enforcing obedience to them.

And what is wrong with that? Nothing at all. In fact, there is everything right and proper about being old-fashionedly strict.

Truly strict parents do their children a great service, in many ways:

• They communicate expectations clearly, leaving little room for misunderstanding.

• They are decisive. England may swing like a pendulum do (as that old song said), but they definitely don't. Their children, therefore, know where they stand.

• They teach their children to expect no more from a situation than they are willing to put into it. Gradually, their children distill a set of tried-and-true methods for living productive, satisfying lives.

• They know their children rely on parents to keep them on the right track, and they correct their children's inevitable wanderings with an even hand.

Strict parents must be disciplined themselves, practicing no less than they preach. Above all else, they understand the importance of rules.

Rules protect. They insure a child's physical and emotional well-being. Rules are the mainstay of order. They regulate and mediate a child's comings and goings in the world. Children are helpless without them. Paradoxically, a rule is both a constraint and a quarantee of freedom.

A rule which is ill-defined, not enforced or enforced only sporadically, is not a rule. It is a fraud, a doublecross, and under this kind of "rule" a child is a victim, a prisoner of uncertainty. On the other hand, a child who tests a rule (as children *always* will) and finds it a predictable quantity is then free to function constructively within its boundaries.

Not long ago my son, Eric (now 11), and I were talking about a friend of his, and the conversation turned to her parents. I asked about his impression of them, and he answered, "They're very nice but, well, *strict*, ya know?"

Intrigued, I replied, "No, Eric, I don't know. I've never heard you use that word before. What does it mean to you?"

He thought for a moment. "It means," he said, "it means, well, like they don't let her get away with stuff she shouldn't do."

"I see. Well, Eric, do you think *I'm* strict?"

"Yes," he said, without hesitation, "but I think you *have to be* when you raise children."

Out of the mouth of babes.

The Sound of One Hand Clapping

I spank my children, or, to put it more accurately, I *have* spanked my children and might, at any time, do it again. Or I might not.

If I do, it won't be because I have given it a lot of thought or believe that children *need* to be spanked or have reached the end of my rope, but simply because I will *feel* like it. I have learned, during nearly 13 years of raising my own children, to trust my feelings.

You see, "to spank or not to spank" is *not* the question. The question, regardless of what you do or don't do, is simply this: "Does it work?"

Two years ago, I wrote in a newspaper column that spanking was not the big, bad thing it's been made out to be. It's not a big deal, but people who are obsessed with children find, in a spanking, the stuff that big deals are made of. After that column appeared, one such maker of big deals told me I had, in effect, endorsed child abuse. Another person said my attitude "disturbed" her because "it plays right into the hands (substitute switches or belts) of people with a 'spare the rod, spoil the child' mentality."

What really disturbed my critics was that I don't share their view of the world, part of which includes a myth that says children who are spanked (a) hate themselves for being such rotten kids, (b) learn to solve problems by hitting people, (c) will someday abuse their own children, (d) become violent criminals or (e) all of the above.

I have good news. Those myths are wrong. The social, economic, political and psychological factors that combine to produce criminals, child abusers, bullies and emotional cripples are far too complex for even a computer to fathom. To suggest that spankings play a major role in shaping that kind of social behavior is ludicrous.

I have more good news. It is possible to spank a child *well*, to do it *right* and to make it *work*. The problem with spanking is that most parents make a sorry mess of it.

The typical spanking scenario begins with a child doing something that is clearly out of bounds — let's say, leaping from a coffee table onto a sofa. Her parents react by jabbering, bobbing up and down at the waist, and flapping their arms. The child notices that, despite their agitated flutter, thay have essentially done nothing. She files this valuable information away in a neuron bank marked "High Priority."

Fifteen minutes later, she climbs up on the coffee table and again propels herself onto the sofa. Her parents jabber, bob and flap as they did before. And again, nothing happens. Remarkable! Fifteen minutes later, she does this leap again, but this time, before her parents stop flapping, one of them says, "If you do that again, I'll have to spank you! Do you understand?"

Of course she understands. She knows a challenge when she hears one.

Her parents, meanwhile, are becoming increasingly frustrated over her "disobedience" or "forgetfulness" or whatever term they use to avoid accepting responsibility for what's happening.

Five more times she leaps and five more times her parents bob, flap and threaten. On the ninth try, she breaks an imported crystal bud vase. Her parents descend on her like furies, flapping their hands against her rear end, shouting, "We told you not to leap, and look what you did!" For several hours following the incident the home is wrapped in a mantle of gloom. No one talks; no one laughs. The child feels cheated. The parents feel guilty. All in all, it's a waste of time, energy, intelligence and imported crystal.

But it wasn't the spanking that was wrong, it was the way it was done.

Rule Number One of a Well-done Spanking: *Don't wait.* For me, spanking is a first resort. This is not to say that I spank for everything or spank a lot. I seldom spank, but when I decide, quite arbitrarily, that the situation warrants it, I do it and that's the end of it.

Rule Number Two: *Don't threaten.* Why the dramatic buildup? A threat is nothing more than a pleading, apologetic way of asking a child to save you from doing "the bad thing." A threat is irresponsible and lazy. *Every* threat is empty.

Besides, the price of not acting is frustration, which builds steadily from threat to threat toward an almost inevitable, and worthless, explosion.

Rule Number Three: *Use your hand.* A spanking is a non-verbal expression of authority and disapproval from *you.* Make a direct connection, person-to-person.

Rule Number Four: *Don't hit and run.* A spanking is not the *end* of something—it is, or should be, the *beginning* of something. After you spank, it is important to talk. Don't offer apologies—just straight no-nonsense stuff: "Now that I have your undivided attention, let me tell you about life with Mommy."

Make a short, simple statement that sums up your feelings about what the child did and clearly marks the behavior as being against the rules. Don't ask for "I'll-be-good" promises or apologies. Say what you have to say, aim the child in a better direction, and let bygones be bygones.

The idea is *not* to cause the child pain, but to (1) quickly terminate undesirable behavior, (2) remind the child of your authority, (3) express, in a relatively low-key way, your anger and (4) grab the child's attention for a moment of plain talk.

My children usually don't know when they are going to feel my hand on their bottom. I don't spank for any one thing in particular, so they can't predict when one is coming down the pike. In general, I spank in response to open defiance, deliberate disobedience or flagrant displays of disrespect. But a spanking is only *one* way I might choose to express myself under any of those circumstances. What matters is that I spank long before I've "had enough." That way, I never get there.

Plain Talk

"Because I said so!" was one of my father's favorite phrases. I argued with him a lot, and that was his stock way of shutting me down.

I was 16 when I vowed upon a stack of rock 'n' roll albums

never to say "Because I said so" to my children. I wasn't going to be *that* kind of parent.

My children were going to be given *responsibility* and unlimited opportunity to make decisions. After all, these were the 1960s, and individual freedom was blowin' in the wind.

A son was born into those uncertain times.

Three years later, the times were no less uncertain for him. These were the 1970s, and tantrums were blowin' in the wind. It eventually became clear that Eric would never acquire enough self-control to make sensible decisions unless I was first willing to act decisively. So I brought the horse around to the front of the cart and moved into the driver's seat.

I still wince a little at the sound of "Because I said so," but I think Dad had the beginning of a sound idea: Young children (and here I refer to the under-five crowd) benefit immeasurably from being given reasons — if the reasons can be expressed in 25 one- and two-syllable words or less. But when the answer to "Why?" is lengthy, complex or arbitrary, the child should hear a clear message that says, in effect, "I will take care of this situation."

The plain truth is, sometimes the most honest, straightforward and authoritative (not to be confused with authoritarian) reason for making a decision or giving an instruction is "Because I said so."

The trouble with Dad was, he didn't know when to quit. I still heard "Because I said so" when I was in high school. But he taught me a valuable lesson: never use fifty words when four will do.

So when my children want to know "Why," I sometimes answer, "Because I don't want you to," or "I have made the decision."

Son of "Because I said so."

The Games Parents Play

There is a game I call "Please?" that parents play with their children. "Please?" begins when a parent wants a child to do something. It's usually something simple, such as wanting the child to sit in the back seat of the car. But parents have the darnedest ways of making simple things complicated and even confusing.

To play "Please?" the parent acts indecisive, as though she doesn't know exactly what she *does* want the child to do. Therefore, she makes no imperative, commanding statements. Instead, she phrases all statements as questions and asks the questions in a small, pleading voice.

For example, rather than, "You are going to sit in the back seat," or "I want you in the back seat," the mother says, "Wouldn't you rather sit in the back seat so Mommy can sit up here? This form and tone tells the child that Mommy needs his help in making this difficult decision. The child is glad to help: "No! I want to sit here. You sit in the back."

At this point, it's a jump ball, up for grabs to the quickest player. Often the parent commits a technical foul by changing the rules and becoming angry: "Look, I told you to sit in the back seat, now get there!" This is not true, since the parent never *told* the child anything. But the foul never gets called, unless the other parent is playing the role of referee.

More often "Please?" does not come to that abrupt an end. The parent usually negotiates a compromise in which the child gets what he wants, and the parent gets to be inconvenienced (having to hold the child on her lap).

Parents play "Please?" to avoid confrontations, showdowns and embarrassment. And it works! But what they get in the bargain is no bowl of cherries. Children are quick to learn when their parents are afraid to assert their authority and can be relied upon to give in. When it comes to a question of "Who's the boss?" if parents won't run with the ball, children will.

There should never be any question about who's running the show in the first place. It is a child's inalienable right and privilege to be informed early in life that parent is boss. "When parent at a loss, child make bad boss," (Bobo, 1980).

Count the times you play "Please?" with your child today. Once is too many.

Parents need to tell children what to do and then stand prepared to enforce their authority (pick the child up and put him in the back seat). Don't ask questions if you don't really intend for the child to have a choice.

Children need to be told what to do by parents who aren't afraid or embarrassed by an occasional showdown. Children feel more secure and comfortable with parents who know where they stand (and where they want to sit).

She Hates Me, She Hates Me Not

This is a transcript of an actual conversation which took place in my house several years ago.

The speakers are my daughter, Amy, then 6 going on 16 (and making me feel 60), and her daddy — yours truly — a real tyrant, as you will see.

Daddy: Amy, I want you to set the table tonight.
Amy: I don't want to. Make Eric do it.
Daddy: I want *you* to do it. And right *now*, by the way.
Amy: I did it last night.
Daddy: Yes, and you did such a fine job that I want you to do
         it again tonight. And right *now*, by the way.
Amy: I *won't* do it. It's Eric's turn.
Daddy: Since you won't set the table, you will have to go to
         your room. You may come down when you decide to
         set the table.
Amy: What if I don't, and it's suppertime?
Daddy: Then *I* will set the table and bring your supper to
         your room, where you will stay until morning.
Amy: I don't care.
Daddy: Well, I do.
Amy: Why?
Daddy: Because I want you to be able to eat supper with us.
Amy: Well, I *will* then, but I *won't* set the table.
Daddy: Amy, go to your room. Right *now*.
Amy: DADDY, IF YOU SEND ME TO MY ROOM, I'LL
         STAY THERE FOREVER!
Daddy: Either set the table or go to your room.
Amy: DADDY, I WON'T BE AROUND HERE MUCH
         LONGER! I'LL RUN AWAY!
Daddy: Either set the table or go to your room.
Amy: I HATE YOU! I'M NOT YOUR DAUGHTER
         ANYMORE! I BELONG TO SOMEONE ELSE!

This was followed by a volley of "YOU'LL BE SORRY!" and
another chorus of "I HATE YOU!"

I'm sure there are times when she really does hate me, such
as when I make her choose between two things she loathes,
like setting the table or banishment to her room.

Feeling hate is predictable, genuine and understandable for
a six year old under those circumstances. Is she supposed to
like it when I put her between a rock and a hard place? Heck,
no!

It's not easy being a person with little power. On the other
hand, it's even worse being a child who's been given, by
default, a lot of power. Children want power, are frustrated by
their lack of it and don't know how to handle it when it lands in
their laps.

So, where Amy is involved, I take firm hold of the reins, and
there are times when she surely hates me for it.

She hates me when I parry her attempts to defy me and win.

She hates me because when she tries to engage me in a power struggle, I refuse to participate. Amy can't win a fight with me because I won't fight with her — not if my authority is at stake.

If I *did* fight with her, I would be encouraging the false idea that she is my equal. She is *not* my equal. She needs my protection and my resources. She will, in due time, be my equal, and I nurture and cherish that potential. But it is not yet ready to flower.

I will not compromise with her regarding my authority until she is more accepting of it. Our relationship is not democratic, and no amount of idealizing can make it so. Amy did not *choose* me for her daddy, and I do not come up for reelection every few years. Amy's voice in the running of the family and the management of her life is not equal to mine, and it will *not* be until she leaves home. Until then, I decide. I even decide when she *can* decide; then I tell her what the choices are. She has a right to hate me. It is, I hope, a measure of the basic openness and frankness in our relationship that she feels able to tell me so.

By the way, Amy *did* set the table. The spoons were on the left, and my placemat was turned at a 90-degree angle. Oh, well.

Commitment: More Than Just a Try

Not long ago, a young woman asked me about a problem she had with her five-year-old daughter. The problem was not anything unusual, but it had hung on in this family for two years, draining lots of energy and wasting everyone's time.

After I listened to this mother's exasperated description of the goings on and asked a few questions, I told her what I thought could be done to settle the issue once and for all.

When I finished, she gave a slight shrug and said, "Well, I'll give it a try."

"Well," I replied, "Giving it a try won't make it work."

"What do you mean?" she asked, coming to life again.

"Excuse me for being so frank, but the best, the most watertight of all possible solutions to your problem won't make change happen if all you're going to give it is (and I shrugged) 'a try.' "

She is by no means alone. Plenty of parents never get past "trying." And that is why so many of them lose control of their children — and themselves in the process.

"I'll give it a try" is another way of saying, "I can't." It is a statement of defeat, surrender and personal ineffectiveness.

That brings us to the point: When you deal with a problem involving a child, more important than *what* you do is the act of *doing*.

Because of my professional credentials and my reputation, parents ask me a lot of questions. Most of them begin with the phrase, "*What* should I do when . . ." (the italics are mine). This manner of asking a question reflects a fundamental, widely held misunderstanding: for every specific problem, there is one equally specific, "best" solution.

Not so. For every specific problem there are countless effective solutions. It doesn't matter which one you select—you can even invent a new one—because for *any* and *all* problems the *real* solution has nothing to do with technique or method.

It's called commitment, or determination, or resolve. It's the sense of purpose you invest in the method of your choice (or invention). The difference between method and commitment, the *what* and the *doing*, is the difference between form and substance. Method is nothing more than a vehicle. Without commitment that vehicle is doomed to stall. Without commitment your method is impotent.

The difference between method and commitment is the difference between saying "I'll give it a try," and "This is the way it's going to be."

Commitment is the backbone of whatever you do. Commitment is the energy of change. Believe me, your children will know immediately when you are "giving it a try." They will sense your ambivalence and your lack of determination, and *they will not cooperate with you because you will have given them no substantial reason to cooperate.*

When a child tests you, she is doing precisely that—she is testing *you*. Not the form, but the substance. And when, in response, you demonstrate your own sense of purpose in what you are doing, you demonstrate also your commitment to her. When she is convinced of *that*, she will cooperate with you.

No question about it.

What's a "Fair"?

"It's not fair!"

I hear that a lot these days. In fact, I've been listening to variations on the same theme, delivered in sundry ways, from statement to scream, for several years.

It's my nine-year-old daughter, Amy. Poor Amy, she must have arrived before her appointed time, because the world was not prepared. The news of her arrival didn't even make a big splash in the media—just a blurred picture and two or three lines to distinguish her from the other fuzzy infant mug-shots in the lineup.

Ever since then, Amy has tried to convince us that a mistake was made. This time around, she was scheduled to do time as a princess. She had, no doubt, paid her dues as a serving wench, a peasant—you know, the usual stuff we all endure before getting to the big time. This fling was to have been different. But something went wrong.

What a disappointment it must be.

Her mother and I can't even buy her everything she wants. She doesn't understand about mortgages and car payments. After all, the castle was supposed to have been paid for along with a villa on the Mediterranean.

But the worst of the worst, the supreme insult, is that there was another child in the family before her. His name is Eric.

The problem, as Amy sees it, is that Eric is sometimes given things before she is, or that he gets something bigger or two of something to her one. Dad may even take Eric to the store and buy him something and come home empty-handed for Amy.

"It's not fair!"

"But Amy," I say, "sometimes you and I go to the store and get something just for you. Why, don't you remember that we bought you a new coat and a pair of shoes yesterday? Eric didn't get anything then."

"It's not fair!"

Come to think of it, she's right. "What is fair?" I ask myself. It's a vague concept that is nothing short of impossible to achieve.

What would satisfy my heir apparent (and most small children) is not for us to be "fair," but for us to give them everything they want. "Fair" means "me first" with the biggest and the best.

When there is more than one child in the family, there is no avoiding explosions over who gets what and whose is the best and the brightest and on and on.

So what are we to do? Should we try to spend the same amount of money on both children or buy the same number of things for each? Do we have to bring Amy something whenever we take Eric to the store?

No. It is not in Amy's best interest for us to encourage the idea that the world can be relied upon to deliver to her an equal measure of whatever she sees someone else getting. Children with this idea are popularly called "spoiled," and spoiled children, when they grow up, are likely to be extremely frustrated and unhappy because the fairy tale *never* comes true.

I usually try something like this:

"It may not seem fair that Mommy and Daddy have given something to Eric and not to you. But you and Eric are different people, and we treat you differently. You will have trips to the store of your very own."

Sometimes the explanation doesn't sit well, and she goes into her dying swan routine. I walk away, refusing to get involved in the drama. Eventually she gets over it.

It's not a question of fair. It's a question of balance.

In Defense of Inconsistency

The solution to any problem simply changes the nature of the problem. I can't recall where I heard that, but it came to mind as I began writing about consistency.

Few people would deny that consistency is a cornerstone of successful child rearing. But I would, because it isn't. It's just another brick.

I used to talk about the importance of consistency as if it were the One True Way. I don't anymore. These days, I'm more likely to say, "There's a time for being consistent and a time for being inconsistent," and then talk about the benefits of inconsistency.

Although it has had extremely bad press, inconsistency has little to do with the problems parents have raising children. If anything, the idea that parents *must* be consistent to be successful has contributed to at least as many problems as it may have solved.

The commandment to *be consistent above all else* has been handed down by well-meaning professionals who, like me, are inclined to be more than a little compulsive. The belief that predictability and routine are what makes people-systems run well is the model they use to guide their own personal and professional lives. Since it works for them, they prescribe it for everyone.

And, to a certain extent, they are correct. Consistency is as essential to the maintainance of our existence as oil is to the smooth functioning of an internal combustion engine.

I'm certain we would all be candidates for the loony bin were we not able to reduce confusion and uncertainty by organizing our lives around a network of routines. But in our enthusiasm, we social scientists have oversold the notion that consistency is the oil that tunes our social engines. And the public has over-consumed the idea in like proportion. The resulting overdose has fouled our plugs and blown sludge into our carburetors.

Yes, children need routine. It simplifies their lives, promotes security and provides a stable framework within which freedom is possible.

Yes, every child needs parents who agree on the rules and boundaries that guide the child's growing.

No, parents do *not* have to agree on how those rules are enforced. To the extent that parents feel they *must* agree on this, they will have problems.

It is unrealistic to expect that two fundamentally different people, who come into a marriage with different ideas about children, can agree on a single set of tools with which to regulate a child's behavior.

Each parent's toolbox is different, and each feels familiar and skilled with his or her own set of tools. Mom is inclined to sit Junior in his least-favorite chair when he disobeys, while Dad is likely to whack Junior's behind parts. So what? There is no conflict here and there need not be disagreement. That Mom and Dad use different means of enforcing the rule is only superficially relevant.

What counts in maintaining harmony in the family is that Mom and Dad agree on the importance of the rule — Do What We Tell You To Do — and are both quick to act when Junior gets out of line. Mom and Dad are acting consistently, even though *differently*, to reinforce the rule.

But parents can get so hung up on the need to be consistent that they begin fighting over their stylistic differences. Meanwhile, as the forest is increasingly obscured by the trees, the rule itself begins to gather dust, and it dawns on Junior that there is no rule at all — sometimes he can disobey and sometimes he can't.

It isn't even necessary for either parent, acting alone, to respond in the same manner every time a rule is violated.

Mom *prefers* to put Junior in the "thinking-chair" when he's a "rebel without a cause," but she is not required to do that *every* time. Sometimes she says he can't go outside, sometimes she sends him to his room, sometimes she simply repeats herself with more emphasis and sometimes she reaches over into Dad's toolbox and pops Junior's behind.

And Dad may not always spank. There are times when he has a man-to-man talk with Junior. Sometimes he takes something away, and sometimes he sits him in Mom's favorite chair.

But no matter what Mom and Dad do when Junior disobeys,

the *rule* is there. It is being consistently enforced by a variety of means, but the end is the same. Furthermore, Mom and Dad's reactions are consistent with how each *feels* at the moment a transgression occurs.

There is even something to be said for being unpredictable in the way you enforce rules. Messages lose their impact when they are stated repetitiously. Being too consistent can evolve into boredom and rigidity.

Too much consistency also prevents parents from seeing changes in their children and adapting to those changes. Too much consistency restricts growth. Too much consistency promotes a simplistic view of life.

Consistency may be the oil, but variety is the spice of living. Don't limit your options by subscribing too literally to *any* single idea. Agree on the rules and agree to disagree over how each parent chooses to enforce them. Appreciate and support one another's differences and let your children know that, yes, Mom has her way of doing things, and Dad has his.

That's consistent with the way the rest of the world turns.

Worry: the Future Game

We influence the future in the way we anticipate it. In this respect, we are all, to some degree, fortune tellers.

This is not whimsy, but a documented principle of human psychology called "the self-fulfilling prophecy." It's the lesson we learned as children from the story of the little engine that could: If you think you *can*, you probably *will*. If you think you *can't*, you probably *won't*.

We not only affect our *own* future in the way we anticipate it, but, in like manner, we influence the lives of others. The stronger the bond between two people, the stronger the potential effect.

Between parents and children, parents wield the most potent influence. On the constructive side are influences such as commitment and optimism. Parents who are not only hopeful, but optimistically *certain* that their children will be all right, seem blessed with children who, by and large, turn out well.

On the destructive side are guilt and worry. Both are forms of negative energy which not only prevent parents from paying adequate attention to the here-and-now, but are also self-fulfilling. Parents who worry about their children always seem to have something to worry about.

Billy-Bob is three years old. He has been tossed out of two preschool programs and is working on being expelled from his third. Few children in his neighborhood are allowed to play with him. Billy-Bob bites.

Billy-Bob is an only child whose middle-class parents want him to grow up without any emotional problems. They have read countless books and articles about raising children. They want desperately to do it right, but something has gone wrong.

They search the past for a reason for Billy-Bob's biting. "What did we do to cause it?" they ask, needing a hook on which to hang their guilt. The more they search, the more they ask, the more Billy-Bob bites.

Billy-Bob bit his mother when he was 13 months old. He was in the throes of a frenzied tantrum which began when his mother took a photograph away from him. The bite set off a guilt-quake inside his mother. It was so big, even Billy-Bob knew something extraordinary had happened. So he bit her again.

Three months later, after sufficient practice on his mother, he bit the next-door neighbor's child. When he was 18 months old, his parents enrolled him in a day-care program, hoping that his being around more children would help. He lasted two months.

Billy-Bob's parents worry so much about what he will be like in 10 minutes, 10 days or 10 years that they don't notice what he's doing *right now*. Whenever he's around other children, they are consumed with anxiety. Billy-Bob can feel their tension and knows just what he's expected to do. So he does. And the more he bites, the more his parents worry.

It's usually impossible to determine, in such situations, whether the worry or the subject being worried about came first. The more parents worry, the more the subject comes up, the bigger it gets, and the more they worry. Until the cycle is broken, there is no resolution, only repetition. And the more the cycle is repeated, the more indelible its imprint on the family.

Worriers cannot be spontaneous, because they are not dealing with things as they happen. Their concerns are scattered somewhere up ahead, in the future, where they will *never* be. The more parents worry, the more they ignore the *real* problem. Meanwhile, the child bears the present-tense weight of the issue on *his* shoulders.

When, and if, Billy-Bob's parents decide to do something about his biting, they might begin by telling him, "Billy-Bob, you have been biting other children, and now you are going to stop. We are going to help you stop, because that's what mommies and daddies are for. Whenever you forget and bite someone, here's what's going to happen, every single time."

It won't matter much *what* they do. What will matter is that his parents will be doing *something*.

Billy-Bob will be *very* relieved, believe me.

Spare the Rod, But Not the Rule

Rules are social boundaries. They outline the limits of acceptable behavior and preserve the stability of human environments. Rules knit society together; they are as essential to our survival as water is to the life of a fish.

For children, rules are an extension of parental authority. Rules are as necessary to healthy development as are stimulation, good nutrition and sunshine. Rods can be spared; rules cannot.

Rules can be communicated to children in a number of ways. A direction or instruction is a rule. A task assigned to a child is a rule. Any decision defining what a child may or may not do or have is a rule.

When the rules of a game are clear, the players know what moves are available and can predict with some degree of certainty what moves the other players will make. Rules organize the game. They reduce uncertainty and anxiety.

And so it is with children. When rules are present, a child knows what is and is not allowed and is able to predict his parents' behavior. Rules are fundamental to feelings of security.

When rules are unclear or enforced sporadically, children can't predict what their parents will do next. Under these circumstances, children become anxious, insecure and sometimes even physically sick.

I do not advocate rules for the sake of rules. Bad rules, or too many rules, can be as detrimental to a child's well-being as poor nutrition. Good rules should meet four basic requirements:

(1) *All rules should be stated clearly*. No dressing or garnish is necessary, nor is a complicated explanation. Preschool children will have difficulty understanding even the best explanation of why a rule is necessary. If you must explain, make the explanation brief and to the point: 25 words or less.

Older children understand reasons and like to argue about them. If parents argue back, the basic issue—that parents set rules and children abide by them—becomes confused. If a child wants to argue, say, "I will not argue. You will have to do as you are told."

Some parents feel guilty about making straightforward demands on their children. So they disguise their demands as requests which require "yes" as the only acceptable answer. "Will you take out the garbage?" is really a rule if the child has no choice but to take out the garbage. Phrased as a question, however, the rule is unclear. The garbage sits in the kitchen, the parents become upset, and the child gets increasingly confused.

(2) *Rules should be clearly defined.* What is meant by "clean up your room"? Parents think their children know, but a child's idea of clean is *never* the same as a parent's. Only Sylvia's mother knows exactly what she wants when she tells Sylvia to clean up her room. To reduce uncertainty and confusion, define tasks specifically, as in, "You must make up your bed, fold your clothes, put them in your dresser, and put your books back on the shelf before you can go outside." If a chore must be done everyday, making a list of the steps involved will eliminate many unnecessary arguments. When a rule is defined clearly, it is easier to enforce.

3. *Rules should be reasonable when they refer to chores.* A child's day should not be filled with chores. There should be plenty of time for rest, study and play. Before assigning a *chore*, be sure the child is able to do *it*. If she's capable, but needs some initial quidance, break the task down into small steps and teach her one step at a time.

For instance, most five year olds don't know how to make beds, but they can be taught. First, have Sylvia watch you make the bed while you describe each step. Then have her help you. Over several days, let her do more and more of the job until she does it alone.

(4) *Parents should only make rules that they CAN and WILL enforce.* When rules are made, children will break them. *That is a rule.* Children *must* break new rules to be sure that they *are* rules. If their parents fail to enforce them, they are *not* rules. If this happens enough, the relationship between parent and child becomes tense and uncomfortable. Parents often become angry at children for breaking rules, not realizing that every child breaks every rule that is ever made. When parents say, "I've tried everything and nothing works," they really mean rules have not been enforced.

Some parents attempt to enforce too many rules. These parents are usually found in hectic pursuit of their children, making up "don'ts" while the child tries desperately to escape.

Don't invent rules on the run. Concentrate on enforcing only two or three at a time. You will be surprised at how quickly other things seem to fall into place once this is accomplished.

We live by rules because without them there would be no freedom. When parents make good rules and enforce them, they create a relaxed emotional climate in which their children are free to be O.K.

Who's on First?

The McZbenburgs are a typical American family — Mr McZbenburg works from eight to five selling recycled groteclusters to Samoan expatriots, while Mrs. McZbenburg takes care of the household and sees to the proper upbringing of their typical three and a half year old, Philigree.

Not long ago, Mrs. McZbenburg decided it was time to teach little Philigree the fine art of cleaning up his room, which was strewn with toys, scraps of paper and a motley assortment of odds and ends after the fashion of a typical three and a half year old.

"Come on, Philigree," she said, "I'm going to teach you how to straighten your room." And down the hall they went, hand in hand.

In his room, Philigree's mom said, "Now you help Mommy pick up everything on the floor and put it where it belongs. Watch Mommy and do what I do."

Mrs. McZbenburg got down on her hands and knees. Philigree watched closely. His mother began picking up toys, talking as she did so, "Now this one goes here and this one goes here and . . ." Philigree kept watching.

"C'mon, Philigree," said Mrs. McZbenburg, "Start picking up some toys. Here, pick up your flimstrum and put it on the shelf."

Philigree picked up his flimstrum and put it on the shelf.

"Good boy!" said his mother. "Keep it up, just like I'm doing!" And Philigree watched his mother pick up several more toys.

"Philigree!" she said, "Your aren't helping! Pick up the bleem and put them in the bleem box."

Philigree began picking up bleem and putting them, one at a time, in the bleem box.

"That's the way!" said his mother as she continued picking up odds and ends. When she had finished putting everything else away, she came over to where Philigree was hunched motionless over a pile of bleem and said, "We're almost done, Philigree! Just a few more bleem and we're done!"

Philigree remained hunched as his mother picked up all but the last bleem.

"Pick up the last bleem and we're done, Philigree!" she said, almost beside herself with excitement.

Philigree picked up the last bleem.

"Good boy, Philigree! Now let's go get some ice cream for all the good work you did."

Final score: Mrs. McZbenburg — 78 toys, odds, ends and scraps. Philigree — one flimstrum and six bleem.

Philigree caught on quickly. He's quite smart, you see, having been born with a cerebral cortex. So every day, just before Mr. McZbenburg came home, Philigree and his mother would go down the hall into his room. His mother would begin picking things up. Philigree would crouch, watching her until he sensed that she needed a reward for her labors. Then he would pick up a bleem or something else and put it away.

This always delighted his mother, and she would continue working while Philigree hunched. When the room was neat, Mrs. McZbenburg always gave Philigree a bowl of scuppernong ice cream for being such a good helper.

When Mr. McZbenburg came home, Mrs. McZbenburg would say something like, "Oh, and Mac, you just wouldn't believe how quickly Philigree is learning to straighten up his room!"

Philigree would just smile.

Rewards and Incentives

"O.K., Junior, I know you don't want to take out the trash, but it you do, I'll give you a dime. How's that sound?" Sounds pretty good, huh Junior?

The notion that children need to be rewarded for obedience has become popular with some unfortunate consequences. Foremost among these is the idea that children perform better when they are promised tangible rewards, such as candy, a toy or a special privilege.

In part, this is true. If you want a child to do something mundane, such as cleaning up his room, offer him a piece of his favorite candy, a new toy or a trip to the neighborhood ice-cream parlor. And then, the next time you want him to clean up his room, be prepared to make the same offer. If you're lucky, the child will only expect more of the same. If luck isn't standing on your side of the street that day, however, he'll want something even better. Yesterday, an ice cream cone; tomorrow a super-deluxe Bicentennial hot marshmallow cream sundae!

Children are impressionable, and nothing impresses them more than stuff for their mouths or hands. (Unfortunately, many adults have the same trait.) It's the "what's in it for me?" syndrome, as much the new American way as Mom's factory-made, frozen apple pie.

Accuse me of being an Adult Chauvinist Swine (ACS), but I subscribe to a double standard — what's tolerable in an adult is not always tolerable in a child.

When a child learns to expect something in return every time he puts out a little effort for someone besides himself, it's obnoxious, but it's not his fault. The child is the addict, but we big people are the pushers. We adults tend to look for the most expedient way to accomplish things, the shortest distance between two points. When we want cooperation from a child, we know that offering some "goody" is likely to get the job done fast. In the child's mind, however, cooperation and the performance of certain tasks or chores become hooked to the promise of special rewards.

This can quickly become a revolving door situation that traps both parent and child. Parent wants the work done without having to deal with the child's excuses . . . child wants the handout and has learned that if he stalls long enough, parent will come through with the goods.

Children need certain tools to meet the challenges of adult life. Extremely important among these are the virtues of industry, initiative and responsibility. All three involve being willing to work, even when the pay-off may be intangible or in the uncertain future. Feelings of pride and a sense of accomplishment are the best rewards of all.

"All right then, I won't ever again offer my child a bribe to get him to cooperate with one of my requests. And he won't ever again lift a finger around here to help me! Now, whose move is it?"

Well, I'm glad you asked. It's *your* move and the sooner you make it, the better. You must play Brer Rabbit and outfox your young Brer Fox.

Begin by listing some privileges your child enjoys and now takes for granted. Any activity which is available to him regularly, but which has not been earned, can be defined as a privilege. The list might include having friends over, riding a bicycle, going out to play after supper or being allowed to stay up later then usual.

Make another list of the chores and responsibilities Brer Fox avoids so cleverly. This list might include putting away his toys, taking his bath, doing his homework, emptying the trash and walking the dog.

Now you have made two lists, and he still hasn't lifted a

finger. Don't get excited. The next step is to look at each item on the lists and ask yourself the musical question, "When?" For the first list, for example, ask, "When does he like to ride his bike?" For the second list, ask, "When do I want him to take his bath?"

Put the lists side by side and there you have it! By connecting the items accordingly, you can make rules such as, "Before you can play your stereo (list 1 item) in the evening, you must take your bath (list 2 item)." Or, "Before you can ride your bicycle after school, you must change your clothes and take the dog out for a walk." Put only one item from the list of privileges into each rule. You can include more than one item from your second list if that seems reasonable. For instance, one rule at our house is that my 12-year-old son must take a bath, do his homework and straighten his room before he works on his models in the evening. It doesn't matter to us exactly when he does the chores or in what order. We don't remind him, but we check to see that his chores have been done and sometimes apply a little "quality control" before he is allowed to play.

So make some rules, because rules are a parent's most indispensible tools. This is also known as the "Godfather Game," because you are making your child an offer he can't refuse.

Or, *can* he? Sure, he can, and he *will*. *Every* child will test *every* rule ever made. Like chemists trying to discover what solution a substance will dissolve in, children will put rules to every conceivable test, but there is one substance in which no rule will dissolve, and that is . . . consistency.

By consistency I mean enforcing rules under all but the most unusual circumstances. I do not mean that a rule must be enforced in the same way every time (see In Defense of Inconsistency, page 38). If a rule has many exceptions; if a child discovers that a rule does not withstand the "stress tests," then it is not a rule, but simply a wish.

Also involved here is the issue of trust. If you establish rules and then fail to enforce them, can you be depended on in other ways?

These methods may not yield the kind of instant results that bribes do, and they require patience, a rather old-fashioned virtue. But, as Brer Rabbit said, "I never promised you a briar patch."

Painless Punishment

Even before they become parents, most people have fairly fixed ideas about punishment. One of these is the notion that punishment must involve a certain degree of discomfort. Extending this idea, many people seem to believe that, within certain limits, as the discomfort increases, so does the strength of the message to the child—ten slaps on the rear will go further toward eliminating undesirable behavior than two slaps; three weeks under "house arrest" will produce more of a lasting change for the better than three days, and so on.

This philosophy has probably filtered down from days of old when "badness" was thought to be a symptom of demonic possession. In those enlightened times, demons were persistent rascals. Once they set up housekeeping inside someone, they would move out only if the person were made to endure intense, and often fatal, scourging.

It is this reputation that causes us so much confusion when the need to punish arises. But punishment does *not* have to be painful. In fact, it is probably better for all if it causes as little discomfort as possible.

We should punish to make two things clear to a child: "I don't like what you did," and "I am in control here." It isn't necessary to say those words. Whether you spank, send the child to her room, or take away a privilege, those are the ideas you communicate.

Furthermore, it is not important that you cause pain in the process. In fact, the more painful the experience is for the child, the *less* likely it is that she will hear the message.

So, let's set the record straight. If a child is "bad," bad things do *not* have to happen to her. Punishment should not be regarded as retribution. It does not have to induce suffering, guilt or remorse. In fact, punishment should, and can, be "good"—for all concerned.

Consider, for example, the act of setting a two year old in a chair after she has committed some dark deed (throwing jello on the wall). Believe it or not, it is irrelevant whether the chair is wooden or upholstered in soft velvet. It does not have to be straightbacked, nor must it face a corner.

It also makes no real difference whether the child sits for two minutes or twenty, except that a two year old forgets why she's sitting after two minutes. Finally, attempts at extracting apologies or promises of "I'll be good" before commuting her sentence are meaningless.

The act of putting the child in the chair says all that needs to be said. Where she is put and for how long have little bearing on whether the child will "do it again." *Every* two year old will do it again. Count on it.

What matters is the parent's willingness to take action and be assertive (as distinguised from aggressive). When the child throws jello on the wall, you respond immediately by putting her in a chair. This communicates strength and authority in a firm, yet gentle, way.

If you invest your energy in trying to keep the child in the chair for any particular length of time, you have missed your own point. Even if the child gets out of the chair immediately, you have still said what you needed to say. If you fight with the child over how long she must sit, you are then saying, "I'm not sure who is in control here, you or me."

By the time she gets out of the chair, you should be facing in some other direction. If you are lucky and she waits for you to give her permission to get down, wait no longer than two minutes. If she looks ready to get down before then, say, "You may get down." Stay one step ahead of the game. If you consistently take the lead, she will learn to look to you for guidance.

A Parent's Best Friend

Question: What are kitchen timers for?
Answer: They alert the cook when the food is done.

Wrong! This simple machine was not designed with the kitchen in mind at all. The so-called kitchen timer is actually a parent's best friend, an indispensable aid in the proper raising of children.

This was known in Biblical times, but the knowledge was lost because of a slight error in interpreting an oft-quoted passage from the Good Book. I'm referring, of course, to "spare the rod, spoil the child."

It is now known that "the rod" was an ancient clock. A rod some three feet long was set in the ground, and its shadow was measured at intervals to calculate the passage of time — hence, a timer. The actual meaning of this passage is clear: The author was exhorting parents to use a timer when things get rotten.

Kitchen timers, the portable kind, should be standard issue to all parents. There is not a more versatile and handy tool for raising children.

A kitchen timer can be used to organize activities. It helps young children understand the concept of time. It will, upon demand, establish routines and define limits. It supplements, enhances and reinforces the parents' authority and helps everyone detour around power struggles.

Last, but not least, it is a virtually infallible way of communicating when "time's up." In other words, a timer can help with all those tasks parents try to accomplish using words alone — the "in-one-ear-and-out-the-other" method, which has never proven reliable, especially not with preschoolers.

The timer makes unnecessary that repetition of oneself *ad nauseam* that has come to be called the "nag" — another way of putting the cart before the horse.

Below are seven suggested uses for timers. Come down off the wall, moms and dads, your troubles are over. Well . . . almost.

(1) Use a timer to signal "when." For instance when the child can go outside. Take the timer on trips to serve as an audio-visual answer to, "When are we gonna be there?" Instead of repeating "in just a little while," set the timer and let the ringer do the talking.

(2) Timers are an excellent way of defining how much time you will spend playing with your child before going back to your chores or taking a much-needed break. Mom or dad says, "I'll play blocks with you until the bell rings. Then I have to stop and go back to my work."

(3) Is there a struggle in your house every morning to get your child dressed and out of the house on time? Play "Beat the Bell!" Lay out his clothes the night before, set the timer when you wake him up in the morning, and make a game of getting dressed before the bell rings. If more encouragement is needed, make him an offer he can't refuse: "if you have all your clothes on before the bell rings, you may ride your bike when you come home." The "prize" should not be something extra special or out of the ordinary. Just a privilege that has been, up until now, taken for granted.

(4) The timer will answer the question, "Can I come out of my room now?" which the child usually begins asking within 30 seconds of being sent there. Stop playing warden. Set the timer when he goes in (five to ten minutes will suffice for most infractions), and tell him that he may come out when the bell goes off. Use the time to call a friend on the phone. After all, how many opportunities do you have for five minutes of uninterrupted conversation?

(5) Use the timer as a prompt for getting chores done. Before: "I've told you twenty thousand times to pick up your toys and take them to your room! If I have to tell you one more time I'm going to do something irrational!" After: "I want to see if you

can pick up your toys and have them put away in your room before the bell rings."

(6) The timer can answer how-much-longer questions, such as, "How much longer can I stay in the tub, play outside, bounce on my bed, play in the toilet, drive you crazy?" For example, my daughter likes to read in bed before going off to sleep. "Yes, Amy," we tell her, "but you must turn off your light when you hear the bell."

(7) The best use of all is when mom or dad (or both) want a little time to be alone (together?). This is known as Mother's (or Father's) Time-Out and is easily set aside with the help of a timer. "Now it is quiet-time for everybody in this house. I want you to play in your room until the timer says you can come out. You may take a nap if you want to (very sneaky)." Nothing compares with a few moments of peace and quiet in the middle of an otherwise hectic day.

Some timers give a barely audible "ding." I'd recommend purchasing what's known in the industry as a "long-ring" model. They're more than worth the slight increase in price. Remember, "A *watched* (timed) tot never spoils."

A Matter of Timing

Of all our many responsibilities as parents, the most demanding is the job of teaching our children the distinction between acceptable and unacceptable behavior. Learning this distinction is, likewise, the most difficult task of childhood. There are no options here — the child *must* learn, and we *must* teach.

Praise and punishment are the two sides of this coin. Praise is good stuff. It feels as good to give as it does to get. Punishment, however, is generally thought of as a negative event, so it often ends up feeling as *bad* to give as it does to get. No one likes to punish, but sometimes it must be done. We muddle through a myriad of approaches (or avoidances) as we grapple with this problem. We reason, threaten, take away privileges, yell, ignore, give menacing looks, spank, confine the child to a chair or room, assign unpleasant tasks, criticize, plead and cry. Each approach works sometimes; none works every time. Our hearts are just not in it.

I would like, therefore, to propose an alternative called Time-out. Time-out is painless, so you need not feel guilty about invoking it. Time-out can be used without fear of damaging a child's self-esteem. Most important, Time-out works! It works for the parent (it teaches!), it works for the child (who doesn't really want or like to misbehave) and it takes the pressure off of everyone.

First, select a safe (child-proofed) place where a child can be isolated for a short (three to five minutes) period. The place itself must not be threatening (dark) or painful (hot, stuffy). Consider half-baths, an out-of-the-way chair, the child's room or any other convenient space.

Use a kitchen timer (portable) to define the period of isolation. This relieves you of playing "warden."

Third, draw up a list of misbehaviors, and post it on the refrigerator door or some other easily visible place (it is irrelevant whether the child can read). The items on the list should be stated concisely and concretely. For example, "*Saying 'No' when you are told to do something,*" as opposed to "*being disobedient*" or "*not listening.*" Start with no more than five items. You can always add to the list later, if need be.

Explain Time-out to the child as simply, specifically and briefly as possible. The explanation must not be punishing. Present Time-out as "the way it's going to be," rather than "the last straw" or "you're in for it now." Go over the list, explaining that when one of the behaviors occurs, she will be taken (or sent) to the "time-out place," to stay until she hears the bell. She may come out any time after the bell rings.

Then, when a list-behavior happens, say, "Running in the house is on the list. You must go to your room for Time-Out."

Disregard apologies, changes of heart ("O.K., I'll pick 'em up"), verbal abuse, promises ("I won't do it again"), tantrums or physical resistance. If the child needs your "help," *take* her to Time-out—firmly but gently.

Disengage yourself from the problem once the door is closed and the timer is set. Do *not* respond to pleading, tantrums, running water, flushing toilets or deathly silence (but don't forget to child-proof). If she opens the door before the bell rings, reset the timer and close it.

After the bell rings, the child may open the door *when she wants to*. Don't position yourself outside, ready to confront or comfort, and do *not* engage in long conversations about the misbehavior.

Remember: no reminders, warnings or second chances. Do not refer to Time-out as though it were something to be dreaded. It is a constructive way of communicating limits and authority to a child.

As is the case with many other things, it's all a matter of timing.

PART TWO

It's Only a Stage

Birth to Eight Months: Infancy

"The first eight months of a baby's life . . . is probably the easiest of all times for parents," Burton White says in *The First Three Years Of Life*. "If they provide the baby with a normal amount of love, attention and physical care," he adds, "nature will pretty much take care of the rest. . . . Nature, almost as if it had anticipated the uncertainties that beset new parents, has done it's best to make the first six to eight months as problem-free as possible."

Dr. White certainly makes it sound easy, doesn't he? Still, some infants are "easier" than others. Researchers who study newborns have found vast differences in temperament, activity levels, how much and how loudly they cry, their reactions to different forms of stimulation, how much and how soundly they sleep and how "sensitive" they are to the environment.

While more generalizations can be made about infants than about children at any other age, their differences far outweigh and are, in the long run, more significant than their similarities.

Every infant applies himself in different ways and at different times to the many facets of growth and development. One baby may develop a true social smile sooner than another. But the baby who was slower to smile may be quicker to crawl. He may still be crawling when the early smiler gets up and walks. In fact, by the time a baby is six months old, it often looks as if he has "chosen" one or two particular areas of his development to concentrate on. Put three six-month-old children in a room together and you are apt to see one working diligently on learning how to creep, another spending most of her time experimenting with sounds, while the third is working intently to develop his finger dexterity and eye-hand coordination. While each baby's timetable may vary considerably, however, the *sequence* of development is fairly predictable.

Personality traits emerge sooner than many parents expect. For instance, by the middle of the second month, babies express definite likes and dislikes, particularly in terms of what they enjoy looking at, how they want to be held and how much stimulation they need and can tolerate.

In short, each and every human infant is fascinating in his own right. He begins to define who he is and what he wants from you during the first few weeks of his life.

The following topics are of special interest and concern to parents of infants during the first eight months of life.

Pacifiers

There are two schools of thought regarding the use of pacifiers. On the one hand (usually the right) is the pro-thumb school (Thumbers), a group of purists who promote the thumb as a natural, built-in tranquilizer. The thumb, they say, is more convenient than a pacifier, and babies who suck this digit practice independence and self-control. Thumbers maintain that pacifiers are artificial and warn that children can become dependent on them.

Proponents of the pacifier (Pacifists), point out that a pacifier can be taken from a child after a certain age. Furthermore, pacifiers do not push against the roof of the mouth and upper gum as thumbs often do.

Both points of view seem reasonable, and each has its merits. There are two reasons for giving a pacifier serious consideration: first, it can supplement an infant's sucking needs and second, it can quiet the "fussies."

During the first months of life, the need to suck dominates the infant's limited behavioral repertoire. Beginning as a survival-oriented reflex, the need to suck comes increasingly under voluntary control after the second month of life and gradually diminishes in strength over the next 10 to 16 months. In most cases, it disappears completely by age 18 months.

The sucking instinct is definitely stronger in some infants than in others. Most infants quickly discover the hand-to-mouth connection and by their second month spend a significant portion of their waking time mouthing various parts of their hands. By this time, they also attempt to put anything they grasp into their mouths.

Except when a child's safety is involved, there is no reason to interfere. An infant's need to suck should never be denied or obstructed, unless, of course, the object to be sucked constitutes a threat to the infant's safety. For an infant whose sucking need is especially powerful, a pacifier can be a worthwhile supplement to her hand, her mother's breast or the bottle.

Until she is six to eight weeks old, baby may have some difficulty keeping the pacifier in her mouth. And some infants, regardless of how fussy they are or however strong their need to suck, refuse to accept pacifiers altogether.

With all this in mind, I offer the following recommendations:
• If your baby discovers her thumb (or fingers), don't in-

terfere and don't attempt to substitute a pacifier. In the first place, it will probably be rejected. Keep in mind that when an infant is sucking on part of her hand, two parts of her body — mouth *and* hand — are pleasurably stimulated. When she sucks on a pacifier, only *one* part of her body — her mouth — is pleasured. Once an infant experiences the added benefit of hand-sucking, she's not likely to settle for less.

• If your baby has periodic bouts of the "fussies," she may be signaling a need for additional sucking time. If she doesn't make the hand-to-mouth connection, try introducing a pacifier.

• Use pacifiers sparingly, perhaps only during baby's fussiest part of the day (this usually occurs in the late afternoon or early evening). The conservative approach will diminish the odds that she will develop a prolonged dependence on it.

• Don't use a pacifier to "hold off" your baby's next feeding. If she's hungry, feed her.

• If your baby isn't particularly fussy, doesn't find her thumb and seems content with the amount of sucking she's getting during feedings, then there's no reason to offer a pacifier. Lucky you.

• By no means should a pacifier be used *every time* a baby cries between feedings. If your baby is obviously uncomfortable or bored, pick her up and comfort her. Pacifiers are not a substitute for cuddling.

Crying

Some babies cry a lot. Some cry very little. But all babies cry. Sometimes fussiness is caused by a readily identifiable source of discomfort: the baby's hungry, has stomach cramps or is in an uncomfortable position and needs rearranging. Other crying is unrelated to physical discomfort and seems to be an attempt at self-stimulation — a way of asking for attention. Some crying can't be explained in terms of discomfort *or* deficiency. Sometimes babies cry for the sake of crying, for the "just because" of it all. Perhaps this is baby's way of reminding himself of his existence — talking to himself, so to speak.

By the end of the third month, most mothers have become quite sensitive to their babies' crying language and can identify the differences in tone and volume that mean "I'm hungry," as opposed to, for example, "I'm bored."

Most babies have regular periods of fussy crying, often in the late afternoon or evening. This daily upsurge in crying usually wanes by the fifth or sixth month.

Here are some suggestions for calming a fussy baby:

• Holding and gently rocking a crying baby will calm all babies some of the time and some babies all of the time. Every baby has his definite likes and dislikes, and you may have to experiment with different positions, rhythms and rocking techniques until you find the right combination for your little one. Music often has a calming effect. If you don't have any recorded music handy, or if you happen to feel creative, sing to your baby while you rock him (singing, because it enhances language development, is actually preferable).

I find that most infants like to be held upright so they can look over your shoulder. Sometimes it's easier for them to fall asleep in that position too.

If you don't have a rocking chair, or if a gentle back and forth motion doesn't seem to do the trick, sit on the edge of a bed and bounce gently up and down. Both of my children preferred this to the motion of a rocking chair.

• Swaddling, or wrapping baby snugly in a blanket, may help him relax. Some infants, however, don't like being physically restricted. Others are soothed by swaddling as long as they are held and rocked at the same time.

• Pacifiers can be helpful with some babies (see Pacifiers, page 56).

• Burping. If no gas is released, try again in three to five minutes. A howling baby tends to swallow air, which adds to his discomfort.

• One of the most useful baby-care products I have tried is called a Snug-Li. Snug-Li is a cross between a knapsack and the traditional Indian papoose carrier. In a Snug-Li, baby can be carried either in front or back. Either way, it leaves the adult with both hands free. Unlike most other backpack carriers or slings, Snug-Li supports even the tiniest head. In addition, Snug-Li grows with the baby (to enlarge the pack, you just take our some of the tucks in the soft, washable corduroy) and can be used comfortably until the baby is eighteen months old or so.

Having used Snug-Li with both of our children, Willie and I know that it's pleasant and satisfying for both parent and child. By the way, the fear that too much cuddling and physical closeness encourages overdependence is groundless. The opposite is true: the more secure a child feels as an infant, the more readily he will move away from his parents when the time comes.

Snug-Li is sold in many infant stores and can be ordered by mail. Write Snug-Li, Route 1, Box 685, Evergreen, Colorado, 80439. This has been an unsolicited testimonial.

Fathers

With the exception of breast-feeding, there is nothing mothers do that fathers cannot do just as well (take it from me). The obsolete notion that mothers can better fulfill their babies' needs has encouraged mothers to feel more responsible for their children than they actually are, while it has caused fathers to feel insignificant and excluded. Without a doubt, there are differences in the ways mothers and fathers interact with their children. Each parent brings a unique set of personality factors into the child-rearing situation, and each contributes invaluably, though differently, to the child's growth and development.

Several studies have shown, for instance, that babies show no innate preference for one parent over the other (with the exception of breast-fed babies). Other research shows that babies whose fathers are actively involved in their upbringing tend to be more outgoing, less fearful of strangers and new situations, more willing to accept challenges and generally more assertive. I suspect these findings have less to do with fathers *per se* than with the fact that it's more stimulating and enriching to have two actively involved parents than just one.

Since males have not generally been brought up to think of themselves in the primary parent role, many fathers feel awkward and inept around their children at first. But a father who *chooses* to be relatively uninvolved, or whose wife discounts his significance, usually ends up feeling as though he is on the outside looking in at the mother-child relationship. Almost inevitably, this father develops jealousy and resentment toward the child. Often his reaction is to put even more distance between himself and his family by becoming increasingly involved in his occupation.

The other side of this coin is the mother who feels overly protective of her role as primary parent. It is usually easier to get a somewhat reluctant father involved with his child than it is to get a possessive mother to loosen her grip. The overprotective mother generally ends up feeling as though she is raising her child in a goldfish bowl—she feels trapped, helpless, isolated, overly responsible and usually ineffective. Suffice it to say that both an uninvolved father and an overly-involved mother interfere with a child's overall growth and development.

Postpartum Blues

It's not uncommon for new mothers to experience a sense of letdown and depression soon after the birth of a child. The "blues" may come and go in the form of mild, infrequent bouts of uneasiness and anxiety, or they may be frequent and intense enough to require professional help.

The postpartum "blues" are probably a combination of several factors including:

• *Disappointment* at discovering that motherhood isn't the earth-shaking, consciousness-raising event it is sometimes cracked up to be. Maybe mom is a little shocked at her baby's wrinkled, rather flabby appearance, having expected her baby to look for all the world as though she stepped out of a baby-powder commercial.

• *Fatigue* at being wakened one or more times night after night and being constantly on call for another human being who is not only helpless but seems to have a talent for making messes.

• *Adjusting to a new lifestyle,* new routines and new priorities (including the fact that her own interests seem to be moving further and further to the back of the bus).

• *Changes occurring in her relationship with her husband.* Perceptions and expectations of one another are modified. Consequently mom may experience a sense of loss and feel that "things will never be the same."

• *Doubts* about whether she is really cut out to be a mother or whether parenthood is what she wants for herself. Almost every new mother goes through a stage in which she feels somewhat resentful toward her baby.

Any or all of these, combined with the rather helpless realization that "there ain't no turning back," can be temporarily unsettling to a woman's self-esteem.

In addition to getting as much rest as you can and saving time for yourself and your marriage, new mothers should talk to other mothers. Express your feelings. You'll be surprised at how comforting and reassuring it is to find that other women experience similar emotional upheavals.

And here's some advice for the new father: get involved! Pitch in! Offer to help with changing, bathing, feeding and everything else that goes into taking care of the baby. If your wife seems reluctant to accept your help, it's probably because she feels she should be "all things at all times" to her child. If that's the case, gently point out to her that the two of you are in this thing together. If you must, insist that she let you help and even at times take over. Her reluctance may also be a way of testing your continued commitment to her. When the baby wakes up in the middle of the night, get up with your mate and talk softly with her while she feeds the baby. If the baby is bottle-fed, take a regular turn at the "night-shift."

The more involved you are with the baby, and the more supportive you are of your wife, the less isolated she will feel and the more resistant she will be to the postpartum "blues." Therefore, the more involved she will be with you. How about that?

Can You Spoil an Infant?

Not a chance. There is no such thing as too much closeness (except in cases where a mother's anxious over-involvement with the baby dominates her life to the exclusion of husband, interests, friends, and so on).

Most experts agree that you can't spoil an infant, but I'm afraid that many parents, and mothers in particular, have taken this to mean that a baby must be picked up and comforted every time he cries. This just isn't so. There are definitely times when baby will cry (see Crying, page 57), not because he is uncomfortable or needs attention, but simply for the sake of crying. When this seems to be the case, it is perfectly all right to let him fuss by himself for a while.

It won't take much time for you to know, from the sound of your baby's cry, what, if anything, he needs from you. If the cry is an attempt at communication, then he should not be left to "cry it out." You should attend to him and make every reasonable effort to comfort him. Your responsiveness to his needs helps him develop a trusting attitude toward the world and toward you in particular. A sense of trust and protectedness gives him the freedom to be curious, explore the world and become assertively independent.

Most babies cry themselves to sleep, at least for a time. Crying at bedtime helps them dispose of tensions that might disrupt the transition from waking to sleeping. There is no reason to interfere with this type of crying either. For your own peace of mind, though, you may want to look in on a crying baby every five minutes or so from the time you put him in his crib until he is asleep. If his crying becomes more insistent, pick him up immediately.

On occasions when you're not sure whether your baby is crying for you or not, always give him the benefit of the doubt. Studies have shown that babies whose parents respond quickly to their cries for attention feel more secure and, consequently, cry less and less with the passage of time. They also tend to less demanding and more self-sufficient as they get older.

Feeding

Most newborns require a feeding every three to five hours. Initially, baby's tummy won't discriminate between daytime and nighttime, but somewhere toward the middle or end of her second month, she may suddenly give up her three a.m. feeding and sleep from around eleven p.m. till nearly six the next morning. Don't count on it, though. She may not sleep through the night for many months to come.

Feed your baby when she's hungry. Although some pediatricians continue to favor a strict four-hour feeding schedule, most child development experts agree the so-called demand schedule makes more sense. Actually, the term "demand" hardly fits. Infants don't make demands. When they are hungry, they cry, simply because that's their way of expressing physical tension. Being made to wait until someone else decides its "time" for them to be hungry only makes them feel frustrated and insecure.

Your baby's internal feeding schedule will be fairly well established by the end of the second month. She will still have her off-days, however, and you will need to stay flexible.

Between baby's fourth and sixth months, your pediatrician will probably advise you to introduce solid foods into her diet. Some babies take quickly to solid food at this age and seem to enjoy experimenting with new tastes and textures. Other babies, particularly breast feeders, reject solid food at this age and possibly for several weeks and even months to come.

Don't ever force feed an infant. Even at this early age, the attitudes you have about food will be communicated to your baby. If mealtime becomes associated with tension, and if questions of *how much* or *what* baby eats become issues, she will acquire a negative attitude toward meals. If this happens, I can virtually guarantee that the family dinner hour will become more and more of a battleground as she grows older.

Introduce new foods one at a time. Baby is less likely to resist a new taste if you offer it near the beginning of a meal, when she is hungriest. Small portions help her get used to a new taste more gradually.

By the time she is six months old, baby will take great pleasure in feeding herself "finger foods" during part of her meal. At this age food is a sensory adventure, and baby will experiment on almost everything you give her to eat—mashing, smearing, crumbling and hurling it to the floor.

Bottle-fed babies are usually able to hold their bottles by the time they are six or seven months old. But even though baby will prefer to hold it herself (and should be allowed to most of the time), it isn't a good idea to let her take a bottle to bed at night or at naptime. Mealtime is for eating and bedtime is for learning how to go to sleep. Babies who take bottles to bed quickly develop a dependence on them which can persist well into the second and even third year of life. In addition, the milk from a bedtime bottle can more easily adhere to baby's teeth, resulting in a form of tooth decay known as "nursing bottle syndrome." Finally, closeness between parent and child at mealtime is important throughout the first year of life.

Breast or Bottle?

Before your baby is born you will decide whether to breast or bottle feed. In making this decision, don't be taken in by the myth that breast-fed babies are more secure and happy than bottle-fed babies. The quality of the mother-infant relationship is enhanced when breast feeding is successful, but nursing is *not* essential to this interaction. No evidence supports claims by advocates of breast feeding that nursing provides a more secure foundation for healthy psychological development. If a woman would rather not breast feed but feels that she *must* in order to be a good mother, she won't do herself or her baby any favors. Furthermore, this unreasonable pressure reduces her chance of successful breast feeding.

In my estimation the advantages of breast feeding are purely practical. It is more convenient. It requires no preparation or paraphernalia. Breast feeding is a lot less time-consuming. Breast milk is pre-heated to an ideal temperature; you never have to worry about storage, and breasts don't require sterilization. Breast milk is free and replenishes itself. Breast milk is non-allergenic; some physicians believe that breast milk may prevent later allergic reactions to cow's-milk products.

Here are answers to some frequently asked questions about breast-feeding:

(Q) Is breast milk healthier than commercial formulas?
(A) Commercial formulas attempt to duplicate the composition of human milk, and overall the similarities outweigh the differences. The differences, though subtle, do favor mother's milk.

(Q) Are breast-fed babies more resistant to disease?
(A) Apparently so. Until an infant builds up his own defenses

against infection, he relies heavily on antibodies from his mother for protection. Many of these antibodies are present in colostrum — the yellowish, protein-rich substance secreted from the breasts for the first few days after birth — as well as in breast milk itself. These protective factors temporarily immunize the baby against a broad range of infectious agents.

Breast-fed babies suffer milder and less frequent episodes of diarrhea and have fewer respiratory and gastro-intestinal illnesses than bottle-fed babies. These effects are more pronounced in babies who have been nursed for more than five months.

(Q) Do bottle-fed babies gain more weight than breast-fed babies?

(A) On the average, bottle-fed babies are larger and heavier at one year than breast-fed babies. This is sometimes seen as a sign of good health; actually bottle-fed babies gain weight more quickly than they grow in length. In breast-fed babies, the two measures tend to be in better proportion. In brief, bottle-fed babies are more likely to be overweight.

Breast-fed babies have more control over the feeding process. When they stop sucking, the mother stops nursing. On the other hand, bottle-fed babies may be encouraged to continue drinking even after their hunger has been satisfied. Bottle-fed babies are usually started on solid foods much earlier than breast-fed babies. Introducing solids prematurely can also contribute to excessive weight gain.

Bottles should *never* be used as pacifiers. Babies should be fed *only* when they are hungry, and not necessarily every time they cry. Having a fat baby is neither cute nor desirable. Excess weight can slow a baby's developmental progress. An overweight baby is more likely to become an overweight child, and later, an overweight adult. Being overweight is not healthy for humans at any age.

(Q) Are there any other dangers in bottle feeding?

(A) Bottle feeding can be extremely dangerous when the water supply is unclean, refrigeration is inadequate or preparation of the formula is not carried out under sanitary conditions. If the formula becomes contaminated, the baby is exposed to serious infection. Diluting the formula to save money can result in malnutrition. Mothers who bottle feed need to be cautious about overfeeding and refrain from adding solids to the diet prematurely. There is nothing *inherently* dangerous about bottle-feeding. In fact, modern formulas are quite close in composition to human milk and promote healthy development.

(Q) Are there women who should **not** breast feed?

(A) Women with active tuberculosis or chronic infectious diseases should not nurse. A nursing mother should consult her physician before taking any kind of medication. Women who commonly use alcohol, marijuana, cigarettes or coffee should ask their doctors whether these substances might have adverse effects on a nursing infant.

Some mothers (very few) have an inadequate milk supply, making nursing difficult or impossible. The most common causes of milk shortage, however, are depression, anxiety and fear of failure. All can inhibit the flow of milk. As I said before, a woman who pressures herself into nursing, but who would rather not, is stacking the deck against success. Don't let your ego get involved in this decision. Do what you feel most comfortable doing.

For additional information about nursing, contact your local La Leche League. There are quite a few good books on breast feeding, including *Nursing Your Baby*, by Karen Pryor (Pocket Books), and *The Womanly Art of Breast Feeding*, published by the La Leche League.

Sleeping

Sometime toward the middle or end of her second month, your baby will probably begin sleeping through the night, much to your delight. In most cases, she will still require an eleven p.m. feeding, after which she may sleep until five or six o'clock the next morning. The first time this happens, you will probably wake up in the middle of the night wondering why you haven't heard from her. Check on her, if it will make you feel better, but don't *under any circumstances*, wake her up.

There is *no* need to whisper or walk on tiptoes while baby sleeps. Your baby will sleep quite soundly and restfully while life goes on at a normal volume in your household. In fact it's more important to turn down the level of stimulation while baby is *awake*. An excess of noise and visual activity can provoke distress in an infant and even overwhelm her defenses, making her irritable and disrupting her schedule. If baby is constantly or frequently exposed to a high level of stimulation, she may fail to settle into a routine.

By four weeks of age, the tonic neck reflex (TNR) becomes established. The TNR, or "fencer's pose," is a characteristic posture of all babies and is in evidence until sometime around the fourth month. When on her back, the baby will turn her head to a preferred side (85% turn to the right) and extend the same-side arm outward. Her opposite arm will be bent, with the hand usually resting on or near the chest. Thus, the "fencer's pose."

In addition to preferring that her head be turned to a particular side, your baby will also show definite preferences in sleeping positions. With some experimentation, you should be able to determine whether she prefers sleeping on her stomach or her back. In either case, it is best to satisfy her natural inclinations. There is absolutely no substance to the idea that babies are more likely to choke when on their backs or smother when on their stomachs.

By the end of the third month, your baby may have eliminated her eleven p.m. feeding and be sleeping about ten hours a night. *Now is the time to begin using a consistent bedtime.* A routine will not only help your baby anticipate when bedtime is coming, but will also give her an opportunity to wind down from the activity of the day. Then she is more likely to accept bedtime when it arrives.

With or without a routine, your baby may cry after you put her in her crib. It's not unusual for babies to cry themselves to sleep, and many seem to sleep more soundly if they are allowed to cry for 10 or 15 minutes after being put to bed. You need not interfere with this unless her cry is obviously distressed.

Many babies continue, even after the third month, to waken for short periods during the night and fuss or make noises. These semi-waking periods are part of a normal sleep cycle. Baby requires no attention during these times, and left to her own devices, she will find her way back to sleep in short order. On the other hand, you can condition your baby to wake up completely and repeatedly in the middle of the night by handling or feeding her every time she does.

If your baby hasn't started sleeping through the night by this time, don't try and force the issue by keeping her up as long as you can in the evening. The best way to encourage a long sound period of sleep at night is to put her to bed in the evening at the first sign of fatigue. When a baby is kept up past the time when she should have been put to bed, she will have more difficulty falling asleep, her sleep will be fitful and she will be more irritable when she wakes up.

At four months your baby will still take two or three naps during the day. By the fifth month, however, there may be days when she takes only one nap. Even so, it is best to put her down for a second rest period, even if she doesn't actually fall asleep. You will certainly need it and an additional quiet time won't do her any harm either.

By the eighth month most babies sleep 12 hours a night and take just one nap during the day. (Some babies, however, take two naps until they are nearly one and a half.) Around the eighth month, many babies, regardless of how cooperative they have been in the past, begin protesting at bedtime. By this time, baby crawls, sits well without support and pulls herself to a standing position. Her mobility stimulates her interest in exploring the environment. This is an exciting time for baby, and she may be unwilling to cease all activity when you call an end to her day. In addition, eight month olds are more likely than either six or 12 month olds to become upset when separated from their mothers, so you may have some problems at bedtime.

This is a time for gentle firmness. Adhere to the bedtime routine you have established, and regardless of her protests, let baby know that bedtime is an irreversible fact of her daily life. Your decisiveness, your firm resolve and the control you demonstrate in this situation will be an ultimate source of comfort and security for your baby.

Eight to Eighteen Months: the Toddler

For children between eight and eighteen months old, the world is changing rapidly.

By his eighth month, a typical infant sits upright on his own, crawls, pulls himself to a standing position and may even sidestep around the perimeter of things (cruising).

Improvements in eye-hand coordination and finger dexterity also take place. For instance, it is now possible for him to pick up small objects (buttons, crumbs, and so on) between his thumb and index finger (pincer grasp). This stimulates his interest in the world of tiny things and correspondingly increases the risk of injury.

During these ten months the child makes tremendous gains in motor, communication and intellectual skills. It is a period of "tooling," when the infant outfits himself with the skills and information he will need to begin mastering the environment.

These maturational events are truly groundbreaking. They are the seedlings of self-sufficiency. For the first time in his life, the child can do a significant number of things on his own.

Driven by an insatiable appetite for discovery, he propels himself from place to place, putting the pieces of the puzzle together into a coherent "picture" of the world as he knows it.

He has become an explorer, a collector of information, an active participant in the overall scheme of things. His one all-consuming purpose is to *know*, to penetrate the mysteries of the universe. Why? Because it's there!

Shrinking Violets

This new freedom, as always, has its price. At the same time the child is experiencing this acceleration in motor, perceptual and intellectual skills, her mother is probably calling the pediatrician asking why her baby is so reluctant to separate from her in the presence of other people. And why, her parents ask, does baby constantly check on them, as if she were afraid they will vanish at any moment.

There are several reasons (or one reason in several parts) why children this age seem so eager to try their wings one moment and so fearful of venturing away from their parents the next.

For starters, the ability to explore the world on their own rearranges their priorities. The qualities of *things* — their texture, taste and movement patterns — are of prime importance to them now. In the short span of several weeks, the world becomes a radically different place, and the prospect of venturing out by themselves into this alien landscape is both exciting and frightening. It's exciting because of the exhilarating sense of accomplishment that goes with opening a new door; it's frightening because taking those first steps into unknown territory is risky. A child of this age wants to take those steps, but not until she makes certain that her primary security-figures are still there. That's you, moms and dads. You are her insurance policy!

Up until now, most of what she has seen, heard or touched has been courtesy of her primary caretaker (usually mother) who carried her, brought things to her, moved objects within her grasp, played with her, and so on.

Mother has been synonomous with gratification of the infant's needs for food, comfort and stimulation. And, from the child's egocentric point of view, their identities have been blended. She has not distinguished "ma-ma" from "me."

As the infant discovers that she can do things on her own, a sense of separateness from mother begins to develop. This is the first stirring of a sense of identity — the beginning of self-consciousness.

For the first time in her life, the infant has a *choice*. Now that she can, to a certain degree, control the distance between herself and her mother, she must decide how close she needs to be. She must balance her need for security and the urge to become ever more independent.

The child is pulled in two directions simultaneously. One voice says, "Hey, kid, you can do it yourself!" If she answers that call, she gives up some of the security that goes with having mom right there to do everything for her.

The other voice pleads, "No! Not yet! It's too much to deal with all by yourself! Get mom over here before she slips away forever!"

How well the child resolves this conflict depends on the answer to one critical question: *How responsive and supportive is the environment to the child's explorations and inquiries? Is her primary experience exhilarating or frustrating? Are her discoveries joyous or painful? Do her caretakers* assist *or* obstruct *her in her playful work? Is her environment stimulating or boring?* Her future is in *her* hands. How often are they slapped?

For a time, the child seeks to restore her equilibrium by gravitating closer to her mother. She seems to intuit that her link with her mother is vital, that mother's presence is essential to her continued security.

Not surprisingly, other people become one of the most threatening elements of the child's universe. They tend to move in on her before she has a chance to size them up, and they often want to snatch her out of her mother's arms and into their own. Her only protection is to cling and scream.

Unfortunately, because few adults understand the reason behind these rebuffs, grandparents often feel hurt, fathers often feel angry and mothers frequently feel responsible for everyone else's hurt feelings.

The following question and answer illustrates the clinging-toddler phase. Throughout the book I will use this question and answer format to elaborate on solutions to typical problems parents may encounter.

(Q) I am the mother of a delightful but very mother-oriented one-year-old boy. He gets upset sometimes if I just leave the room. He won't let anyone else hold him, if I am in sight. Sometimes, not even his daddy. Needless to say, this gets very frustrating for me at times. I nursed him until he gradually weaned himself at eleven months, and I wonder if this contributed to his being so clingy. I thought letting him nurse for as long as he wanted would promote independence.

(A) When you leave the room, panic sets in because *he* is not controlling the separation. It's one thing for him to crawl away from you; another entirely for you to walk away from him.

And yes, breast feeding can promote the growth of an independent spirit, but so can bottle feeding and being held and comforted and so on. But, before a child can take those first tentative steps toward independence, there must be no question, no lingering doubt whatsoever in his mind, about whether you will remain close at hand. He must reassure himself that you will stay there until he doesn't need you to be there any longer.

If he wants to cling, let him cling . . . if he wants only you to hold him, *you* hold him. The more receptive you are to his expressions of need, the shorter this phase will last.

The evidence clearly shows that the harder the child has to work to keep mommy close, the more clinging he will ultimately become. This does not mean that putting a child in day care or leaving him with a sitter must be traumatic. At those times it is best for mommy to hand him over quickly. The longer mom hangs on and hangs around, the worse things become.

If, instead of closing in on him with outstretched arms, people will just sit and wait, he will eventually get around to approaching them. If they make no sudden movements, he might hang around long enough to make friends. At this somewhat fragile time in his life, he will feel most comfortable when closeness happens on *his* terms.

Magical Mischievous Tour

Sometime between eight and fifteen months, a child discovers that the world is full of magic and that she is one of its foremost magicians. When a child becomes a magician, the old saying that "The hand is quicker than the eye" is never more true.

Around this time, parents find cryptic messages scrawled on the walls in lipstick, pages torn out of the family Bible, the contents of the toilet in the tub, all the books out of the bookshelf, all the clothes out of the dresser, and the kitten in the refrigerator. The magician's quick hand is, of course, the child's. The slow eye belongs to the parent.

Parents don't seem to mind at first. They laugh and praise the young magician for her tricks. "Isn't she cute?" they say.

Then they become jealous because the child's magic is better than their own. They make their faces go red, their eyes grow cold, and begin applying the old quick-hand to the slow-rear, just to prove they haven't lost their touch. "Isn't she awful!" they say.

The young magician tries in vain to make the old ones understand. She invents more tricks, pulls more pranks, performs more and better feats of legerdemain, only to be reminded of her slow-rear. The young magician learns fear, and this is her Waterloo. Fear will slow the best hand down. The old tricks stop working. In years to come, when all magic is forgotten and the eyes get slow, she will be ready to become a parent herself.

Toddlers and parents live in different worlds. Toddlers live in a wonderland of enchantment, where every sight, sound and touch is new. Everything that happens in a toddler's world happens for the first time ever. And it all happens just for her, and no one else.

The small child does not have words enough to explain the amazing things that happen in her world: no words to tell why paper shreds and glass breaks. There are no reasons for anything except "just because." No wonder children believe in magic.

The Cookie Tree, a children's book by J. Williams, (out-of-print, Parent's Magazine Books), should be required reading for all parents. It begins:

> The village of Owlgate was quiet, and tidy, and nothing surprising ever happened there. Everything had a place, and everything was in its place. Everybody knew why things happened, and everything happened just as it was supposed to. Nothing surprising ever happened because nothing surprising was *allowed* to happen. "That way," said the people of Owlgate with satisfaction, "You always know where you are."

Parents live in Owlgate. They have reasons and places for everything. They work hard all day long giving reasons and finding places and making sure things stay put. Words have taken the place of wonder, and if something cannot be explained, then it isn't there.

When an egg falls on the floor, a twelve month old may see a piece of the sun spill out. A parent sees a mess. Tiny fingers reach for things that come apart or fall and bounce and break or splatter and spread out in all directions. In Wonderland, it's magic. In Owlgate, it's mischief, and mischief is the reason for messes. But in mischief, there is also the thrill of discovery, and therein is the reason for Learning, with a capital "L".

The young child does not have enough language to understand the "Whys" and "Why Nots" of things in Owlgate. She discovers the world by experiencing it directly. The splat, bounce and break of things are defined by the child's own action, and it is through action that she discovers all the different things the world is made of, how it comes apart, what's inside, what happens to what, and when, and how, and so on. She must experience *all* of this before she can ever make sense of the words we use to describe the "Why." And so, messy, magical mischief is also the reason for Language, with another capital "L".

Children who are allowed to roam about being mischievous learn that words can also be used in magical ways. They learn language quickly, and they learn to use it well. Mischief also flowers into imagination and creativity. A scientist is, after all, nothing but a grown-up magician, making the mischief of progress.

The mischievous nature of a child's curiosity is the force underlying all learning and accomplishment. At the same time, it is also the source of many childhood accidents.

During this critical developmental phase, it is essential that certain physical boundaries be established, both to insure the youngster's safety and to provide an environment which encourages exploration, learning and creativity.

The toddler cannot predict what objects and situations in her surroundings could be harmful, nor is she able to appreciate the value of irreplaceable or expensive household objects. Her nature *demands* that she touch, feel and taste everything within reach. Powered by an insatiable appetite for discovery, she is most alert when in motion, exploring for novelty everywhere.

At some point, it is inevitable that this exploratory drive will aim her toward fragile ceramic figurines, antique glassware, the African violet collection, and everything else within reach.

By far the easiest, least expensive and most sensible way to reduce the obvious risk is to put treasures well out of her grasp, as soon as she is able to reach them. By child proofing your house in this way, the boundary between "can touch" and "don't touch" is established by the child's own physical limitations. Parents who fail, or refuse, to child proof must constantly watch where their toddlers are and what they are doing. These parents never have a moment's rest, and their children cry a lot.

I can hear you now: "But Michelle has to learn what she can't have, and besides, it took me years to collect all these things." You have a point. A child must eventually be taught the difference between what she *can* have and what is out of bounds. But the connection between reaching for a certain object and a slap on the hand or a loud "No!" is established (maybe) only at great cost to the parent's peace of mind and the child's sense of confidence and capacity for learning.

Protect your valuables and breakables by putting them up and away. Chasing a child around the house, frantically trying to cover all the bases, is a losing proposition. You cannot win, because a child has more energy and determination.

Relax and enjoy your parenthood. Feed your child's curiosity, but not with African violets. Provide her with a variety of objects around the house of different colors, shapes, and textures (but not a lot of toys). Let her "discover" things that are unbreakable. When she finds them, teach her to play "put-and-take" with you. Play *with* her, not *against* her.

Before you visit friends or relatives, call and ask if they would help make the visit a more relaxed and pleasant one for all concerned by gathering up their treasures and closing off certain rooms. "Please don't think me rude, but I'd so much rather talk with you than worry what Michelle is doing behind my back."

Child proofing is even more essential when objects and substances that are potentially harmful to children are involved. Cleaning fluids, paint, medicine, pins, glass bottles, plastic bags, aerosol sprays and tools must be out of a child's reach. Electric sockets can be fitted with child-proof plates. A lock on the door to the basement steps is a deterrent to broken bones and concussions. Lower cabinets can be fitted with child-proof latches or cleaned out and made safe and fascinating to crawl into.

Playpens

Playpens have their pros and cons. Used wisely and sparingly, a playpen can perform a service for parents and provide baby with a safe place to play. If misused, however, a playpen can be an obstacle to normal development. When left unattended in playpens for long periods, children become bored and frustrated and even depressed.

Use of a playpen after a child is old enough to walk is even more damaging. There is evidence suggesting that children who spend lots of time confined in cribs or playpens suffer delayed speech and are less coordinated. A handicap imposed on a child in this way is not easily undone.

As your child grows, use the playpen less often and for shorter periods. When he begins crawling, give him plenty of free time to roam and explore. The more a child is able to exercise his curiosity, the more intelligent and creative he will become. If you use the playpen while ironing, washing or cooking, set it up near you and talk to your child while you work. This keeps him alert and stimulates language development.

Protect your child's health by providing a safe environment for him to explore without having to experience frequent frustration, boredom or punishment. By establishing these physical boundaries in a loving, sensible way, you not only insure his safety, but promote his development and provide a more relaxed atmosphere for yourself.

(Q) My son is eight months old. I've kept him in a playpen for short periods during the day ever since he was three months old. Until recently, he occupied himself quietly until I returned, but those days seem gone. Lately, as soon as I put him down in the playpen, he screams bloody murder and doesn't stop until I pick him up. This poses a dilemma. I can't be with him every minute of the day. There are times when I'm busy and can't give him any direct supervision, which he definitely requires since he's already pulling himself to a standing position and sidestepping around furniture. In other words, I can't leave him alone, and I can't not leave him alone, but he hates the playpen, so what can I do?

(A) Before we go any further, you need to understand that playpens aren't for play, not in the real sense of the term. They're boring. Boredom is about all that's possible in a fenced-in area no larger than 20 square feet. The more stuff a parent heaps in to occupy the child, the more cluttered the pen becomes, further restricting the child's ability to play.

Before they begin crawling, most children will endure the relative isolation of a playpen for brief periods during the day. Crawling, however, stimulates an infant's desire to explore the world. Once a child discovers what constant excitement there is to be had by moving from one place to another and then another, getting his hands in the stuff of what's happening, he's not likely to sit quietly in the confinement of a playpen. Add to his curiosity the fact that a young toddler (between eight and twelve months) isn't at all clear on how much closeness he wants with his mother. This business of getting around on his own is a barrel of monkeys, but it also takes him further away from the one he loves the most.

So this age child is caught in his *own* dilemma. He wants to be with you and he wants to be away from you, doing his own thing. He feels a bit better if he's in control of how much distance there is between you and when separation happens. If *you* walk away, he yells, but if *he* crawls off, it's goodbye. Just to make sure you haven't vaporized while he wasn't looking, he checks on you every few minutes. If a stranger's about, he makes straight for you. When you put him in a playpen, his anxiety level goes up. Not only is he not controlling the separation, but he can't get to you.

Now, I'd like to digress a moment and tell you a true story about baby ducks. Several days after they hatch, a brood of ducklings will line up behind their mother and follow her wherever she goes. This is called *imprinting*. After a few weeks of parading about in this fashion, they break away. Ethologist Nikolaas Tinbergen wanted to see what would happen if imprinting was tampered with. Small barriers were placed around a controlled course the mother duck walked. The baby ducks had to scramble over the barriers. The result: these frustrated ducklings persisted in following their mothers long after other ducklings had moved off on their own.

Before a child can begin making motions of independence, he must know, beyond any shadow of a doubt, that his mother will be easily accessible in time of need. Playpens frustrate the newly mobile child in the same way Tinbergen's barriers frustrated the ducklings. Frustration makes a child all the more determined to keep his mother close.

So, by using a playpen to get away (for whatever reason) from a child who is moving under his own steam, you increase the likelihood that he will cling to you long after most children are becoming more self-sufficient.

One of the nicest gifts you can give you and your child once he begins crawling is a child-proofed living area where he can crawl and putter and get into safe, unbreakable things to his heart's content while you relax, knowing he's all right. He'll experience the same insecurities as other post-crawlers, but instead of getting stuck, he'll go right on through them.

The rule is a simple one:

> After crawling, don't confine,
> Childproof for your piece of mind,
> Allow your child to freely roam,
> In the safety of his home.

Biting

During the first year of life, biting is almost exclusively exploratory in nature. An infant's mouth is as primary an organ of discovery as her eyes and hands. Furthermore, the sensations that arise from using her mouth to explore things are extremely pleasurable, so nearly everything gets put in there.

An infant learns to discriminate tastes, textures and

temperatures with her mouth. She finds out what is food and what isn't by chewing on everything from ash trays to zwieback.

She finds answers to the same questions about people: "I wonder what Mommy tastes like. Uhmmmmm. Not bad! Hey, she does interesting things and makes new sounds when I do that. Wonder if she can do that again?" As an added bonus, infants discover that biting relieves teething pain and feels plain ol' fashioned good (by gum!).

Sometime close to the beginning of an infant's second year, biting becomes a way of being playful and affectionate. It's a way of saying, "Hey! I love you! Wanna play?" Biting continues to feel extremely pleasant and the child doesn't know that you are not sharing her ecstasy.

As your toddler grows into her second year, she encounters an ever increasing number of frustrating situations. She may well make the discovery that by biting down very hard on something, she can release the tension she builds up in these encounters. A likely target is the someone most closely associated with her frustration.

Here's the tale of a typical biter and my advice to the bitee:

(Q) I have a fourteen-month-old son who bites me several times a day. Sometimes he is clearly frustrated at me, but sometimes he bites for no reason whatsoever that I can see. This has been going on for the past three months and is getting worse. I have tried spanking, putting him in his crib and biting him back (on the advice of my pediatrician), but nothing seems to get the message across. He only bites **me**, and I don't understand what I could be doing to cause it. What should I do?

(A) Don't take it so personally. He's not biting you because he hates you or because you deserve it—he bites you because you're *there*. You are the person most available to him. You frustrate him more than anyone else because you share more time with him than anyone else does. Throw in the fact that toddlers are easily frustrated, have no self-control and love to sink their chops into things, and you have a typical fourteen month old biting his typical mother.

Your son bites you at different times for different reasons, but he continues to bite because you have never insisted that he stop. Thinking about what you might be doing to "cause" his biting has prevented you from acting on the biting itself.

Put yourself squarely in the present tense and *do* something about it. As much as possible, prevent his toothy attacks, even playful ones. Surely you can tell when one is on the way. Every time he tries to bite you, regardless of whether he succeeds, face him and say "No!" Then pick him up, turn him around so he faces away from you and take him to his room. Put him down on the floor (*not* in his crib) and walk away, leaving the door slightly ajar as you go. He will "hear" the message clearly.

When he emerges, he will probably come straight to you. If he wants the reassurance of being held, hold him, but do not talk about the incident. If he is still agitated and tries to bite you again, repeat the sequence.

When he learns that you are not a willing victim, he may try biting someone else. Again, whether or not you are able to prevent that from happening, say "No!" and put him in his room. If you aren't at home, improvise with an out-of-the-way chair.

By the way, biting a child back sometimes works, but more often it makes the problem worse. I don't recommend it because it confuses the child, puts parents in the position of modeling the behavior they want eliminated and is likely to start a lets-see-who-bites-harder contest.

This method should bring noticeable improvement within two or three weeks. As usual, commitment is the key. And that, my friends, is the honest tooth.

Weaning

(**Q**) I'm having trouble getting my 15-month-old son to give up drinking from a bottle. He drinks from a cup during meals but cries for his bottle whenever he is upset or sleepy. Should I refuse to give it to him?

(**A**) There is much to lose and nothing to be gained by struggling with your son over a bottle. When we make issues out of things like bottles and thumbs and security blankets, children are likely to become more desperate in their attachment to them.

Allow your son to drink from a bottle whenever he expresses a need for that source of comfort. Insist, though, that he follow your lead and drink from a cup during meals.

I strongly advise against filling a bottle with milk or any sugar-sweetened liquid, such as iced tea or fruit punch. The sugar in these drinks greatly increases the risk of tooth decay. As his parent, the decision regarding what goes in the bottle is yours. Fill the bottle with unsweetened (strained) fruit juices or water only, and stand firm on this decision.

Your son will probably lose interest in the bottle quickly if you begin to water down the juice and gradually (over several weeks time) increase the proportion of water until you have eliminated the juice altogether. During this process, leave the bottle, filled with water or the water-juice mix, where he can reach it without asking for your help. He will eventually forget about the bottle, and so will you.

Just the other day, I read an article by a pediatrician which dealt with weaning. His opinion was that continued use of a bottle beyond the twelfth month will almost surely "stunt" (my translation) a child's social and emotional growth. Consequently, he said, the child might continue to "baby talk," require diapers long after the time for potty training was due or indulge in some other infantile fixation.

This is malarkey, genuine and undiluted. There is no clinical evidence to support such a claim, and the doctor's statements will ultimately create more problems than they pretend to solve.

That these statements were made in a national publication by a man of medicine virtually assures their acceptance by the average reader as fact. Chances are that readers who are parents of toddlers who still suck an occasional bottle will become scared that the bottle is warping the child's psyche.

Thereafter, when the child wants a bottle, the parents will become anxious. They will fabricate excuses, diversions and persuasions, all to little avail. Having met with no success, they may become upset. At this point, the child will become upset too, because his parents' behavior is confusing. Lacking the words to express his confusion and frustration, he may well have a tantrum. Predictably, his parents will feel guilty and give him a bottle.

Nervous, insecure parent . . . confused, screaming child . . . and an issue that will continue to cause distress in their relationship—that Dr. So-and-So is able to manufacture so much out of so little attests, perhaps, to his skill. On the other hand, one might recall a comment, attributed by some to Bobo: "The difference between experts and the rest of us is that experts are forever talking about things we can't see, while the rest of us see things they never seem to talk about."

By no means should a child who is capable of drinking from a cup be encouraged to continue drinking from a bottle. Nor should parents offer a bottle as a pacifier. Allow a child access to the bottle, simply and naturally. As with so many things, the more of a problem you make of it, the more troublesome it will become.

Strange Fruit

At this age, everything in the environment is fascinating; everything must be explored. Infants will touch everything they can, and anything that passes inspection by the hands goes to the mouth. Then, after being tasted, chewed and mashed, if the tongue says, "Yes!" it is swallowed.

(Q) My daughter, 13 months old, has begun playing with her b.m.'s. If I don't catch her in time, she scoops it out of her diaper and smears it all over herself. What is most upsetting, however, is that she also manages to eat some of it. The word "aakey" usually keeps her from putting certain things in her mouth but hasn't worked with this. I try to keep my cool, but I'm just about at my wits' end. What can I do?

(A) Given the opportunity, most children will play in their bowel movements, just as they will play in the dirt from your potted plants, the sugar bowl, oatmeal or whatever. To an infant, b.m. is no different, except she made it! How delightful! Another bit of magic from the world's greatest magician.

Rest assured, however, that there is nothing abnormal about this behavior (at this age), and nothing is wrong with your child. Furthermore, aside from what we might *think*, there is nothing dirty or unhealthy in what she is doing. Granted, it's a mess, but no more than a rather exasperating example of recycling.

Nor is there anything especially significant about this behavior. The trap, however, is that we big people have an outstandingly negative reaction to it. We are repulsed, disgusted and infuriated at having to "swab the decks" afterward. No matter how we try to keep cool, it's difficult not to let our true colors show, thereby tipping the child off to how significant the whole business is to us.

Make a big deal out of something, and it will become a big deal. Any exaggerated reaction on your part (spanking, screaming, fainting, throwing up) is probably going to set the stage for a repeat performance.

I would suggest that you maintain as much cool as you possibly can and wash her up without any special to-do. If you need a break to recover, then put her back in her crib and "take five" (or fifteen).

Eighteen to Thirty-six Months:
The ~~Terrible~~ Twos

TERRIFIC!

The "Terrible Twos." I have this image of children screaming, throwing things, playing in make-up, eating soap, breaking china figurines, saying "No!" to everything — running amok while mommy and daddy chase, grab, spank, yell, scream and run amok.

To be honest, it's not exactly an image. It's a vivid memory starring the inimitable, one-and-only Eric!

To live with Eric today is to wonder if this is the same child who didn't sleep through the night until he was two and a half years old. Can he be the same child who was dubbed "Mr. Mad" or "Mr. Tough," depending on his mood, by two of our best friends? Ten years ago no one could have convinced me Eric would be sane when he was 12, much less the mellow, thoughtful, delightful person he is today.

It took me several years and another child to learn that two year olds can be terrific. There's no question about it, their reputation for terrible-ness has, to some extent, been earned. But the difference — terrible or terrific — is not primarily a matter of child. It's a matter of parents.

The most dramatic and significant transition in the development of an individual occurs between 18 and 36 months. It is a revolution, involving sweeping changes in the child's experience of both himself and the world. Naturally his behavior takes some dramatic turns as well.

It can be one of the two most stressful periods in the overall life of a family (the other being pre- and early adolescence). *But it doesn't have to be.* As with most endeavors, the key is understanding, which can help make the "Terrible Twos" *terrific.*

"I'm a Me!"

Infancy is a time of almost total dependency: Infants must rely on parents and other people to feed, bathe, dress, change and even move them from place to place. Between eight and eighteen months, children make rapid gains in cognitive (problem-solving), motor and communication skills. They begin to experiment with cause-and-effect relationships, discovering in the process that they can manipulate the environment. Children between eight and eighteen months old are collectors of information. They are constantly on the move, harvesting information with their hands, eyes and mouths. At this stage the process is random. The child has no blueprint — just an irresistible urge to know everything there is to know about every "thing."

Throughout her meanderings, the toddler absorbs an incredible amount of information without, however, knowing how to use it. Then sometime around her eighteenth month she realizes she can act upon the world to *make things happen.* At this point, her guidance systems switch from automatic to autonomous pilot. Before she was an explorer; now she is an *experimenter,* an alchemist, out to create history — her own, at the very least.

From this moment on, things will happen the way *she* wants them to happen, and people will do what *she* wants them to. Full speed ahead and damn the torpedos!

As the "sense" of her environment is revealed, the toddler begins interacting with it to *solve problems.*

A 14 month old, seeing a jar of cookies on the kitchen counter, will reach in vain and point and yell until someone comes along to lend a hand. Several months later, this same child pushes a chair to the counter, climbs up and gets the cookies for herself.

As her mind expands, so does the world. In no time she is consumed with excitement, with no way to express her exhilaration except through activity. She is "on the go" constantly, "getting into everything," climbing up on counters and bookshelves, climbing down out of her crib and carseat, always one step ahead of you. She won't take "No" for an answer. After all, what does a "No" amount to when everything else around and inside her says "Yes!"

One of the limitations nature has imposed on two year olds is a gap between physical and intellectual development, favoring the latter. Their bodies have not caught up with their minds. They may be able to "see" the solution to a problem but may *not* be able to make their bodies perform the movements required to carry it out.

For example, a child may know that a certain shape fits into one certain space in a puzzle but be unable to make her fingers work well enough to maneuver it in.

This frustrating disparity is often expressed in sudden, violent and sometimes destructive tantrums. If someone tries to lend a helping hand, the child usually becomes more enraged. She would rather do it herself and fail than watch you succeed. That's understandable. Whose growth is this, anyway?

Sometime around the middle of her second year, a child realizes, in one relatively sudden, insightful moment, that "I'm a Me!" It's the flowering of individuality, of self-consciousness. It's the biggest "Aha!" of all.

For the next 18 months or so, the child is aborbed in defining who "Me" is and establishing clear title to that psychological territory. Much to her dismay, she also has to accept that her boundaries are not all-encompassing. She is not the only "Me" in the world, but one of many.

At this age, children must learn that independence means less than being able to do as they please. Just as the task of the child is to establish her autonomy, her parents' task is to begin the process of socialization, of communicating and enforcing boundaries, limits and rules governing the child's expressions of independence.

It gradually dawns on the child that in order to become a separate, independent person, she must give up a corresponding measure of her attachment to her parents, mommy in particular. These sacrifices and disappointments can be overwhelming. For all these reasons, the third year of life is a relatively uncertain time with few dull moments.

Dominated by the central question of whether it is more advantageous "to be or not to be (independent)" the child is a study in paradox: clinging and cuddly one minute, demanding and defiant the next. She wants the best of both worlds and slowly, painfully realizes that there is no middle ground.

This is the second time the infant has had to deal with issues of separation, the first time having occurred between 8 and 12 months (see Shrinking Violets, page 68).

"Don't Leave Me!"

It isn't unusual to see 18 to 24 month olds respond to the temporary uncertainty of this internal revolution by demanding more visual, physical and verbal contact with their parents. For a short time they may need someone to hold on to, a port in the storm.

If parents are fairly tolerant of the child's determined clinging, the child will, within several weeks or months, gain all the reassurance he needs to move through this metamorphosis.

(Q) My son is 20 months old. He has been a delightful baby, but has recently started clinging to me somewhat more than before. He follows me around the house and wants to be held a lot. How should I handle this?

(A) His need to cling expresses, paradoxically, the realization that he is a person in his own right. He has made the discrimination between "me" and "you." He now knows you are not a blend: you are *two* people, and that fact places "psychological space" between you. This distance allows him to begin testing his wings — to move farther away from you and into the environment.

This metamorphosis, however, carries with it a certain degree of uncertainty at first. You no longer seem as available and accessible as before. He doesn't know how great the distance between the two of you will become. He wants to fly, but he does *not* want to give you up. He doesn't have the words to express his anxieties, so he follows you from room to room, reassuring himself that this change is not the beginning of some disappearing act. In other words, before he can take one giant step forward, he must take one baby step back. In this game of "Mother May I?" your answer must be, "Yes, you may." If he wants to be held, hold him. If he wants to follow, let him. The fewer obstacles in his path, the less disruptive this transition will be for everyone in the family.

The Roots of Rivalry

The birth of another child into the family during this period of transition can be very disruptive. The older child often acts as if the new baby were a tiny trespasser who sneaked into the picture while her back was turned. Feeling that this small someone will take her coveted place next to mommy and not yet fully committed to giving it up, she rushes back to close the gap.

(Q) We have a two-and-a-half-year-old daughter and a six-month-old son. Off and on, ever since the baby was born, the oldest has asked us to rock her at bedtime. She has also asked to have her bottle back. We have **not**, in spite of several tantrums, given in to these requests, but now there's an additional problem. We began our daughter's toilet training about five weeks ago, with success at first. A couple of weeks ago, however, she began refusing to go if prompted and now she has more accidents than not. They seem to be almost deliberate, and this disturbs us. She now says she wants to be put back in diapers. Should we stop for a while, put her back in diapers and try again later?

(A) One thing your daughter does *not* need, regardless of what she asks for, is permission to backslide.

The problems you describe are typical of what can happen

when less than three years separates one child from the next in a family. When the second child was born, your daughter's position in the family shifted, creating anxiety and distracting her from the basic task of growing up. The reasons for this kind of developmental stall are not at all mysterious, and such problems are generally short-lived. The arrival of the baby reminded your daughter, at an inopportune time, of how wonderful it was to be carried and rocked to sleep and bottle fed and have mommy change her diapers.

Your task is to reassure her that her place in the family, while different and changing, is still secure and protected. And you must convince her, firmly but gently, that she has no choice in the matter.

The time for bottles, being rocked to sleep and wearing diapers has passed. She is obviously ready for training, and it should proceed. Keep her in training pants, except at night. She probably won't stay dry at night for another year. *Do not* follow her around asking if she needs to use the potty. When she gets up in the morning, take her into the bathroom, point to her potty and say, "Remember to put your wee-wee and poo-poo in here today. If you want mommy to help you, just call me." If she asks to be put in diapers, tell her that she is a big girl who wears pants during the day and diapers only at night. If she has an accident, change her without a fuss. Then take her into the bathroom and remind her once again where to put her business in the future.

Continue, even in the face of resistance, to relate your expectations to her in a clear, calm voice. I've said it before, but it deserves repeating: the more effectively authoritative the parents, the more successfully autonomous the child.

(Q) We have two boys: one has just turned three and the other is 16 months. My problem is with the older one. He wants my attention almost constantly throughout the day—hold me, read to me, play with me, help me. If I can't go to him immediately, he whines and cries until I do. He's been this way since shortly before our second child was born, but it seems to be getting worse. It is extremely frustrating for us all. What could be the problem, and what can be done about it?

(A) It sounds as though his demands are beginning to dominate the family. It is in everyone's best interest, including his, for you to act, before the problem gets firmly rooted in your lives.

Set aside two specific times during the day: a time with him and a time without him. Perhaps your time with him could be during the younger child's nap. In any case, set aside at least 30 minutes to spend totally with him, doing what *he* wants to do. Take the phone off the hook, and don't answer the door.

For your time away from him — at least 30 minutes — stay out of his sight and relatively inaccessible to him (it may help to have another adult take over during this time). Go to your room and lock the door. Take a drive or a walk. Mom's time out — just for mom.

The rest of the time let common sense tell you whether to comply with his requests for attention. If you can give him your attention without interrupting something else, fine. But if giving him attention means stopping what you are doing, say, "No," (assuming he's not in dire straits). If he acts as though he can't live with that, take him to his room with the suggestion that he "cry here."

I suppose it's the need parents have to be all things to our children that works us into holes like this. "Good" mommies don't make their children cry. "Good" mommies sacrifice everything for their children. Those are the sort of whips we flog ourselves with. But there is a difference between being a "good mommy" and being a slave.

As you dismantle his present set of expectations and start to build new ones, he will yell. He has learned that sobbing brings you around in short order. His crying also means he senses a change in the rules and rituals that govern his relationship with you. The uncertainty of not knowing what's going on or where you are headed will stimulate a healthy amount of distress.

Nonetheless, the best way to help him deal with his discomfort is to chart your course and stay confidently on it.

You might also consider finding a preschool program for him to attend several mornings a week. The break from one another would do you both good.

James Dean

As the second birthday approaches, the child's personality clamors ever more presistently for recognition. Young children have little, if any, appreciation for the virtue of moderation. They tend toward extremes in their behavior, so when the self is discovered, it emerges in exasperating ways.

"I don' wan' to! . . . No!"

Rebellion is nothing less than an expression of the toddler's need to be a separate person and assert her flowering identity to its utmost. It is important for parents to realize that this behavior, in its many manifestations, has a definite place in the

overall scheme of things. However infuriating, it is an exclamation of growth and becoming.

If all this is put in its proper perspective, parents are less
likely to overreact. Keep in mind, parents run the show,
regardless of the child's protests and contrariness. It is our
responsibility to establish limits and enforce them in firm, yet
gentle ways. When we respond to these small mutinies out of
fear or anger, we have, in essence, lost control of ourselves.
This not only increases a child's anxiety, but feeds the fantasy
that she is more powerful than we are. The power struggle that
inevitably ensues leads nowhere.

The patterns established at this early stage in the parent-
child relationship will tend to endure, and as the mold sets, it
becomes more and more difficult to break.

(Q) My two year old has recently started ignoring and testing me
whenever I ask her to do something. Can you tell me anything
about handling this behavior?

(A) What you describe is typical of two year olds. In fact,
rebellion is a healthy ingredient in any child's developmental
process.

Encourage your daughter to recognize your authority and
cooperate with the limits you set by using more than just your
voice when giving directions. For instance, if she ignores you
when you ask that she come away from the television set, move
her away gently. At the same time, repeat your request and
give her something else to do, such as, "Sit down here, and I
will get you some pots and pans to play with."

This "show and tell" technique can even be used with commands such as "Pick up your toys." A child's resistance can be
overcome by gently moving her through the paces, as though
you were physically teaching her what you expect.

Aggression

Two year olds are extremely territorial. The space immediately in front of them, and everything in it, is "mine!" In-
trusions into that territory threaten the child's self-concept
and, therefore, provoke distress. The more passive child cries,
while the more assertive child strikes out in some way. Brief,
but intense, clashes over space and toys are commonplace in a
group of toddler-twos.

As if that weren't enough, they are virtually oblivious to one
another, insensitive to each other's feelings and incapable of
remorse. A two year old can give and take on a limited basis
with adults and older children, but has a difficult time doing

the same with another two year old. Put two or more children of this age together and you have all the makin's for a good fight. But this is nothing to lose sleep over. In a way, their willingness to tangle reflects healthy, expressive personalities.

(Q) We are best friends, writing to you about our children, two girls, ages twenty months and two years. Both children are fairly easy going—until they are in the same place at the same time, that is. When they get together, which is almost every day, they fight constantly. It looks as though they dislike each other. They pull hair, snatch toys away from each other, hit, scratch and refuse to share. This is all the more puzzling because with other children they get along fine most of the time. What's going on, and what can we do to stop it?

(A) You have inadvertently stumbled upon the recipe for Instant Tot-bash: Take two toddlers between 18 and 36 months old. Blend them together for two or more hours almost every day. Sit back. Watch them bash each other. (Warning! This mixture is highly volatile and will, in almost every instance, undergo spontaneous combustion. Onlookers are advised to maintain a respectable distance from this event. The manufacturer assumes no liability and will not accept returns for refund or exchange.)

The level of aggression you describe is not only typical, but heralds the flowering of two healthy, demonstrative personalities.

The most important thing to keep in mind is your friendship. It is the catalyst to the conflict: the friendship brings the youngsters together frequently. The more children this age are together, the more likely they are to do battle. It is actually better, when pairing two year olds, to select ones with similar temperamental characteristics. Two passives or two actives will mix far more compatibly than an active and a passive.

Don't let the friendship be an obstacle to letting the problem solve itself, which it eventually will do. Both of you have an investment in the children's liking one another. Their relationship, had it been affectionate, would have affirmed and strengthened your own bond. But if you want their relationship to be an extension of your own, then their conflict may become threatening to you.

Use your friendship as a way of coping with their rude interruptions. As much as possible, let them have enough space and time to work things out for themselves. At the same time, give each other permission to intervene whenever the warfare seems to be getting out of hand. Two year olds can, and will, hurt each other without ever "intending" to.

When a toy is snatched, gently take the toy away from the snatcher and give it back to the snatchee. Then keep the screaming snatcher away from the snatchee. If need be, remove her to another place until she calms down. If they both go bonkers at the same time, separate them until they relax.

Above all else, keep your sense of humor about you, and be an example of harmony for the children to follow.

(Q) When my two year old has a friend over to play, they fight over toys almost constantly. Today he pushed a little girl down for no reason. I spanked him and sent him in the house. Did I do the wrong thing?

(A) I was intrigued with your use of the phrase "for no reason," because it illustrates how we big people often misunderstand the behavior of children.

When your son pushed the little girl down, he did so for no reason of ours, but just "because." That is the way toddlers are. They fight over toys because they want everything *right now*, and there is only one way to skin a cat, and there are no rules — just things to want — and waiting is not fun at all. That is why at this age, and in this situation, neither a spanking nor any other form of punishment will make any connection. "Reasoning" won't complete any circuits either.

Take time to comfort both the pushee and the pusher. They are both upset, so reassure them that their world is still safe. Then, involve yourself in their play, showing them, with your own actions, how to play side-by-side without a battle. Be a facilitator, a moderator, a Henry Kissinger of the sandbox. Remember, however, that the game is *theirs*, not yours. If things flare up, hold them both on your lap and say soft things.

Will this solve the problem? Not today. But, in time, they will learn moderation and reason. Meanwhile, remember that you are the only one with patience, and use it.

(Q) We have two girls, who are four years and eighteen months old. I've heard that the second born is more aggressive, but this is ridiculous! I actually have to intervene to keep the baby from hurting Audrey, our oldest. If Audrey is playing with something and will not give it up when Molly wants it, Molly will kick and bite and throw things at her. I know that an eighteen month old has very little self control, but what can I allow Audrey to do in her own defense?

(A) It sounds as though Audrey is very tolerant, patient and gentle with Molly, especially in light of the abuse she takes from her. Molly is entering her "first adolescence." During this stage, children tend to be extremely demanding and rebellious and, when frustrated, will often react with a tantrum or some form of aggression. So the situation you describe is not at all unusual.

You are, in some ways, fortunate that Audrey is not younger. If that were the case, both children's self-centered territorial instincts would clash dramatically, and you would be having an even more difficult time.

From this point on, Molly needs, as much as anything else you can give her, the constant presence of a firm, yet gentle, hand. It is time for her to begin learning who is the proper authority in her life and what is appropriate behavior with you, other adults, peers and Audrey.

Audrey should *not* be made responsible for protecting herself against a toddler who knows little about restraint. As much as possible, however, allow the children to work out their own arrangement concerning toys and other things. Tell Audrey that you do *not* want her to strike back when Molly attacks, but that she should protect herself by first getting away from Molly, and second, asking for your help in resolving the conflict.

When a toy is involved, see that Audrey gets it back and attempt to substitute something for Molly. This will not always sit well with her. If she throws a tantrum, take her to her bed or crib (with the side down) or put her on the floor (if carpeted) and walk out of the room. By doing this you will let her know that there are definite, constant rules concerning expressions of frustration that occur when the world does not turn according to her whim.

"The Dracula Syndrome"

Biting, relatively common to toddlers and two year olds, strikes an especially dissonant chord among adults. It is, from our civilized perspective, irrational and barbaric.

When there's a biter in a group, we tend to lose sight of other aggression that might be taking place. The biting becomes the focus of attention and the child who bites becomes a scapegoat. If another child begins to bite, the blame falls on the original biter, who must have "infected" him.

If the biting takes place in a nursery, as is often the case, parents may develop the mistaken idea that the teacher, through neglect or ineptitude, "allows" children to bite. What we need to realize is that toddlers give no warning when they are about to attack — they just attack.

Not long ago, for example, I was asked into a day-care center to observe an 18-month-old "biter." There were five toddlers in the group. I had been in the classroom for about 45 minutes when this child did his "thing." There were three adults in the room at the time. None of us could have anticipated his attack, and we were not able to prevent it.

The child's parents can't do anything about what takes place in the classroom either. In fact, the more responsible the parents feel, the more likely that biting will be talked about in the home and during the ride to and from the center. This attention only increases the odds of his biting again and again.

There is nothing "wrong" with a toddler who bites. He simply has learned, probably through a chance combination of instinct and accident, that his teeth are an effective weapon. Now he must be taught to restrain this impulse — one of many lessons in self-control.

(Q) I am the director of a day-care center and would like your comments on a situation in our toddler classroom, in which there are six energetic and assertive children, ranging in age from 17 to 24 months. Three months ago, one of the children began biting occasionally, usually when another child was trying to take a toy away from him. Despite our efforts to stop him, he still bites once or twice a day, generally when the activity level of the group is high. The biting has triggered a reaction from this group of parents that has been difficult to handle. All of them are up in arms over this and insist that we do something to stop him. He is not an unusually aggressive child in other ways and is not the only child in the room who has bitten. Both the teacher and his mother are beginning to feel defensive. Can you offer any suggestions?

(A) His parents must not talk about biting with him or around him (unless, of course it also takes place at home). It is not even necessary to keep them informed of incidents in the classroom. The less they know, the less fuel they bring to the fire.

Biting is more likely to occur during periods of general excitement, so separate the biter from the group when the activity level goes up. Provide him with a less active alternative until things settle down. When he does bite, or even *tries* to bite, the teacher should face him immediately with a firm "No," then sit him in a chair facing the group. She must do this as quickly as possible, *before* tending to the wounded child. The biter may be allowed out of the chair after the victim is calm and has returned to the group.

More than that, only time can take care of.

Tantrums

I will now demonstrate my truly unremarkable ability to em-
compass past, present and future, all in one ordinary vision.
As I close my eyes and concentrate, the message rises slowly
through the murky waters of time, revealing itself in a burst of
clear light . . . Yes! It is revealed! The Spirit speaks!

*"Two year olds throw tantrums. This has been so since time
began and will be forever . . . so what'sa the big'a deal, anyway?"*

That's a good question, Spirit. Parents tend to exaggerate the
significance of tantrums. Suffice it to say that when adults
make mountains out of a child's molehills, the child will learn
to build mountains.

For instance, some parents feel that tantrums occur because
they have made some mistake in dealing with the child's
demands (which they mistakenly interpret to be expressions of
need). It then stands to reason, if they *are* to blame for the
child's tantrum, that they must right the wrong as quickly as
possible. So, having said "No," they say, "Yes." Or having spanked, they then give the child more than she originally demanded, to keep their guilt at bay.

These maneuvers work. The tantrum stops, the parent is
relieved and the child learns that tantrums are a successful
means of obtaining anything she wants. So she throws more
and better ones.

Other parents react to tantrums with anger rather than guilt.
To them, the tantrum is evidence that the child does not accept
their authority. They see the tantrum as a mutiny and react by
demonstrating their authority on the child's rear end.

The paradox is that a spanking, in this situation, is *not* an expression of authority. It is a display of fear, panic and desperation. Parents who are truly in control and secure in their feelings of authority are aware that an occasional tantrum is normal for any young child. If spanking stopped tantrums, the
tantrums would stop. But they don't; both continue, more and
more often.

Between 18 and 36 months, tantrums are almost a reflex
response to anything that is frustrating. And two year olds are
easily frustrated. They want more than their stomachs can
hold or their arms can carry. In fact, an occasional tantrum is a
healthy expression of the child's need to experiment with being a rebel.

Keep tantrums occasional by reacting to them calmly and
matter-of-factly, in the manner of an authority who is in
control.

When a child of one or two makes a tantrum, simply pick her

up and carry her to her bedroom. Deposit her in her bed. If she still sleeps in a crib, leave the side down so she can get out. If she can't get out, put her on the floor. Then leave, because there is nothing to discuss. If you *must* say something, say, "You may have your tantrum in here."

As you leave, pull the door partly closed. If she comes out before her frenzy has subsided, gently put her back in. When she is quiet and comes out, do not mention the tantrum. It's not important.

It's neat and simple. Do this whenever a tantrum occurs, and they will never become a major issue. Parent is still boss. Child is still child. Molehills are molehills.

Jaws II

(Q) My two year old occasionally bites himself when he is mad because he can't have his way. What can I do to stop him? Does this mean he is insecure, or that something is troubling him emotionally?

(A) To your first question, my answer is, do nothing. Children of this age are largely uncivilized, and the ways they express their anger are, likewise, quite primitive. They scream, throw things, roll on the floor, strike out at objects or people nearby . . . and sometimes they bite. Their targets include toys, furniture, parents, other children and themselves. It is possible to "cure" a toddler of biting other people, but virtually impossible to prevent him from biting himself. In the first place, you can't predict when it's going to happen. It is somewhat like lightning, except this bolt will often strike more than once in the same place (usually the arms or hands).

Parents become alarmed and confused by self-biting and generally respond with one form or another of uncivilized panic. They shriek, run for help, struggle to separate "Jaws" from arm or faint. They are also likely to feel guilt at having "caused" the child to bite himself, in which case the child ends up being held and pampered.

All those reactions send this message from parent to child: "I lose control when you bite yourself." Biting becomes an issue of great significance, and the child capitalizes on the issue as a source of power and reinforcement. Giving a child attention for biting himself makes it more likely to happen again.

So do nothing. Pretend to be busy with something else. If your child shows you the bite marks, tell him how sorry you are that he hurt himself and go about your business. If he breaks the skin, calmly help him wash and apply antiseptic to the area. If there is any doubt about his being adequately protected from infection, call your pediatrician. Watch the wound for festering or failure to heal. By reacting calmly, you lessen the chance that it will happen again.

The answer to your second question is no, he is probably not insecure or emotionally troubled. Many children bite themselves (more than parents are willing to admit). Two year olds "teethe" on themselves purely to play and test your reaction. There are many superstitions about the meaning of "odd" behavior, but often the behavior occurs initially because children are simply children. It continues because parents over-react.

On the other hand, if you live with an older child who has developed this practice into a habit that occurs whenever he is frustrated or a child who bites himself more than occasionally, I recommend a talk with a therapist.

The Bedtime Blues

(Q) We have an 18-month-old girl who has, until lately, always gone to bed (at nine o'clock) very pleasantly, fallen asleep quickly and slept through the night. In the past several weeks, she has become a monster at bedtime. She screams, becomes rigid and goes into a rage when we leave the room. I have always rocked her for several minutes before putting her down. Now, the moment I stop rocking, she starts yelling. This went on for three and one-half hours last night, as we did everything we could think of. Finally she wore herself out in my arms. She has also been waking up briefly in the middle of the night. What have I done to cause this, and what can be done to stop it?

(A) You haven't done anything to cause her screams. Her Jekyll to Hyde transformation at bedtime is the first stage of a revolution commonly called the "Terrible Twos."

Gone are the days when she would smile and coo pleasantly as mommy and daddy put her to bed. Cribs are confining and not compatible with her new way of thinking. Gone are the days when a few minutes of rocking was enough. What right does mom have to stop rocking? None!

She has also figured out that life goes on in the house after the lights go out in her bedroom. It's a trick! How dare you!

To make bedtime go more smoothly, you must first rid yourself of the paralyzing idea that she screams because you have done something wrong. She screams because *you* have done something to *her*, and she will not stand (or lie) for it. There may be no way, short of letting her sleep with you (*don't* do that!), to put her to bed without screams for a while.

Next, keep it firmly in mind that her bedtime exists solely for *your* sake. The importance of putting a child to bed is so daddies and mommies can be husbands and wives again. Bedtime is an exercise in learning how to separate the child from the marriage (see Bedtime Is for Parents, page 161). With that in mind, I recommend that you move bedtime back to eight o'clock. Between 7:45 and 8:00, move her through the preliminaries. Then put her in her crib and, screams or no screams, leave the room. Remember that "in hesitation, all is lost."

I realize how difficult it is to forget you are parents when there's a child screaming in the house. So put yourselves on a schedule. Take turns "checking in" with her every ten minutes. Walk with feigned casualness into her room, say a brief something about going to sleep, lay her back down, give her rigid body a kiss and walk out. As she begins to get the message, you can extend the time between checks to 15 or 20 minutes.

While she rages, you and your husband can talk, play backgammon, read or do whatever you enjoy doing together. Support one another and help one another make the transition from parent to spouse. Real people again! Now *that's* something to look forward to.

(Q) Our 20-month-old son is putting us through some changes. He is becoming more active and refuses to take an afternoon nap. In addition, he has learned how to climb out of his crib. Bedtime is becoming a battle. What can we do?

(A) Before you do anything, you need to understand how important these changes are to your son's growth and development. On the surface, this behavior may appear to be symptoms of rebelliousness, so it's no surprise that you've engaged him in "battle."

But there's more going on here than meets the eye. The transformation taking place is more accurately described in terms of an underlying process—the fertile soil from which this "rebellious" behavior grows.

The metamorphosis from caterpillar to butterfly has begun. Caterpillars fly and babies climb from their cribs. As your son's sense of himself expands, so does his view of the world. Everything takes on new and exciting dimensions, stimulating his wonder *and* his activity level. Who can blame him for not wanting to stay in a crib?

The not-so-simple act of climbing out of the crib is much

more than an athletic event. It requires and expresses a feeling of trust, an irrepressible confidence in his ability to accomplish new things (scale new heights, so to speak), and most of all, it acknowledges the permission he has given himself and senses he has from you to begin uncoupling from you and becoming independent. He no longer has to stay put just because you put him there.

Take the path of least resistance. Instead of trying to make him stay where he is determined not to, begin a gradual change-over from crib to bed. Dismantle the crib (let him help) and put the mattress on the floor. Let him sleep there until he learns the boundaries of the mattress and no longer rolls out in his sleep. Then move him to a regular bed.

You might want to put up a child-proof gate at his doorway, especially if you live in a two-story house. The gate will secure him in his room after you put him to bed, but will allow him to roam within reasonable boundaries until he's ready to sleep. In this way you aren't forcing him to lie down, but you are setting limits on his activity after bedtime. If he stands at the gate and screams, return to his room at regular, lengthening intervals (begin with ten minutes) to calm him down and tuck him in with a firm message about going to sleep. This will take some effort for several days but will eventually pay off.

The best solution to his increasing activity level is to child proof your home, if you haven't done so already. This not only guarantees the child's safety but your peace of mind as well.

As for naptime, trying to make him sleep is a losing proposition. You can still require that he remain in his room for one hour every afternoon, though. Continue putting him to bed for a nap as part of his daily routine. If you must, use the gate to keep him in his room. Once he gets accustomed to this regular downtime, he will probably start napping again. Whether he sleeps or not, use the time for yourself. For the next few years, in fact, the more time you can make for just *you*, the better off *he* will be.

Einstein Didn't Talk until He Was Three

(Q) We are the parents of an active and alert 20-month-old boy who doesn't talk. He has a limited, single-word vocabulary which includes "ma-ma," "da-da" and "bye," but whenever he wants to say something to us, he acts it out with gestures. He has no trouble understanding anything we say to him, but we wonder if he has a problem. Up until now, we've put no pressure on him to talk, but it has been suggested to us that we not do things for him unless he uses words to tell us what he wants. What are your thoughts on this?

(A) A three-word vocabulary at 20 months is not cause for concern. In one sense, your son's vocabulary sounds fairly extensive.

We all have two vocabularies: one active, or expressive; the other passive, or receptive. Our active vocabulary consists of words we use when we talk (or write), while our passive vocabulary includes all the words we understand. We generally understand more words than we use, and in children the difference is marked. Your son's passive vocabulary is probably the more accurate reflection, at his age, of how well he is progressing in language development. From this point of view, he is obviously doing fine.

Well, then, why doesn't he talk more? Probably for several reasons, all having to do with his age.

He stands on the threshold of the "Terrible Twos," a traumatic 18 months in the lives of most children. It is the agony and ecstasy of childhood—and parenthood as well. The child who is almost two views and acts on his world as though he were the center of all experience. He also takes his first, tentative steps toward independence. And tentative they are, since his need to be cuddly and close is still powerful. His need to feel independent is satisfied by being in control of situations—and people. His continued dependency needs are met through involvment with you, his parents. All these needs are, paradoxically, satisfied by not talking. He is able to control certain situations, prolong your involvement with him and receive plenty of attention in the bargain. Isn't he clever?

So cooperate with him, casually and matter-of-factly. Don't try to force him to talk by ignoring his pantomimed requests. That would create a useless and frustrating power struggle. He is, after all, becoming adept at gestural language, an art which will enhance his overall communication skills in the long run.

Talk to him, but don't require him to talk back. When he's ready and has found other ways to satisfy his need for attention, he will no doubt discover that talking works better than charades.

When a child is 24 months old, a speech and hearing evaluation might be appropriate if several of the following indicators are present:

• The child uses less than a 20-word expressive vocabulary.
• His expressive vocabulary is not increasing, or he shows no interest in talking.
• The child is becoming increasingly dependent on gestures.
• He is becoming visibly frustrated in his attempts to com-

municate.
- He does not respond when spoken to nor seem to understand simple directions.
- The child does not show an understanding of what you want him to do when you show him a picture and say, "Point to the puppy," "Show me the ball," or "Where's the hat?"

Three Year Olds

A child's growth, like that of every other living thing, proceeds through a sequence of stages. Each stage, or phase, is defined by new ways of interacting with the environment, and each successive theme is an extension and elaboration on previous ones.

A three year old begins to build a sense of initiative, or purposeful self-confidence, upon the trust and autonomy acquired during the "Wonderful Ones" and "Terrible Twos."

During the 18 months prior to her third birthday, the child was busy forging a clear sense of who she is. As you might expect, her young self-image is fragile, like a clay pot that hasn't yet dried.

The omnipotence she felt as a two year old has turned inside-out. Once upon a time, she ruled the world. Now all she can lay claim to are a few toys and a vague, shifting sense of her identity, and even that small territory is a struggle to maintain. Is it any wonder, then, that three year olds are so easily threatened by such things as the dark, loud noises and bumps on the head?

Owies

Physical injuries, no matter how minor, strike too close to home for the three year old's comfort. Even the slightest pain from a tiny scratch can dislodge the tentative grasp he has on the "me" he feels he must guard so carefully, lest it slip away as mysteriously as it came.

Furthermore, a three year old has no way of knowing that wounds heal, which inflates his fear and feeling of helplessness.

(**Q**) Our usually easy-going three year old has recently started acting more sensitive to pain than he used to be. He gets almost hysterical over a little scratch or scraped knee. I won't even attempt to describe his reaction to a cut. We have tried to get him to realize that his injuries aren't that bad, but it doesn't help. We don't know what more we can do. What suggestions do you have?

(A) Threes (and young fours) have a reputation for over-reacting to mild pain in the manner you describe.

It will do no good to try to persuade your son that his perception of these traumatic events is inaccurate. There are some things only time can teach. The more you do, the more you talk, the more exaggerated his reaction is likely to become. Simply tend to his wound, put your arms around him and sit quietly until he calms down. Your being there is all he needs to restore his misplaced sense of "togetherness."

Isn't it nice to know we don't always have to talk so much?

Fears

Fears are common to three year olds. Leading the list are fear of the dark, of being left alone and of "things that go bump in the night."

Three year olds often misinterpret ordinary events as threatening because of the interaction of three characteristics:

(1) Their need to protect their recently acquired and still fragile sense of identity. As children grow in self-sufficiency, they must come to grips with the anxiety associated with letting go of their parents. Fears dramatize this process. They are symbolic, fantasy-laden expressions of the young child's feeling of vulnerability.

(2) The flowering of imaginative thought. Threes have the ability to conjure up mental images of things real and unreal but lack the ability to control the process.

(3) Their inability to separate *word* from *thing*. If there is a word for something, then it *must* exist. Threes can't separate fact from fiction because both are represented in the same medium — language.

Parents often misinterpret a child's fearfulness as a symptom of insecurity or upcoming emotional problems. They react as if the fear were the child's way of saying, "You guys aren't taking care of me." They feel responsible for the child's anxiety, so they try to protect him from it. Unfortunately the parents communicate their anxieties to the child and actually *increase* his sense of helplessness.

Trying to reason the fear away usually doesn't work either. The rational explanation and the imaginative fear are on separate, incompatible wave lengths. A reasoned approach only heightens the child's sense of isolation: if his parents can't see things as he does, then he really is at the mercy of whatever he thinks is "out there."

The most effective approach is to first acknowledge the fear ("I know the dark can be frightening when you are three years old."). Then identify with the child ("When I was three, I was afraid of the dark too."). Finally, reassure him of your ability to protect him ("I'll be downstairs in the living room and I will take care of you".).

Stay close enough to make the child feel protected, but not so close that your presence validates the fear.

(Q) Believe it or not, my three-and-a-half-year-old son is afraid of newspapers. He says he doesn't like the way they smell and refuses to enter a room if one is there. He is also afraid of other paper products. He won't sit at the table if there is a napkin at his place, won't blow his nose in tissue paper and wants me to clean him after he uses the bathroom. He has become quite insistent about all this and has a tantrum if we do not cooperate. What should we do?

(A) Newspaper is a new one to me, but it isn't any more significant than garden-variety fears of the dark or frogs.

Young children do not see the line we draw between fact and fancy. Their playful innocence makes them vulnerable, for the same process that turns bathtubs into sailing ships can also bring shadows alive in the night. With a bit more exaggeration the child sees himself as a victim of sinister forces beyond his understanding or control.

By accommodating his demands and rearranging the world in order to protect him, you inadvertently become part of the drama, thereby giving validity to his fright. "Newspaper can hurt me. I know it can, because Mom and Dad protect me from it. Other kinds of paper can hurt me too." He can also use this issue to manipulate you and gain control of certain family situations. It is no surprise, for instance, that his fears have disrupted mealtimes and hooked you back into helping him use the bathroom. Power struggles between children and parents almost always involve conflict over bedtime, mealtime or the toilet.

Your son is saying, "I will come to the table only on my terms. I will only go so far in using the bathroom by myself." However, he is not actually in control of himself or the situation. He is convinced his fear is real. The more you cooperate, the more his original insecurities increase, and the more fearful he becomes.

You must help him distinguish between what is real and what is not. It is essential that *you* define for him the way the family functions. While I see no harm in letting him choose for himself whether to enter a room in which there is a newspaper, you must not let his panic persuade you to remove it. About meals and the bathroom, make no concessions. Tell him, "You are one person in this family, and your place at the table will look like everyone else's." Insist that he sit with the family during meals and use his napkin appropriately. Firmly refuse to assist him in the bathroom.

Give the problem back to him. After all, *he* invented it.

Intellectual Growth

Three year olds gradually learn to deal with delay of gratification. A two year old will always choose the immediate reward — even if it is less attractive — over one she must wait for. A three year old can hold off for a short time provided she has something else to occupy herself with in the interval. This ability to postpone gratification indicates a strengthened tolerance for frustration and increased self-control.

Three year olds demonstrate a remarkable memory for past events. When my children were three, they continually amazed me with their ability to describe, in precise detail, events that had happened months before — ones I had almost forgotten and could not recall with comparable clarity.

Threes are also able to retrieve information selectively for problem solving. For these reasons, children of this age show more variety on their approaches to problem situations. If a two year old's first attempt to solve a problem doesn't work, she will often fly into a rage. She sees no other alternative. A three year old, having experienced the same initial failure, is more likely to try one or two other strategies before she gets overwhelmed with frustration.

A three year old learns from her mistakes and uses this feedback to modify her problem-solving techniques. The emergence of trial-and-error thinking is one of the two most significant intellectual events occuring at this age. The other is the flowering of creative, imaginative thought. Threes are suddenly interested in making things. They enjoy coloring, painting, working in clay and building things out of whatever material is available. But more than anything else, three year olds *pretend* and, if left to their own devices, will spend a major portion of their day engaged in self-directed imaginative activity. This timely happening is a perfect compliment to their growing independence and initiative. For the first time in her life, the child is capable of occupying and entertaining herself for relatively long periods.

The three year old uses her intellectual freedom to explore and come to grips with her initiation into the social side of life. Her almost constant imaginative play is a way of practicing and preparing for greater social responsibility. The three year old is literally playing at growing up. This ability to mentally represent entire social scenarios also allows the three year old to keep enough distance between herself and actual events to keep her anxiety level under control and protect her still-fragile self-image.

Imaginary Playmates

One day shortly after my son's third birthday, I sat downstairs listening while he and another child played upstairs in his room. After nearly two hours of animated conversation and much activity, Eric bounded down the stairs. Alone.

"Who were you playing with?" I asked.

"My friend," he said, a gleam in his eye.

"And what is your friend's name?"

"Jackson Jonesberry," he said with obvious pleasure.

I have no idea where he got the name and like to believe it came from the same place Jackson did.

When my daughter was three, she created not one, but a whole group of imaginary friends, including "Soppie," "Honkus" and the inimitable "Shinyarinka Sinum."

The appearance of imaginary playmates is an unmistakable sign of the three year old's interest in peer relationships. With a Jackson Jonesberry or a Shinyarinka Sinum, a child can satisfy this strong need for peer affiliation while at the same time practicing her social skills in a safe and controlled context.

When Eric was three and four, we lived in a rural area where there were few opportunities for play with other children. For nearly two years, he played with Jackson and several other invisible friends. Invisible to Willie and me, that is, for to Eric they were very real. I am certain he could "see" them.

There is no need to worry about the amount of time children spend in this sort of play. Adults should not interrupt or intrude when a child plays in this manner. When it is necessary to interrupt for practical reasons, do so with utmost respect for his "guest." Adults should *never* question the existence of such an invention.

In light of the importance of imagination to social and intellectual growth, I strongly urge parents to keep children this age away from television. It can distract and eventually overwhelm the young child's imagination.

A child watching television learns to depend on something outside herself for creative stimulation. She does not learn to be creative. A child watching television is not preparing for a larger role in life. She learns how to be a spectator instead of a doer, a follower rather than a leader. A child watching television is not practicing independence or exercising any initiative. She learns how to be complacent, dependent, resourceless and irresponsible.

This is true regardless of the program—"Sesame Street" included (see Television, page 207).

Kid Klutz: He Trips, He Spills, He Stutters, He Walks into Walls

During the fourth year of life, children may act as though they are becoming *less* instead of *more* coordinated. Typically, they trip and fall more often, their feet get tangled when they run ("He's got two left feet") and they drop and spill things and generally play the role of Kid Klutz. They may also begin stuttering—repeating themselves, backing up and holding on to certain sounds.

Paradoxically, this physical and verbal awkwardness arises because the three year old is trying to orchestrate thought, language and movement. Up until this time, the child focused on each of these developmental areas in relative isolation from the other two. Now, he is putting them together in a coordinated system.

Whereas before he concentrated separately on learning to walk and to talk, he now tries to walk and talk at the same time. This example, while oversimplified, expresses the essential character of this stage in the child's growth. It is a time of reorganization and integration, and at first the pieces don't work as well together as they did individually.

Unfortunately, parents often react as though the child has suddenly developed a problem. They become anxious, lose patience and try to help the child overcome his "difficulties." All of this makes a problem where there was none. His parents' anxiety tells the child something is "wrong," and minor difficulties become traps. This is particularly true in the case of stuttering.

The general rule is, have patience and be supportive. If the child spills his milk for the thirteenth time in 12 days, instead of blasting his self-esteem ("What's the matter with you! Why can't you do something as simple as blah, blah, blah!"), say something like, "Oh, oh. Here, take this rag and help me clean up. I remember spilling my milk when I was three years old, too."

Stuttering can usually be prevented if parents take the time to listen and show interest in what the child is trying to say. If he starts stuttering, here is what *not* to do:

- *Don't* complete his sentences for him.
- *Don't* say things like "slow down" or "take a deep breath and start over."
- *Don't* discuss his stuttering when he can hear you.
- *Don't* interrupt him or tell him to come back when he is calm and can talk "better."

Talk slowly to a child who stutters. If he has trouble telling you something, ask him questions he can answer in three words or less. If he complains about his stuttering, let him know that sometimes even big people have tralking tubble.

Social Growth

By the age of three, the child's almost intolerable self-centeredness gives way to a more social view of herself in relation to others. She learns to take turns (which preceeds true sharing) and to play *with* (instead of simply around) other children.

Three year olds occasionally act as though they can look at a situation from someone else's point of view. Expressions of empathy are rare, though, to anyone except their primary caretakers and children with whom they are familiar. Three year old playmates comfort each other and are sometimes even penitent when they bruise one another's feelings.

Three year olds can form transient play relationships with other children their age or slightly older. Proceed with caution, however, when mixing three year olds for the first time. They don't understand the value of social foreplay. Instead, they rush into intimate and risky interactions with one another. This causes as many disastrous first encounters as rewarding ones. And first impressions definitely count with three year olds. Children who hit it off well generally continue to do so, while children whose first encounter was filled with friction are likely to have subsequent difficulty getting along.

But close encounters of the worst kind can be prevented if adults are sensitive to the risks involved in putting children of this age together, and if they give the children adequate supervision, structure and guidance until they are playing smoothly with one another.

This is a good age for introducing the young child to group day care. Be careful when selecting a preschool, because the value of the experience depends on the quality of the program. By and large, however, research indicates that developmentally-oriented group care produces (1) an increase in constructive, goal-oriented behavior, (2) an increase in cooperative play, (3) an increase in assertive behavior, (4) improvement in conflict-solving skills and (5) improvement in the child's ability to adapt to new situations (see Choosing A Preschool Program, page 228).

Three year olds carefully observe other children and imitate them. This "monkey see, monkey do" tendency, although exasperating at times, is important to the growth of social skills. On one level imitation is a game, an almost ritual exchange between children which forms positive, cooperative social bonds. On another, it is a way of acquiring problem-solving skills. Researchers have found that once a three year old watches another child cope with a stressful event, she can employ similar strategies to deal with the same situation. On yet another level, imitation is a low risk way of experimenting with new forms of behavior. If they are nothing else, three year olds are experimental and therefore, somewhat unpredictable, little people.

It's a try-anything-once age. They go through this phase of their lives trying on any and every behavior imaginable, seeing if it fits or adds something interesting to either their own image of themselves or that image they see reflected in other people's reactions to them.

The first three years of a child's life are spent building a relatively enduring personality — a basic wardrobe. For the next two years or so, the youngster window shops for "accessories" — bits and pieces of behavior to add variety and spice to her act.

She's likely to borrow these tidbits from anyone, but playmates and older children figure heavily in what she brings home. The three year old's love of mimicry is clearly a sign that she is beginning to identify with other children, and that they are exerting considerable influence as role models for one another.

Episodes of regression to behavior reminiscent of infancy are also common, and all the more so when there's a new sibling involved. These include increases in bowel and bladder accidents, asking for a bottle, using baby talk and wanting to be carried and held more than usual.

Most of these harmless excursions back in time are best handled by looking the other way. However, if several repeat performances in a short period tip you off that a pattern is developing, then it's necessary to intervene authoritatively before the mortar sets.

(Q) My husband and I would appreciate your suggestions on a situation that has us puzzled. Our three-and-a-half-year-old son taught himself to use the toilet when he was just two. Since then, he has enjoyed playing with his diapers, training pants and various articles of toddler clothing, which we let him do. Recently, after being at the home of a friend his age who is not toilet trained, he came home, put on several pair of training pants and wet them, just slightly. He has done this twice since, and we aren't sure what it means. I've also noticed that, on occasion, his penis gets hard when he is playing with putting on diapers or training pants. Should we forbid him to wear them? I might add that we are expecting a new baby in four months. Could this have anything to do with it?

(A) I don't get a sense of anything unusual from your letter. Your son sounds like a typical three year old. Not that lots of threes dress "down" in diapers and old clothing, mind you, but typical in the sense that this age child is imaginative and experimental and enjoys role play.

There is no need to forbid him to play in his old clothes. I would suggest, however, that you convey clearly your rules and expectations about them.

It is probably unwise to let him play with the diapers. He may think he has permission to wet them, especially after the new baby arrives and he notices that his younger sibling enoys this prerogative.

As for the arousal of this penis, keep in mind that a three year old's sexuality is diffuse and capable of responding to any form of pleasurable stimulation. In this case, putting on his diapers and training pants must arouse warm feelings associated with the many pleasurable experiences of infancy—being held, having diapers changed, wetting his pants and so on. Similar physical responses are fairly common in boys and girls (although in a less obvious manner) who suck their thumbs or nuzzle favorite blankets.

This is not cause for concern, and there is no connection between the sensual feelings he has for his diapers and my suggestion that you repossess them.

Lies

A three year old's sense of fantasy is so much a part of her personality that the distinction between what is truth and what is not is hazy. The meaning of "truth" is not *really* clear until a child is nearly seven.

A young child doesn't completely understand the concept of responsibility either. To her, things simply happen, and the extent of her involvement is not always clear in her mind. Therefore, don't expect threes (or even fours, fives or sixes) to be completely truthful. And don't regard it as a moral weakness when they aren't.

This age child is easily frightened into concealing the truth. If the threat of punishment is present, the child's natural defense is to try and avoid pain by saying, "Not me." If this works, the child will feel relief at having been spared from her parents' wrath.

There is also a certain rush of exhilaration at realizing that a concealment has "worked." This exhilaration can be habit forming. The greater the treat and the more risky the concealment, the greater the thrill of getting away with it. And so the child rolls the dice again the next time and keeps on rolling.

Occasionally, the concealment falls flat, and the parents "score" with a spanking. Some of the time, though, it works to at least confuse her parents, and so the child "scores." If the child tries five "hoodwinks," and only one is successful, chances are she will go on playing the odds.

(Q) Our little boy, who is three years old, will misbehave and then when we confront him, deny he did anything. We punish him anyway, but it makes us upset, because he acts so hurt. We wonder if he knows why he is being punished, or if he really believes he did nothing wrong. How should we handle these situations?

(A) Remember that "an ounce of prevention is worth a pound of cure." Don't give a child an opportunity to conceal something you already know he did. Instead of asking, "Did you tear all the leaves off my African violets?" make a firm, positive statement, such as, "You tore the leaves off my African violets. I am very angry. You must clean up the mess and then go to your room." Ask a child no questions, and he'll tell you no lies.

If you see a child misbehave, or if circumstantial evidence points to him as the culprit, don't open the door for argument by asking the obvious question. Extracting admissions of guilt or apologies is not necessary. Save time and trouble by making statements that tell the child you know what happened. Ignore his protests and alibis. You'll be doing him a favor.

When several children are playing together and something goes wrong, it's not worth the effort to play "Who-done-it." Besides, children are quick to make a scapegoat of one child in the group, usually the smallest, or one who has taken lots of blame in the past. They cannot be relied on as impartial witnesses. Where siblings are involved, say, "This happened while you were playing together, and you will both be punished for it." In cases where your child is one of a group, break up the action and direct the disciplinary lesson at your own.

Concealments are less likely if the threat of spanking is not an issue. Punish by taking away privileges — bicycle, outside play, having friends over and so on. It's true that spankings take less time, but in this case they seldom have a lasting effect. On the other hand, it's too easy to let "You can't go outside for three days" slide after the first day, so make the consequence short but meaningful.

Punish the act, and disregard the concealment. Don't promise a child that things will go easier if he tells the truth, or that he will be punished doubly if he lies. This sort of "plea-bargaining" is extremely confusing, and it tells the child you *expect* him to lie. Unless you want the seed to grow, this idea must not be planted in a child's mind. A child who misbehaves should be punished immediately. No deals or legal mumbo-jumbo should divert attention from what happened.

"Mine?"

Until recently, from the child's egocentric (self-centered) point of view, there was but one territory and one set of possessions — hers. Part of growing up is accepting the disappointing fact that everyone else owns a piece of the pie too. This requires that she civilize her view of the world by learning what is implied by the words we use to define "possession."

This is a difficult task, because the lines separating "mine" from "yours" are largely invisible. There is, for instance, nothing distinguishing about the "my" in "my firetruck."

The possessive pronouns — mine, yours, his, hers, theirs, ours — are abstractions referring to ownership. Three-and-a-half-year-old children find it difficult to comprehend abstractions, which are one step removed from the world of color and sound and touch and taste and smell.

To a three and a half year old, "This firetruck is red" makes sense because red can be seen. It can be experienced *directly*. "This firetruck is *mine*," however, makes no sense. "Where and what is a 'mine'?" puzzles the child.

Attempting to understand abstractions, the youngster translates them into behavior. Oftentimes, this behavior runs counter to the intended message. For example, the word "don't" is also an abstraction, referring to the *absence* of some action. "Sit on the dog" makes sense to a three-and-a-half-year-old because the message is concrete, down-to-earth. On the other hand, "Don't sit on the dog" complicates matters considerably. The child is perplexed, and in an attempt to resolve his confusion, does the obvious, which is to plop down on the dog. Because we fail to see the child's behavior in its proper

context, we say the child is "disobedient" and "knows better."
Far from it.

(Q) During the past three months, on four separate occasions, our three-and-a-half-year-old daughter has shown me objects which she has concealed and taken from a playmate's house and the day-care center. After each incident, I have talked calmly and tried not to make a "big deal" out of it, but I'm not sure this is the right approach. Is this more serious than I'm willing to admit? Should I have punished her? How would you suggest I deal with it if it happens again?

(A) Not to worry. Nearly every child this age tries the "sticky fingers" routine. This is not to be confused with stealing. The motives are anything but similar. In fact, your daughter is, in the most literal sense of the term, *innocent*.

During the preschool years, "taking" is an experimental behavior — no harm intended. She is, first of all, testing your reaction: "What will momma do if . . . ?" I applaud your daughter for inventing such a clever and ingenious way of defining the difference between "mine" and "yours." By taking what she has been told is someone else's, or what rests at someone else's house, your daughter is attempting to define the concepts of possession and ownership.

So whaddaya do now? Help her out. She's asking a question. Give her the answer. React calmly and directly. "Oh. You took a toy from Bobby's house. This toy belongs to Bobby. This toy is *his*. You and I are going to take the toy back to Bobby's house and give it to him."

It is extremely important that you return the item immediately, while the question is fresh in her mind. It is equally imperative that your daughter accompany you on this mission.

It is *not* important that she confess, apologize or hand the item back herself. These requirements only serve to punish the question and muddle the answer. It is sufficient that she see you apologize and transfer the item to its owner. Keep the lesson simple and straightforward. No need to spice it with either guilt or grief.

"Play wif Me!"

For the most part, three year olds have resolved the conflicts surrounding the issue of dependence versus independence. But not completely. There are still times when they are tempted to give up the ground they have gained and retreat to a lifestyle that guaranteed comfort and security. Independence involves risks and, remember, the three year old has no map to show him the way. Dependence, on the other hand, is secure and addictive. One way of expressing this internal tug-of-war is to pull on mommy and say, in essence, "Be my playmate."

(Q) About how much time each day should I spend playing with my three year old? I don't work, so I've got just about all the time he needs.

(A) A very tricky question, for which there are no definite answers. At this age, there should still be plenty of time when the two of you sit down together just for the fun of it, but your responsibilities do *not* include being his playmate.

In fact, although he may want you to spend your day playing with him and be rather insistent about it, that is exactly what he does *not* need from you at this stage.

He does not require that much or that kind of attention from adults. He needs adults for protection, affection and control. He needs adults to read to him, to organize and arrange his play space, to reinforce his initiative, to encourage his independence and to give him ideas he can use to take off in new, self-sustaining directions.

Burton White, author of *The First Three Years of Life* and an authority on preschool children, has said that one of the most accurate indicators of developmental health in a three year old is an ability to occupy and entertain himself for significantly long periods of time.

That doesn't mean parents should stop playing with their children after their third birthdays. Three year olds need to know that their parents are still available to them. Keep in mind, however, that the more of a playmate a parent is, the more his authority and the child's autonomy are undermined.

Set limits on when you will play with him and when you won't. Don't be afraid to say "no" even if he screams. Find a morning preschool program and enroll him three days a week.

And while you're taking care of *his* independence, don't forget about your own.

Naps and Bedtime

(Q) My daughter is now three and a half. Even when given an hour's opportunity for an afternoon nap around two o'clock, she doesn't fall asleep. Then by 5:30, she falls apart. She cries and is touchy and can hardly sit up and eat her supper. If she goes to sleep around 3:30, I try to wake her after an hour or so, or she will be up until 9:30 or ten. Is this just another stage?

(A) It sounds as though your daughter may no longer need an afternoon nap. This transition from nap to no nap won't happen overnight though. For a while there will be days when she will obviously need a nap and days when she will not feel the need as strongly.

During this transition stage, she is likely to resist taking an afternoon slumber, for the simple reason that being awake is far more exciting than being asleep. Remember that children become upset when their routines are disrupted. This transition, then, because it involves shifting bedtimes back and forth, may be unsettling. You can count on her being cranky and out of sorts at times.

A routine would help her make this difficult adjustment. You must establish the routine, and you must enforce it in the face of occasional resistance. With this in mind, establish a bedtime. This decision should take into consideration such factors as work schedules, what time everyone needs to leave the house in the morning, where the child spends her days and so on. In the end, however, parents should decide when *they* want the child in bed. Every child needs parents who spend private time together regularly. So let's say that you choose 8:30 as the time when you want your daughter tucked away.

To make this happen, begin at eight o'clock to prepare her for bed. Turn off the television, turn down everyone's activity level to idle, give her a warm bath, send her to the potty, offer a small (preferably sugar-free) snack, read a story (in bed), talk softly with her about pleasant things that happened during the day, kiss and cuddle her, turn out the lights and leave the room. If she resists sleeping, make it clear that she must stay in her bed with the lights on. Enforce your decision calmly, but as firmly as necessary.

If her biological clock is turned to the norm, she will sleep until about eight o'clock the next morning. Depending on how active her day is, she may or may not want to nap. If she falls asleep of her own accord, allow her to sleep no more than one hour. In the evening, whether or not she takes a nap, begin again to wind things down at eight o'clock, aiming for that 8:30 bedtime. The most important thing to remember is that *you* establish the routine and *you* program her to fall into it through calm, consistent enforcement. The pattern will eventually become fixed, and she will make her own adjustments concerning naps according to her own needs.

Fours and Fives

The play of a three-year-old child is open ended and improvisational. He is a self-starter and can occupy himself for relatively long periods of time, but he is playing solely in the present—the here and now. He has no objectives in mind; he plays simply for the sake of playing.

Four and five year olds begin to establish goals and direct their activity toward accomplishing them. If you ask a three year old, "What are you doing?" you will usually get this answer: "Playing." A four or five year old answers the same question more specifically, telling the purpose of his activity: "I'm building a boat."

This ability to conceptualize and work toward a predetermined goal is the next step in the child's drive to master the environment. It signals the emergence of achievement motivation—the focused desire to accomplish, to create, to do.

Fours and fives express their need to achieve in a variety of ways. They begin to form definite interests, and, more often than not, these interests are gender-related. Typically, boys identify with the role model their fathers present—showing an interest in similar things (sports, automobiles, gardening and so on). They express more need for daddy's approval and companionship and engage in activities associated with their fathers (playing with tools, cooking and so on). At the same time, little girls are forming close ties with their mothers and exhibiting clear preferences for behavior and activities which are—relative to the standards in the home—feminine in nature.

This age child's gender identity also stabilizes. Four year olds realize that boys grow up to be men and girls grow up to be women. The emergence of precocious "sexual" behavior in this age children is their way of exploring and, thereby, understanding all that is implied by the mysterious difference between males and females.

As you might expect, the strategies they use to obtain answers to their questions are direct and unself-conscious. It's the age of "Let's play doctor" and "Show me" and it's bound to cause parents some consternation.

"You Show Me Yours, and . . ."

"I heard them all giggling and laughing upstairs in my daughter's room and went upstairs to see what was so funny. They all had their clothes off, every stitch! They were all hopping around the room, hitting each

other with pillows. I just stood there. My mouth wouldn't work."

"Bobby had been in the bathroom for a long time, so I went to see if he needed any help, and there they were. I thought I had prepared myself for anything — but two boys?"

"Every time I look around, Julie has her hand inside her pants. She does it everywhere. I've tried everything I know to stop her, but it only gets worse. I'm embarrassed to take her any place."

It happens in the best of families. There you are, managing things smoothly, coping with the occasional, expected hassles, but at least there's one thing you don't have to deal with for another ten years — or so you think. Then one day you happen to look in on the little ones who have been playing so quietly together for a half-hour, and . . .

Sometime between their fourth and sixth birthdays, most children discover that their bodies have pleasure places where touching feels almost as good as a chocolate ice cream cone tastes. There's nothing perverted or wrong in a child's liking ice cream, and there's nothing unnatural about her wanting to know about her own — or someone else's — body once she discovers the mysteries within.

A child's curiosity does not readily obey the green and red lights that adults set up to define what is "right" and what is not. It never occurs to a child who indulges in immature sex play that she is doing something wrong, and the idea that this delightful discovery is forbidden can be confusing and destructive. After all, it's her body, and it feels good. When adults look sickened, shout, slap the offending hand, or say it's bad, the message is that making oneself feel good is wrong. She hears people saying there's something wrong with her body — that it mustn't be touched.

Eventually, what the child finds delightful and good about her body is scrubbed from her thinking and words like "disgusting" and "nasty" are written in. Embarrassment, shame and guilt can easily become attached to her body-image and translated into ideas concerning herself. The final conclusion: "I'm *bad* to want to feel good."

There's a further danger in punishing or showing disapproval of such self-discovery. If a child's interest in her body is punished; if it becomes tinged with shame, then she will hide it from sight.

It is essential that our children feel free to talk with us about

sex and related matters. If a young child's unashamed openness is punished, then later, as a teenager, it is unlikely that she
will feel comfortable approaching her parents with questions,
doubts, or problems concerning sexuality.

So, what to do? There are no easy prescriptions, but here are
some general guidelines.

A child, like anyone else, has a need for, and a right to,
privacy. Don't intrude on her world, at regular intervals or
simply because she is being "too quiet." If you happen to find
your child exploring her body in the privacy of her own room,
let it be. She is doing no harm, physical or psychological, to
herself and certainly no harm to anyone else.

Children who explore themselves in public places must learn
that bodies are a private, personal matter. Tell them something
like, "I know that feels good, but the living room is not the
place to do it. If you like, you may go to your room where no
one will bother you." This will help the child develop self-
control without defining the act as "forbidden." In public, the
straightforward approach is also best: "Please take your hands
out of your pants while we are in the store. You may do that in
your room when we get home." When there are two or more
children together, simply divert their attention and briefly
mention that what they are doing is not allowed: "You two are
not allowed to play together like that. I want you to put your
clothes on and come downstairs. I need your help with
something."

Keep in mind that it is natural for young children to show an
immature interest in sex in one way or another, and that there
is no difference at this age between curiosity displayed toward
one's own body and curiosity displayed toward other bodies of
either sex. Be honest and simple when answering the questions
that may come up. Keep a straight face even if you feel
bewildered or shocked. Respect the child's right to privacy, but
at the same time teach her that there are appropriate times and
places for everything.

Moral Development

Four and five year olds are forming an elementary sense of
moral values. They aren't capable of abstract thought,
however, so they define "good" and "bad" in terms that are
closely related to their need for approval. "Good" is doing what
their parents approve of, and "bad" is what they disapprove of.

They are not yet able to apply moral concepts to a wide
range of situations. For example, a four year old may be able to
tell you that it would be wrong for him to take something from

his friend's house (the concept of possession being fairly well established by this time), but he would not be able to apply the general principle that "stealing is wrong." If asked the question, "Why shouldn't you take a toy from Bobby's house?" he would probably answer, "Cause it's Bobby's toy."

Furthermore, he doesn't understand why certain behavior is acceptable in some situations and not acceptable in others. He relies almost exclusively on signals from his parents and other adults to make these subtle distinctions and adjust his behavior accordingly.

For these reasons, it is essential that parents establish rules and guidelines solely in terms of what will and won't be allowed under each specific set of circumstances. The more talking and explaining parents do, the more the essential message — the rule — gets lost in the torrent of words.

Talk, Talk, Talk

Mikey is four years old. He's a smart little fella, full of mischief and stubborn as a mule. His parents are very conscious of the way they are raising him. They don't want to make *any* mistakes.

They believe the best way to teach Mikey the difference between right and wrong is to reason with him, thereby helping him to understand all the complicated "whys" and "why nots" of the world. Let's look in on the Mikey household to see if we can find an example. Ah, yes, his father is "reasoning" with him now:

"How many times do I have to tell you, Mikey, it's not nice to hit someone who is a guest in our home and then call him a 'pooh-pooh.' Reverend Diggs is our minister and he deserves to be treated with respect when he comes to visit. Hitting people and calling them names is bad manners. It's not polite, and you know better, don't you?"

Mikey nods.

"I thought so. When you hit someone who is a guest in our house and call them a name, they feel bad because they think you don't like them, and mommy and I become angry when you do things like that because we've talked with you about hitting and name-calling before and blah, blah, blah. . . ."

Poor Mikey. He hasn't the vaguest notion of what his father means, but he knows enough to stand there and pretend to take it all in. He knows he's in trouble, but what's this about someone's name being called?

The truth is, Mikey isn't old enough to understand most of what his father is saying. In fact, the more his father talks, the *less* Mikey understands.

His father is well-meaning enough, and he certainly has a point—Mikey must learn to express his affection in some other way. But Mikey didn't know. He got carried away in his excitement. Unfortunately, at the end of his father's monologue, Mikey won't have learned much. In fact, the monologue is so confusing to a four year old that by the time it's over, Mikey will probably have forgotten how it all started in the first place.

The process of learning to talk involves more than learning to make certain sounds. It's like building a house, except this "house" takes at least twelve years to build and another six or eight years to put on the finishing touches. Talking involves learning thousands of associations between patterns of sound (words) and the things (nouns) or actions (verbs) they represent. Then the child must learn how and when to use all the qualifiers (adjectives and adverbs) that assign values to the nouns and verbs. Then he learns how to classify and organize words into larger units of meaning. Finally the child develops an appreciation for words which refer to ideas rather than objects. And through this entire process, the child is also learning a complex set of grammatical rules without which none of this makes any sense. Complicated, isn't it?

Mikey's "house" has a foundation. The walls for the first floor are slowly being put together. His father is throwing roofing shingles at him.

At four years, the Mikeys of the world can understand only words referring to things and actions—stuff they can see or feel with their senses.

Words like "respect" and "polite" evaporate in Mikey's brain. The key to understanding is *not* practice, it's *maturity*. Mikey's parents could drill him for a week on the meaning of "respect," and he still wouldn't know what it meant. He won't be able to understand "respect" next year or the year after that. In fact, an understanding of words like "respect" won't begin to emerge until Mikey is about seven or eight years old.

Let's go back to Mikey and his dad for a moment.

"Do you understand what I'm saying, Mikey?"

Mikey Nods.

"Good. Now I don't want you being disrespectful to our guest and that includes name-calling. Do you understand?"

Mikey nods.

"Good. Now I want you to go tell Reverend Diggs you're sorry."

Mikey is a clever little munchkin. He has learned to escape the firing squad by nodding his head at just the right moment.

He can tell when to nod by the changes in his father's tone of voice and facial expression.

Mikey will even apologize to the Reverend, but he won't know why he's saying, "I'm sorry." He doesn't know what "sorry" means either. So, the next time there is a visitor, Mikey is just as likely to get excited and hit and say "pooh-pooh," and then everything will start all over again. Mikey's father will talk a mile a minute, and Mikey still won't know what he is talking about.

If you *must* reason with a young child, remember that you are helping him build a house. Make sure it's a solid structure. Don't try nailing on the roof before the walls are up. Observe three rules of thumb:

First, speak with the child immediately, before the memory fades away.

Second, use simple words that refer directly to *what* was done, *who* did it and *who* or *what* was done to. Don't use words that refer to morals or ethics (such as "deserve," "respect" and "polite").

Third, do your reasoning in 50 words or less. Say your piece, and (if you feel it is necessary) assign some form of punishment. "Mikey, you hit Reverend Diggs and called him a 'pooh-pooh.' We don't hit or call people 'pooh-poohs.' Go to your room. Your timer is set for five minutes. You may come out when the bell rings."

Enough said. Mikey understands.

Do You Believe In . . . ?

(Q) I have a five-year-old daughter with whom I feel I have an open and trusting relationship. The problem that I am at a loss to deal with involves my religious views. Through family members, kindergarten and friends my daughter is exposed to a belief system that I do not share. I am not necessarily opposed to this, but I feel reluctant to share my religious views with her for fear that if she repeats my thoughts and ideas, she will be ostracized at a time in her life when she is not able to deal with it. And yet, she is beginning to ask me questions about my beliefs. In the past I have responded to her questions with, "Yes, lots of people believe that." Now, she asks "Do **you** believe that?" How do I maintain the openness we have without endangering the relationships she has with others?

(A) More important than the need to protect your daughter from having differences of opinion with other children is her need to know exactly where you stand on these issues.

At this time in her life, her need to identify with you takes precedence over peer affiliations and peer approval. You are her primary role model and she is consciously striving to pattern herself after you — your behavior, your interests, your ideas. She looks to you to set the standards and wants only to follow your example. And yes, she *will* identify with your beliefs and claim them as her own.

You are also her primary source of security and will continue to be for the next seven years (or thereabouts) as she goes about finding a comfortable place for herself within her own generation. Before she ventures into new social territory, however, she must have a blueprint for behavior, and the directions must be clear. She depends on you to show her the way, but in this instance, it sounds as though she's having some difficulty "reading" you.

If you make it difficult for her to pin you down (remember, she doesn't know that you are trying to protect her), she will become "hung up" on the question, "What does mommy believe?" The vague, evasive quality of your answers will frustrate her and stimulate feelings of insecurity. In an effort to reduce her anxiety, she will fixate on the religious issue until you clarify matters for her.

Furthermore, she may interpret your discomfort as a sign that you are ill-at-ease with your own beliefs — that perhaps *you* feel something is wrong with them. Otherwise, why the game of hide-and-seek?

I also think you may be overestimating the significance of her religious beliefs to her acceptance among her peers. A child's religious views, or the religious persuasion of her parents, is relatively insignificant to the social process at this age. Young school-age children don't ostracize one another because of differences in race, religion, politics or what-have-you unless their parents encourage them to. The exception would be the child who wore her differences "on her sleeve."

Answer her questions. I would suggest, however, that instead of telling her what you *don't* believe, you answer her primarily in terms of what you *do* believe. Keep in mind that five-year-old children cannot understand philosophical abstractions. Explain your beliefs clearly, concisely and concretely.

For the sake of trust.

Six to Eleven: Middle Childhood

The psychology of the young school-aged child can be summarized in two words: acceptance and achievement. Her self-esteem hinges on her success at creating a secure place for herself in the social matrix of her peer group and at establishing and attaining specific goals of excellence.

A child must now learn to apply herself to a variety of challenging, and often demanding, tasks. In doing so, she draws on the trust, autonomy, initiative and imaginative playfulness she acquired during her preschool years.

Children whose preschool years were a success are prepared to meet the social, intellectual and emotional challenges of middle childhood. They are able to take reasonable risks with confidence; they are increasingly self-rewarding and self-motivated; they accept, and even seek, increased responsibility, and they continue to experiment with new expressions of independence and autonomy.

On the other hand, the child who arrives at this crossroads with a burden of "unfinished business" may have difficulty in the new roles expected of her by her parents, teachers and peers.

Going to school introduces a child to new social, emotional and intellectual pressures. For the first time she must adapt to a new set of intellectual and behavioral expectations. Being a "student" requires greater independence of thought and behavior, places greater distance between the child and her parents, introduces her to new authority figures and brings her into closer proximity with her peers.

As a child broadens her social base and expands her range of interests and activities, she establishes significant and relatively enduring precedents for herself within her peer group. Her social personality is negotiated through interaction with other children her age and defined in large measure by the roles she is assigned or acquires within the tribe.

Most children, by the time they are six years old, have internalized the behavioral limits taught them by their parents. From this time on, a child's attention shifts toward learning the implicit and explicit rules that mediate behavior within the peer group. Her moral judgement is further elaborated through participation in rule-governed activities — competitive games, structured play and so on — and the relatively formal atmosphere of the classroom.

Although she is capable of applying moral and ethical principles across a fairly wide range of situations, a school-age child's moral judgements tend to be dogmatic, rigid and egocentric. Typical peer conflicts at this age involve arguments over whose point of view is "right," who behaved correctly, who broke a rule and so on. Young school-aged children compare themselves to each other in every conceivable way. Everything is a contest, from the absurd to the trivial.

Super-Sensitive

(Q) I have an eight year old who is super-sensitive. He believes everything other children tell him. Recently, he proudly told one of his friends that he had sold 20 tickets to the school fair. The other child said that **he** had sold 100 tickets (which wasn't true). My son believed him and felt terrible because he hadn't sold as many. I've explained how and why children sometimes stretch the truth, but my son continues to believe everything he is told. What can I do to help him understand?

(A) In any competitive situation, there is a risk that someone may experience emotional pain. Learning how to compete involves learning to accept and deal with losing in such a way that it doesn't threaten self-esteem.

In this respect, the "super-sensitive" child is at a disadvantage. Super-sensitive, however, is a label *you*, his parents, have selected and attached to him. It actually says more about *you* than your son. Because you think of him as "fragile," you are inclined to react protectively when the competition puts him down.

It is understandable for parents to feel protective when their children hurt, but reacting protectively is not *always* in children's best interest. Super-sensitive becomes a self-fulfilling prophecy when parents' reactions prevent children from confronting situations on their own and learning from them.

In other words, you may be doing too much *taking care of*, when what your son needs is enough space to learn how to take better care of himself. An overdose of sympathy can be addicting.

I suggest that you simply reflect the content of these situations back to him in a fairly objective way, while acknowledging his feelings and helping him explore more successful ways of handling these problems. For instance, "Mark wants to be better at selling tickets then you, and you want to be better than Mark. When Mark told you he sold one hundred tickets, how did you feel?... Do you think Mark really sold one hun-

dred tickets?. . . Why did he tell you that? . . . Let's talk about
what you can do next time something like this happens, so you
don't end up feeling so awful. . . . Have you got any ideas?"

Take the emphasis off self-pity and focus his energy on solving the problem. His self-confidence rests on being able to do
that for himself, and he needs to hear you saying, "I know it's
hard, but you can do it."

You may have to settle for a "sensitive" child, but he can still
be "super!"

Pecking Orders

(Q) We recently moved into a neighborhood where there are many
children about the same age as our eight-year-old daughter. The
other children gang up and pick on her almost constantly. I have
watched them take things away from her, tease her until she cries,
make fun of her, exclude her from their games and call her names.
She comes home crying several times a day. I have talked and
talked with her about staying away from them, but as soon as we
talk and she stops crying, she wants to go back for more. She gets
along fine with each of the children individually, but as a group they
are mean to her. Should I handle it by not letting her play with them
for a while or letting her play with them only if I supervise? Or
should I talk with the children or their parents?

(A) Don't do any of the above. The correct answer is, stay out
of it.

Something needs to be done, but the doing needs to be done
with your daughter. There is more going on than meets the eye.

The treatment she is getting comes with being the new kid in
town. Her arrival threatens to rearrange the fragile structure of
the group as well as to break up some of the tenuous alliances
the "old-timers" have with one another. So the group reacts
protectively. You said it yourself: individually, the children
have nothing against her — collectively, she is regarded as an
untouchable. She is being slowly initiated into the group's
pecking order.

The more serious problem is a paradox: you must act to prevent your daughter from growing into a victim role, but you
must not interfere in the victimization. The role of "victim" is a
seductive one because it evokes a potent, yet destructive, rein-
forcer — sympathy.

Furthermore, by accepting the underdog's definition of
herself, along with the notion that she needs you (and only you)
to help her, you can become that person's "lifeguard." You get
to feel competent and needed; a strong temptation to resist.

And finally, the "villain," by virtue of the "victim's" helplessness, gets to feel powerful. Each role compliments the other two. Villains need victims who need someone else to give them sympathy and a helping hand. This triangular drama is addicting and self-perpetuating because everybody gets something out of the arrangement. It's a soap opera, every bit as enticing and repetitious as any you can find on the tube.

Back off. A victim without a "lifeguard" must either sink or swim. When a victim starts swimming, she's no longer a victim. I'll bet your daughter can swim. Obviously, she is in no real danger and wants to be with these other children, so let the problem be hers.

If you don't have a kitchen timer, get one. Every time your daughter comes home crying after an encounter with her tormentors, tell her she needs a "rest" and that she must stay indoors for 30 minutes. Set the timer to signal when she can go back outside. During this time, you can listen and reflect her statements back to her, but don't discuss her anguish in sympathetic terms. Persistent crying should be done in her room, alone.

If she is playing outside, and you hear her crying, go out and bring her in, with the same instructions (these suggestions do not apply to cuts, bumps, bruises, and other injuries to the body.) She may want to know why you aren't doing something about the horrible way the kids treat her. You can say something like, "Those aren't *my* playmates. They are *your* friends, and *you* will have to learn how to get along with them. I can't do anything except talk to you about it. Do you want to talk?"

Perhaps the most difficult thing about being a parent is having to make certain decisions that force your children to stand on their own, even when they tell you they can't.

Junior Jeckyl and Master Hyde

(Q) My son is six years old and in first grade. At home he is a real problem—disobedient, boisterous and generally hard to handle. I went for my first conference with his teachers braced for the worst. Instead, they told me he is one of the best-behaved children and one of the best readers in the room. I had no idea. Since then, I've tried to get him to read to me at home, but he refuses (as usual). I don't get it. What am I doing wrong? Or, what are *they* doing right?

(A) Children are far more likely to engage in conflicts with their parents than their teachers. This is number thirty-nine of the time-honored Fifty Ways to Grieve Your Mother: Be the teacher's perfect precious and bite mommy on the leg — or her ego (whichever is more vulnerable).

There are at least five reasons why number thirty-nine has become a tradition with children:

First reason: A teacher's role is more clearly defined than a mother's. Teachers are for teaching, which they do from 8 a.m. until 3 p.m., Monday through Friday, nine months a year.

Mothers are for . . . everything, which they are expected to do . . . always. There's vast territory for a child to explore in his relationship with his mother, because the limits of that relationship are vague. So, anything goes — or can at least be tried.

"Teacher" is an occupation. Her status as an authority figure is clear and has institutional support. But, if it makes you feel better, consider that plenty of teachers who have no problem managing 30 children in a classroom can't get a handle on the one they have at home. A teacher's a teacher and a mother's a mother, and never the twain shall overlap.

Second reason: Mothers tend to take out one heck of an emotional mortgage on each of their children, with lifetime payments and no insurance. This investment makes objectivity almost impossible. A mother's self-esteem, sense of competence and well-being are all too often tied up in her children and their behavior. There can be a problem of separating who is who.

Teachers are paid to be objective. Aren't they lucky?

Third reason: Rules are more clearly defined at school than they are at home. Parents often expect "good" behavior without defining exactly what "good" means. Furthermore, parents are more likely to make exceptions, overlook things (hoping they will go away) and fight with one another over how to enforce rules.   Parents often act confused, which is not lost on children.

A teacher's rules are usually few and clear. She enforces quickly, makes few exceptions and her spouse is not in the classroom. She is clearly "The Boss."

Fourth reason: In school, a child can observe the behavior of other children and follow their example. This *can,* and does, work both for good and ill, but the group usually pressures its members to behave in ways that enhance its image. Classmates expect every child to contribute to the collective identity and shun children who detract from that image.

Fifth reason: At home, within the family, the entire course of a child's upbringing is charged with the issue of autonomy and independence. The basic question of how much independence is possible, and by what means it is obtained is central to a child's participation in the family. By its very nature, this issue *demands* that children be somewhat rebellious. Some conflict between parents and children is not only inevitable, but healthy. It is the parents' responsibility *to the child* to contain that rebellion within safe, reasonably appropriate limits.

At school, on the other hand, the central issue is achievement, which often requires cooperation. Because rebellion is incompatible with the expectations of the classroom, the likelihood of conflict between teacher and student is considerably lessened. Children who rebel in school are those for whom the challenge is too great or not great enough, those who have not been able to rebel effectively at home and those who have difficulty fitting in the social configuration of the group.

Your little James Dean is a rebel *with* a cause at home because he has developed a consuming sense of autonomy and an appreciation for his own individuality. He cooperates with the teacher because he has developed a sense of initiative and will to achieve.

Congratulations on a job well done.

Organized Sports

(Q) What do you think about organized, competitive sports for children? Our son is eight years old, and the current craze among the neighborhood children his age is Pee-Wee Football. Actually, the adults appear at least as excited about it as the kids. The way the parents behave at the games makes me wonder whether they haven't got big money riding on the outcome. The same mania sweeps through the neighborhood in the spring, during Little League season. We are caught between wanting our son to feel that he's part of the group and not wanting him to learn, at this age, that winning a game is the most important thing in life.

(A) Organized activities of this nature are inappropriate during middle childhood (ages six to ten). Though organized sports might seem ideal for children at this competitive age, it's not so.

To begin with, adults are overly involved in these activities, both in terms of their presence and their emotional investment. Adults organize, raise the money, draw up the playing schedule, pick the teams, coach, referee, give out awards and make up the biggest share of the audience.

But it doesn't stop there. Not only do big people play too prominent a role in planning and organizing these events; they can also be found defining and mediating social issues, encouraging rivalries, confering status as they see fit and resolving conflicts.

Adults have no business being that entangled in the play of children. Their involvement is a complicating factor that prevents the children from learning to resolve certain critical issues on their own. Instead of being activities for children, Pee-Wee Football and Little League Baseball become theaters where youngsters are manipulated for the ego gratification of adults.

That these sports are competitive is not, in itself, disturbing. This age child needs and, left to his own devices, will seek out appropriate competitive experiences. What *is* disturbing is that children who are caught up in these sports don't play simply for the sake of the game — for the fun of it, that is — but play to obtain adult approval. In fact, they don't really *play* at all. They *work*, performing for the crowd.

The difference between competitive play and competitive work can be measured in terms of emotional outcome. When children band together to play a sand-lot game, one group wins and one group loses, but everyone usually leaves the field feeling O.K. When adults direct an organized sports event, the children on the losing team often end up feeling angry, dejected, frustrated, ashamed and depressed. This isn't play. This is serious business, and the stakes are high — too high. Under pressure from adults to perform, the child athlete's sense of achievement and self-esteem becomes defined in terms of winning and losing. Process and participation take a back seat to outcome, which isn't what being a child is about. Everyone suffers, including the children who don't get to play because they aren't "good" enough.

The basic problem — and one that isn't limited to this issue — is adults' tendency to act as though children will botch the job of growing up unless we engineer the process for them. The opposite is true. When we place ourselves *between* the child and the challenge of growing up, we are no longer in a helpful position. Instead, we are interfering and, to that extent, the child is ultimately less capable of dealing with life.

Guidance, support, encouragement, supervision — these are things children need from us. Carry them too far, however, and they become pure meddling.

Allowances

No one has more right to complain about inflation than this country's children. Recent trends have conclusively proven what old-timers in Maine have been saying all along — "As the economy goes, so goes the allowance."

Since the first of the year, this key economic indicator has plunged a record twelve points. In the wake of management's refusal to negotiate the level of this peculiar dole, episodes of panic bubble-gum buying have been reported in several junior high schools.

Concern over the effects this allotment can have on the economy is reflected in the increasing number of questions I've been receiving on the subject, including the following:

(Q) At what age should a child be started on an allowance?

(A) As a rule of thumb, it makes sense to start a child on a small allowance at the same time her teacher begins instruction in the mathematics of money. Preschool children are generally unable to grasp that the amount of money they have places an upper limit on *what* and *how much* they can purchase. In the child's eyes, there is no correspondence between the size or desirability of an item and its cost. Until a child is old enough to understand the idea of exchange and deal with the complexities involved, I recommend that parents limit her experience with money to certain exercises in *paying* for things.

(Q) Should a child be required to earn his allowance by doing chores around the house?

(A) Absolutely not. The question of how much the child is expected to contribute to household maintainance is *completely* unrelated to the allowance issue.

The child's allowance should be for the sole purpose of giving him opportunities to practice efficient money-management. It should *not* be manipulated to persuade the child to carry out his assigned duties, nor should it be suddenly withdrawn to punish him for inappropriate behavior.

Chores are for developing responsibility, self-discipline and other essentials, but it takes the better part of childhood for this lesson to take hold. Given a choice between developing some responsibility and riding a bicycle, most children will choose the latter. Therefore, parents must make the choice, and once made, enforce it.

It boils down to a simple matter of obedience, for which there is but one effective incentive — parental authority. In the end, children do chores because they are *told* to do them.

Parents who exchange money in return for chores are unwittingly undermining themselves. When money is used to mediate this aspect of the parent-child relationship, people lose sight of the basic issues of authority and obedience.

Every child needs to learn the value of chores, and every child needs to learn the value of the dollar, and parents need to make sure the lessons don't get mixed up.

(Q) Is it all right for parents to give a child a chance to earn extra money by doing special work beyond what's expected of her?

(A) Certainly. Chores are those jobs which are part of the household routine — taking out the garbage, feeding the pet iguana and so on. It's perfectly acceptable for parents to contract with their children for work other than regular chores, though deals of this nature should be the exception rather than the rule. No one should forget that, within the family, work is *not* done for money, but simply because it needs to be done.

(Q) What should children be required to spend their own money for?

(A) That's an interesting question. In the first place, the child's allowance is *not her money.* It is the *parents' money,* which is shared with the child to teach her how to use it.

Parents should keep tabs on how the child intends to use the money and retain the right of refusing to let the child spend it irresponsibly or in ways which are incompatible with the values of the family. Parents need to teach their children how to be intelligent consumers — how to recognize quality, how to compare, how to shop for value and so on.

It goes without saying that a child should *not* be required to spend her allowance on essential food, clothing, books or school supplies. The allowance is not meant to *establish* the child's standard of living, but to *supplement* it.

(Q) How much should a child receive each week?

(A) Something between too little and too much. If the amount is either insufficient or excessive, the child may not learn to set responsible limits on his own spending.

Determine the actual figure by taking into consideration the socio-economic level of the family and peer group, the child's age, how involved he is with activities outside the family, where the family lives and, last but not least, the current rate of inflation.

Eleven to Fourteen: the "Tweenager"

> *"Whenever I ask him to do something, he just sits there, as though I don't exist. He's unpredictably temperamental, too — swings back and forth between joy and misery as if he's riding an emotional seesaw. And when he's in misery, watch out! Nothing I know of or have tried will satisfy him. But the worst thing to deal with is this idea that he can do whatever he pleases, without regard for anybody else. And stubborn? Hah! If I say go, he wants to stay. If I want to stay, he wants to go. Loving one minute, 'don't touch me!' the next. To tell you the truth, I've about had it. There are times when I feel this urge to throttle the little monster, but I always snap back to reality moments before my hands wrap around his throat. Sometimes I think it's either him or me."*

Another two year old, right? Wrong. The monster this parent is complaining about hasn't worn a diaper for ten years.

Introducing the large, uneconomically-sized version of the "Terrible Two": he pouts, he stomps his size-seven feet, he bellows at the top of his lungs. . . . Ladies and Gentlemen! A big Bronx cheer for that second-most terrible of all terribles — The Tweenager!

(Author's note: the insertion of a "w" between the "t" and "e" in "teenager" is not a misprint. The term "tweenager" refers to an eleven, twelve or thirteen year old person. I coined the phrase to distinguish this three-year period in a youngster's life, which is completely unlike the years immediately before and after. Most eleven, twelve and thirteen year olds are no longer children, but they are not quite adolescents. They are betwixt and between definition; therefore, the term "tweenager.")

The tweenage years can be a miserable time for both "tweens" and anyone else who has to deal with them day in and day out — parents and teachers in particular. There are many outward similarities between the "Terrible Twos" and the equally "Terrible Tweens." So much so that many writers now refer to the second 18 months of life as the *"first* adolescence."

Like the two year old, the tweenager is a rebel in search of a cause. His defiance of parental (and most other) authority is blindly reflexive. However, the tremendous growth of language during the intervening decade has replaced the monosyllabic "no!" with a peculiar form of self-centered ranting which makes no sense to anyone but the speaker.

And, like his predecessor, the tween is an emotional basket-case, careening wildly from one passionate extreme to another—a bull in the china shop of feelings.

It's another two years of almost certain temper tantrums, which burst forth any time the tweenager's inevitably unreasonable wants are not catered to. The more unreasonable they are, the greater the force of the explosion.

This volatile character was portrayed brilliantly by young Michael Landon in "I Was A Tweenage Werewolf," Hollywood's in-depth study of pre-adolescence. (Regrettably, the "w" was left on the cutting room floor by a junior editor who read it as a misspell.)

The two year old is also father to the tween in his maddening self-centeredness. The tweenager is willing to inconvenience anyone to get what he wants. And excuuuuuuse *you* for leaving your foot where his royal tween-ness would step on it. Any empathic weaknesses which might interfere with this "me-first" obsession are suspended for the duration.

Again like the two year old, the tween cannot seem to make up his mind whether he prefers to be dependent or independent. But whichever role he chooses—Freddy the Freeloader or James Dean—it's darn sure going to be on *his* terms and no one else's. He will, for instance, curse his parents for having the gall to restrict his freedom, insisting that he's capable of taking care of himself, come what may; then he will ask them for money, a ride somewhere or (more likely) both.

But there is method to this madness. Just like the two year old, whose behavior is the echo of a consciousness which is rapidly expanding and propelling him from explorer to experimenter and observer to doer, the tween is making a similar leap in his ability to flush out the mysteries of the universe. His mind, after ten years of grappling with the logic of concrete, measurable relationships, is beginning to grasp the abstract, the hypothetical, the stuff of no-stuff-at-all. Not surprisingly, the tween is as hopelessly drunk on this process and its attendant revelations as the two was in his time.

Add an overdose of hormones, put the mixture under ever-increasing peer pressure, and you've got a guaranteed two or three years of katy-bar-the-door-and-jump-back-jack.

Ah, but amid this mayhem are two reasons to rejoice—most tweens are potty trained and very few of them bite.

The tweenage years are a time of transition—a symphony, or more aptly, a *cacophony* of change involving the whole child and dramatically altering his definition of himself and his world.

Changes in the structure and chemistry of the child's body and corresponding upheavals in his emotional nature bring him face to face with his emergent sexuality.

About this time, a child's brain begins to process and organize information in a radically different manner, adding new dimensions to his perception of the world and further complicating his view of himself.

Pre-adolescents tend to be introspective; that is, they think a lot about themselves, sometimes to the point of obsessiveness. They reflect upon and evaluate their own behavior, feelings and even their own thoughts. This ability to look within brings into clearer focus not just the person-that-is, but also the person-that-could-be—the *ideal self*. Comparisons between the real (present) and ideal self generate either aspiration or anxiety, depending on factors which include how much discrepancy there is between the two and whether the pre-adolescent has basically positive or negative self-regard.

Because they scrutinize themselves so carefully and speculate on the thoughts of other people as well, pre-adolescents often believe that they are constantly watched, usually by peers. Therefore, and quite understandably, they are given to "performing" for their imagined (but not necessarily imaginary) audience. This explains why tweens are so generally self-conscious about their personal appearance, spending hours (at least it seems like hours when *you're* waiting to use the bathroom) primping before every "public appearance," however routine.

During this critical period the child transfers most of his security needs from parents to peers. The peer group bridges childhood (when the child relied on his parents) and adulthood (when the healthy individual is primarily self-reliant); it is a social laboratory where rules and roles can be practiced, evaluated and incorporated. Gradually, the clique becomes a thing of the past as the pre-adolescent turns his attention toward forming stable friendships and participating in large group activities.

Early adolescence is a time of great psychological vulnerability. The young person's self-concept is ambiguous, and therefore fragile. From a developmental standpoint, the child's task is to establish identity—an enduring sense of who he is and is becoming. This is not so easy for someone caught, for the moment at least, between the comfort and security of childhood and the uncertainty of adolescence.

I Was a Tweenage Misanthrope

When I was 12 years old, I hated everything. There was so much to hate I couldn't remember it all. To keep it straight, I wrote it all down. In keeping with this stark, no-frills view of the world, I entitled it my "Hate List."

My Hate List filled several pieces of lined notebook paper, both sides. It was in my possession at all times so I could refer or add to it at a moment's notice. Nothing and no one was immune. Naturally, my parents were at the top of the list—in CAPITAL LETTERS, surrounded by exclamation points. I hated every one of my teachers, even the ones who were tolerant of my abrasiveness. I hated them if they gave me a C, and I hated them if they gave me an A. I couldn't be bought.

I hated my brother. I hated my sister. I hated my neighbors. I even hated my friends. Each one took a turn on my list. I hated books, homework, the guy who ran the neighborhood store, the barber who cut my hair too short everytime, grass because it had to be mowed, leaves because they had to be raked, cars because they had to be washed, my room, girls, white socks, white Levis, police and all food except for hamburgers, french fries and cokes. I hated my mother's hamburgers. She made them awful just to punish me for spending my meager allowance at the Burger Palace. I hated having an allowance. It was demeaning. I hated having no money.

I hated acne medications, my clothes, my shoes, my jacket, the stupid hat my mother bought me and the galoshes my father made me wear when it snowed. But most of all, I hated me. I couldn't stand the sight of myself in the mirror.

"Yuk! Look at that face. No wonder Linda avoids me. I'm ugly! I hate Linda. I'm short, I'm skinny, my face breaks out, I've got freckles, my biceps are concave, my ribs show, I have dandruff, my hair is red, I can't suntan, there's no hair on my face . . . Oh Lord, please don't make me put on shorts for gym any more—my legs are too skinny and my knees are too knobby. Why do I have to wear glasses? Why do I have to wear braces? My arms are too long, my nose turns up, my ears stick out, my chin is too pointy, I can't play football, I can't fight, nothing good ever happens to me! I'm a reptile! I'm a worm! I'm a bug! I deserve to be squashed!!!"

What a dirty trick it is to be twelve. You ain't nothin.' You aren't a child. You aren't a teenager. You aren't an adult. You need your parents, and you wish they'd leave you alone. You want friends, but you don't know how to be friendly. You want to be one of the crowd. You want to be different. You're always on guard, protecting a fragile sense of who you are or wish you were.

Confusion. Resentment. The victim of a cosmic joke. Twelve is the pits. But there is one way out.

Thirteen.

Keep Both Hands on the Wheel

Pre-adolescence can be emotionally tumultuous and confusing for all concerned. Unfortunately, in many families it is a time when limit-setting begins to break down. It is easy for parents to let themselves by intimidated by the child's emotional upheavals and begin allowing her more responsibility than she can handle in order to avoid confrontations.

Exactly the opposite is called for. This is a time for reaffirming your authority rather than allowing the child to dismantle it. Although she will surely reject the notion, it's also a time when the child needs to know that hands other than her own are ready to take the wheel.

(Q) Six months ago, we moved from the East Coast and settled in a nice community in the Midwest. The adjustment has been somewhat difficult for all of us, but it seems to have particularly affected our 12-year-old son. This once outgoing and popular child has formed no close friendships since the move. In fact, he seems to avoid children his own age and has taken to associating with children several years younger. We have spoken to him about making more of an effort to find a friend, but he stays put, spending most of his free time in his room, watching television. He has also become more dependent and attached to his father and me. How can we help him?

(A) I suggest that you start by talking with your son about how generally upsetting the move has been to everyone in the family, how difficult it was to leave old friends and find new ones, and so on.

The disruption of a move often causes the pre-adolescent to regress to earlier forms of behavior. He may seek out younger children because they are more accepting, and because his status among them is virtually guaranteed. He is also likely to act more dependent on his parents.

Be understanding and supportive. Encourage and help him expand his activity away from home. A gentle assist from you in the form of arranging for his involvement in activities sponsored by the church, Y.M.C.A. and so on may be helpful.

Finally, I can't urge you strongly enough to remove the television from his room and limit his access to the family set to a maximum of one hour in the evening. His absorption in the television is a way of retreating from the challenge of carving out a niche for himself in his new surroundings. Every hour spent staring at the tube further dampens his initiative and increases his inertia.

(Q) Our thirteen year old has recently started threatening to run away from home. He is the second of three children and is almost exactly three years younger and three years older than his brothers. He complains about everything—we expect too much of him, he never has anything to do, we are "easier" on his younger brother, his older brother gets to do more than he does and so on. It seems as though he's miserable nearly all the time. He can be loving and cooperative—but has not been for at least three months. Should we be concerned about his threats? We hear them two or three times a week. What should we do?

(A) I don't think there's much possibility that he actually will leave for good—not anytime soon, that is. The ones who run with the intention of staying gone don't talk about it much beforehand. They just *go*, and the pressures which push them to that extreme are far more serious than the typical "Tweenage Blues" you're describing. In a similar vein, people who repeatedly threaten suicide are seldom the ones who (except through miscalculation) end up in the morgue. In both instances, the threat is a dramatic way of calling attention to oneself: "Hey! You better look at me, 'cause it might be your last chance!"

There are victims and there are "victims." Included in the former are real-life runaways and real-death suicides. A "victim," on the other hand, is nothing more than a caricature of tragedy—too involved in wearing this particular mask to even consider playing a lesser role. Included in the latter are, quite often, middle children and "tweenagers." Congratulations! You've got two for the price of one!

In one sense, the middle child is a "tweenager" throughout his childhood. Born both too late and too early, he rails against the injustice of having an older sibling who enjoys more freedom and a younger one who seems to get more attention ("You let him get away with murder!").

The middle child wants the best of both worlds, without having to pay the price. He wants to be gloriously independent and securely taken care of at the same time. The lure of becoming a victim is almost impossible to resist in this irreconcilable dilemma. "I'm gonna run away!" is a frustrated, exaggerated expression of this conflict. It is both a battle cry for freedom and a plea for more attention.

As the middle child moves into his "tweenage" years, his middle-ness is compounded. Woe is him! Insult upon injury! The straw that broke . . . and all the rest.

I would be less concerned about his threats than the feelings behind them. Understand that this is a particularly stressful transition in his life and an equally important time in the life of your family.

Keep communication open, but beware of allowing the child too powerful a voice in defining crucial issues. The questions (or challenges) children of this age raise are often superficial or irrelevant, only distracting from, and preventing resolution of, more important problems facing the family.

For instance, concern over threats of running away can mask the more salient issue of, "What does being a member of this family mean when you are 13 years old?"

(**Q**) Several times in the past six months, we have found panty hose, usually several pairs at a time, in our 12-year-old son's room (he will be 13 soon). He says he took most of them from his aunt's house (he sometimes baby-sits for her children). He denies ever wearing them, but can't (or won't) explain why he is so interested in them. We don't understand what his problem is, since he seems like such a typical, well-rounded boy in every other way—he is active in sports, makes good grades and has lots of friends. What do you think is going on, and how should we handle it?

(**A**) You're right. What you have is a typical, well-rounded twelve-year-old boy expressing his emerging sexuality in a rather unusual, but by no means abnormal, way.

And *he's* right, too. He probably *doesn't* know why he's attracted to panty hose; he just knows he is. Let's face it—part of the mystery and magic of sex at any age is that words are inadequate to express why it feels so darn good. It just does, and that's enough. For instance, if I try to explain why I'm sexually attracted to my wife, I end up describing *her.* Fine, but why am I attracted to that particular combination of characteristics? I dunno. Just am.

The only problem with the panty hose is that most adults are narrow-minded about expressions of sexuality by a child. We tend to have definite ideas about what is and is not appropriate. So when a 12-year-old elopes with a pair of panty hose, we freak out because it doesn't fit our preconceived notions of what is O.K. Another facet of the problem is that we think of the differences between children and adults in purely quantitative terms. A 12 year old possesses less "adultness" than a thirty year old—he is smaller, less practical, and so on.

But childhood is not just the lower 18 rungs on life's ladder; it is a different ladder altogether. Children play at a different game, particularly when it comes to things like sex. In fact, the basic difference between children and adults is that children learn about such things *by playing*, while adults think of learning as a very serious undertaking.

For the past year or so, your son has been increasingly, irresistibly, attracted to the female body. He can hardly contain his curiousity! But he has to. The average 12 year old has enough presence of mind to know that the female body is off limits for another few years. But it just so happens that there are these things called panty hose that women wear over a very intriguing area of their anatomy. So . . .

He's only playing. Just learning, in a safe and harmless way. In this case, panty hose are "transitional objects" — items the youngster uses to help him come to grips with the changes taking place in his body, in his mind and in his emotions. He is interested in them because the "real thing," besides being off limits, is too threatening for the moment.

If your son were not "typical" — if his behavior were extremely unusual in other respects or if he isolated himself from other children his age or seemed depressed — then more concern would be appropriate. But even in that context, panty hose would be the *least* relevant detail.

Take this ideal opportunity to let him know that you understand how panty hose could be so intriguing (but *don't* analyze his interest for him). Tell him that as his body matures and his feelings about women change, you are there to help answer his questions and discuss his concerns. If the door is open, he will walk through it, and when he discovers that you're willing to listen without judging or criticizing him, he will seek your counsel more often.

PART THREE

Toilets, Tantrums and Other Unmentionables

Toilet Training
Readiness Signs

"My pediatrician says that parents shouldn't even *think* about starting to toilet train before a child is at least two and a half," a mother once told me.

Any doctor who makes such a statement, should be sentenced to hard labor in a diaper laundry. There is no such truth. In fact, there are no general "shoulds" at all pertaining to the age when a child can learn to use the toilet. Some children are ready to develop this skill when they are 15 months old. Others show no signs of readiness until nearly age three.

Both these examples are exceptional. Most children are ready sometime between the ages of 18 months and two and a half years. In any case, there is no "normal" age for toilet training, and there can be no prescriptions for when this learning must take place or how long the process should take. The important variable is *not* age. It is the child and the signals she will send to let you know when she is ready to give potty sitting a try.

Don't hold your breath waiting for your child to say something akin to, "Mom, I believe it's time you told me about the legendary great white water-chair." She might not say anything. Chances are, however, she will begin by dropping little hints that can be translated to mean essentially the same thing. These hints, or readiness signs, include (but are not limited to):

• waking up dry in the morning for several weeks,
• being dry after naptime fairly regularly,
• staying dry for more than two hours between diaper changes.

This tells you her bladder is holding more, and she is developing some ability to work the muscles that control urination.

To continue our list:

• telling you when she is about to release
• taking her diaper off when it is wet or soiled
• asking you to change her when she is wet or soiled
• imitating you when you use the toilet
• showing a definite interest in the toilet and some indica-

tion that she knows what it's for
• asking to sit on the potty

When these signs will emerge depends on both the child and her environment. One important question is, "Does Jennifer have the opportunity to express her readiness?" For instance, is the bathroom door left open? Is she allowed and even encouraged to watch the big people in the house use the toilet? Does she have a seat her own size to sit on and pretend?

Another important question, follows closely on the heels of the first: "If Jennifer exhibits several of these signs, will someone pay attention?" Sometimes a mother isn't ready to listen, because she wants the closeness and affection that spin off the diapering ritual to last longer.

At some time during the second or third year of life, a child's toileting readiness peaks. This peak lasts for several weeks. Parents who initiate toilet training during this critical period will probably find that the child will master the process quite smoothly.

It is important, therefore, that parents be sensitive to the child's expressions of "I'm ready!" If the critical period is not responded to, the child's natural eagerness will wane. Later, it will be difficult for everyone to paddle back upstream.

On the other hand, if parents act too pushy and eager to get the whole business over with, the child will become negative and uncooperative. It's just her way of saying, "I'd rather do it my way!" You can lead a child to the water-chair, but you can't make her sit.

Every child is unique, and every home is different. No two children will show the same signs at the same age, nor are there any methods which can guarantee success.

Give your child ample opportunity to discover why mommies and daddies and brothers and sisters sit on the water-chair. Don't push the process, but be aware of the readiness signals and prepared to initiate toilet training when they appear. Remember that once the readiness signals occur, several weeks of hesitation may let the best opportunity slip away. Above all else, watch the child—not the calendar.

A Family Affair

(Q) One of the psychologists in the town we live in will come into your home and toilet train your child for about $300. He uses a method which he claims virtually guarantees complete success in one day. We have a 26-month-old daughter who seems ready to use the potty, and we want to know what your thoughts are on having the psychologist perform this service for us.

(A) Frankly, the whole idea is profoundly disturbing to me. I do not believe it is within the legitimate province of a psychologist to offer such a service.

Learning to use the toilet is a normal part of every child's socialization. Given time, the child's readiness and gentle encouragement from the parents, it will happen without undue stress or any great investment of effort. In this respect, it is no more significant a skill than learning how to drink from a cup, use a fork or get dressed.

Toilet training does, however, involve more of a mess and a smell than buttoning a shirt, and after two or more years of changing diapers, parents are usually eager to get it over with. It is this eagerness that your friendly neighborhood psychologist is capitalizing on by offering his tidy service.

Any specialist in child development should be able to comment on the acquisition of this skill and identify, for instance, factors which facilitate the child's success. However, except in cases where either the child or the circumstances are exceptional, the first-hand, on-site services of a specialist are not necessary for the actual learning.

In fact, it is probably better for both parents and children for professionals to keep a respectful distance from natural developmental processes of this nature.

There is more going on during toilet training than meets this psychologist's eye. Apparently, he has little appreciation for the transition which toilet training brings about in the parent-child relationship.

Not only is the child learning where to put his b.m.'s, but he is learning to be less dependent on his parents. This usually involves some ambivalence. Does he really want to give up the creature comforts that come with being an infant in exchange for dry pants? This ambivalence and the anxiety that accompanies it, can be resolved successfully *only* with his parents.

For parents, toilet training means readjusting their manner of relating to the child and their perceptions of him. It is crucial that parents and their children work through this transition together, in their own way and their own time.

You want your child to use the potty? Here's how, in less than 55 words (see pages 137-8 for readiness signs).

Buy her a potty and some training pants, consign her diapers to the rag bag and tell her where to put her business. Help at first with the details. Then, stand well out of the way so she can experience this as an exercise in independence.

Simple, yes? You don't need a Ph.D. to do that.

This psychologist-person probably had enough candy up his

sleeve to persuade a toddler to use the potty, but most children are smart enough to go poop in the corner as soon as he leaves.

Better Late Than Never

(Q) My almost four year old shows no interest in using the toilet. When he was two, I decided I would let things be until he showed me he was good and ready. Now it's almost two years later and all he shows me is wet, messy training pants. When he was about three, I became panicky and upset at his lack of progress, but then I felt bad about having made such an issue of it and backed off entirely. When he has an accident (five or six times a day), he is very good about cleaning himself up and putting his wet clothes in the right place. At night, he still wears diapers. He goes to a day care program (which he lives for) five mornings a week, and while he's with other children, he controls himself. He has even used the toilet there on several occasions. But as soon as we get home, he floods. Don't tell me to withhold privileges, as there is **nothing** he cares enough about to make him cooperate. The nurse at our family doctor's told me that this is a sign of emotional problems and that we need to make an appointment with a psychologist. Do you agree?

(A) Nope. He doesn't have emotional problems—he's a four year old who has never been given a straight message about using the toilet. He has probably never heard you clearly say, "I want you to put your wee-wee and b.m.'s in the potty . . . and no where else, mind you."

There is a difference between making an *issue* of something and making a *statement* about it. Unfortunately, toilet training has become a major issue, full of myth, anxiety and misinformation. Consequently we have difficulty *thinking* effectively about it, much less making effective statements about it to our children.

Only in America, for instance, will you find entire books devoted to the subject. Several of the more recent ones come complete with stories to read to the child. One has drawings showing a fireman, policeman and a teacher, all sitting merrily on toilets. What a production!

Only in America would someone think to write, for a public hungry to buy, a book entitled *Toilet Training In Less Than A Day* (Azrin and Foxx, Simon and Schuster).

Only in America will you find behavioral psychologists with impressive credentials offering, for a modest fee ($300 and up), to come to your home and, with the aid of a doll that wets, toilet train your child in one day while you sip coffee and watch "As The World Burns." You can trust your kid to the man who has his Ph.D. (pronounced "fid").

It's the Twentieth Century Medicine Show: "Amazin', just amazin'. Yesiree, folks, just step right up and watch as I demonstrate in front of your very eyes with a real live two year old just like the one you've got at home how you too can toilet train your child in one day. . . . That's right! One day! Not two, but one! You heard me . . . no more poopy pants, no more ammonia smell clogging up your nostrils, no more disposable diapers clogging up your septic tanks, and all accomplished in one amazingly short day."

Amid all the hocus-pocus, confusion reigns. We have made a mystery out of something that is simply a practical, unamazing exercise in self-sufficiency — like learning how to eat with a spoon. Think about it. First, the child sees you using a spoon, and he experiences what it's like to have you feed him with a spoon. When you see that he has developed enough manual dexterity to hold a spoon and guide it to his mouth, you give him his own little spoon. Initially, he slops his food everywhere — he has "accidents," which you patiently, and with words of encouragement, clean up. And lo and behold, in time he learns to eat with a spoon. Through this whole process of learning to eat with a spoon runs the message, "You can feed yourself." And so he does. I never yet heard of a child who was psychologically traumatized by spoon-training.

Two years ago you could have shown your child how to use a potty his own size and said, "You can use the potty just like everyone else does." And he would have done his business there and everywhere else for a while. And you could have been patiently encouraging. And he would have learned.

But he never got the message. Then, a year later, he sensed your anxiety, heard conflicting statements and said to himself, "Well, if *they* don't know what they want me to do, then I don't know what I want me to do either."

So now? Now you gotta convince him. But first, convince yourself. Do you want him to use the potty like the rest of the world's four year olds, or do you want to continue acting confused and paralyzed by words like "emotional problems"?

Don't tell me there's "nothing he cares enough about," because you also said, "He lives for day care."

So here's a four year old who knows what to do but won't. Convince him! Say to him, with no uncertainty, "I want you to put your wee-wee and b.m.'s in the toilet . . . and no where else, mind you."

Give him an "allowance" of one accident a day for the first two weeks: "If you have two accidents, you don't go to school the next day." At the end of two weeks, take away the "allowance."

During this time, keep an accident scorecard posted in a prominent place (such as on the refrigerator). Put a check in the box-of-the-day for each accident.

Oh, and don't ever, ever, ask him, "Do you have to go to the bathroom?" Make *him* responsible. And he will be.

The most delightful story I ever heard about toilet training was of a mother who gave her two year old a set of training pants and a potty of his own and said, "Use it."

Well, the little fella just flat refused. "NO!" he said. "I wanna poo in my didee."

"Fine," his mother said, taking a diaper and laying it in the bottom of his potty. "Poo in your didee — right here."

It was all the convincing he needed.

Don't Ask, *Tell*

(Q) Our almost three-year-old son absolutely refuses to use the toilet. He responds with a firm, amplified, "NO!" nearly every time I ask him if he would like to use the potty. If I try coaxing him, he wails. Actually, I have caught him "off guard" several times during the past six months, and he has shown me that he does know how to use it. Otherwise, he refuses to cooperate. I am looking forward to getting rid of the diaper pail. Help!

(A) Why should he cooperate? Obviously, you have yet to tell him, in definite terms, exactly what it is you expect of him. As long as you continue to ask, in whatever way, "Won't you *please* use the potty instead of using your diapers?" He has your permission to say, "No!"

Children spend nearly the first two years of their lives viewing the universe as though they sit at its center. Because of their obvious limitations, we wait on them hand and foot — we carry them, bathe them, powder them, comfort them, feed them and dress them.

It should come as no surprise to any of us that almost every child emerges from this cocoon feeling as though he is the world's most significant person, rightfully in control of everything and everyone. This fantasy has obvious appeal, and most children are reluctant to give it up.

For parents to survive the "Terrible Twos" they must develop an uncanny ability to sense and avoid power struggles. Whenever we react to the two year old's natural inclination to oppose us (after all, from *his* point of view, *we* are the ones who are stepping out of line) by attempting to force cooperation, the game is lost.

The struggle itself is our undoing. A person in control has no need to struggle.

So far, so good. You are definitely *not* in a power struggle with your son over the use of the toilet. You say, "Please?" he says, "No!" and you back down. Under the circumstances, he has no need to struggle. He is in control.

Ah, but *avoiding* power struggles is only part of the picture. The real trick is to learn to maneuver *around*, rather than retreat from, opposition. In other words, you don't fight, but you don't run away either. Up until now, you have not taken an assertive stance on the question of whether your son uses the potty or not. Because of your indecision, your son has seized the opportunity to proclaim, "I'm more powerful than you are."

For seven days, make no mention of the potty. Change his diapers on schedule, without protest or impatience. If he tells you he *wants* to sit on the toilet, give him an assist and then excuse yourself. If he calls you to see his accomplishment, acknowledge what he has done in a positive, but matter-of-fact way: "That's very good. I'm going to put your diapers back on now."

During the week, purchase several pairs of heavy cotton training pants. On the morning of the eighth day, greet him with this announcement: "Today is a brand-new day! Today you begin to use the potty. You are not going to wear diapers any more. You are going to wear these big-boy pants and learn how to keep them dry. Come with Mommy. I want to show you something."

Take him to the bathroom and show him an alarm clock you put there the night before (as an alternative, the timer on your stove will do).

"This clock has a bell that will tell you when you need to sit down and use the potty. It's called the potty bell. When you hear the potty bell, *I want you* to come in here and sit on the potty. The bell will ring four times today (set it to ring in the morning, after lunch, before dinner and before bed), but you may use the potty any other time you need to. You aren't wearing diapers any more. *I want you* to keep these big-boy pants dry."

Set the alarm to ring at the same times every day for the next few days. When it rings, tell your son, "It's time for you to use the potty. Call me if you need some help." Don't become overly involved. Prompt him when the bell rings and then keep your distance.

If he tells you he doesn't want to sit right then, don't push, but gently remind him that he needs to keep his pants dry.

Respond to his successes with encouragement, but without unnecessary razzmatazz. Deal with accidents (and there will be some) in a calm, direct manner: "You forgot to use the potty. That's all right. You will do better next time. I'll help you put dry pants on. Remember, *I want you* to keep these pants dry by using the potty."

By using an alarm to signal "potty-time," you are gently turning his resistance away from you. At the same time you are making clear, authoritative statements which convey what you expect of him.

Instead of giving him permission to say, "I won't," you can give him an opportunity to grow. It's an offer he can't refuse.

Power Struggles

(**Q**) My four-year-old daughter holds her bowel movements. Her pediatrician assures us that there is nothing physically wrong with her. She lets out only a little at a time and therefore is still in diapers. I have been playing it cool and not forcing the issue, but she has a younger brother who is an infant, and the thrill of changing diapers is wearing thin.

(**A**) I would not hesitate, with a four year old, to communicate some firm expectations about where to put b.m.'s. Young children are quite intuitive and can sense when their parents have a big investment in an issue. I suspect that your daughter has seized on this passive form of rebellion to keep attention focused on her, rather than on her younger brother. In this way, she continues to get her importance confirmed. What you need is a method which will get her to use the toilet and at the same time reassure her that she is important.

Tape a sheet of paper daily to the refrigerator door or some equally visible place. Tell her firmly that she is not going to wear diapers anymore and that she will use the toilet for b.m.'s. Inform her that when she has an accident, she will receive a large check (✔) on her score card.

Now consider what privileges she enjoys daily. Playing outside after supper? Riding her tricycle? Going to a friend's house? Make a list of three activities she values most. Tell her that you will eliminate one activity for every accident, starting with the activity that is most important to her.

Then explain that an accident-free day will earn her a special privilege. Make a list of five activities she likes, but doesn't get to do often (go to McDonald's, go to a park, go to bed at 9:30 instead of 8:30). Let her choose one at the end of every "perfect" day and deliver her reward the following day.

Expect two to three weeks to pass before you see steady progress. Don't be discouraged by a relapse after a good start. Stay firm, but gentle, and always be encouraging. Your confidence in her, combined with a steady attitude of authority, will make more of a difference to her than anything else.

It's None of Your Business

(Q) Bobby, our four year old, is not bowel trained. He holds his b.m.'s and constipates himself for several days at a time, sometimes nearly a week. When he can't hold any longer, he usually releases in his pants. Sometimes he tells us when he is about to go, and one of us literally runs him to the bathroom, but once we get there he usually loses the urge. Later he will have his inevitable accident. We have tried laxatives, and they made him somewhat more regular, but no more cooperative. We have him clean himself with supervision after every mistake. He also needs help taking his pants down and getting up on the potty. We've tried everything.

(A) Wow! I'm exhausted! Frankly, your son is not putting his b.m.'s in the toilet because you are doing all the work. He may not be trained, but *you* certainly are. And by the way, he *is* cooperating — in the confusion.

You are investing a tremendous amount of energy in monitoring, supervising and helping him with something he should be in charge of by the age of four. This long-term investment has created a climate of chaos and confusion concerning "Bobby's b.m.'s."

No one, including Bobby, knows exactly what to do when Bobby feels like having a b.m. The statement, "we've tried everything," probably means that over the years there has been an accumulation of inconsistent responses and messages in reaction to his gestures, requests and mistakes.

Your son is confused. He is probably wondering, "Who's having the b.m., me or my parents? Is a b.m. something that should or shouldn't happen? Can I have one by myself? Who am I doing it for? Am I really four years old?" Because there are no clear definitions, the confusion has never been resolved.

It is essential that you back out of the picture. First, define the situation.

Teach him, if he *really* does not know, how to pull his pants down or off and position himself on the toilet seat. If he has difficulty, dress him in elastic-waisted shorts. A wooden stool will give him any additional boost he needs.

Most four year olds are capable of cleaning themselves *without supervision*. Some initial guidance for Bobby will help to define this as his responsibility. Take the time to teach him exactly what he should do when he soils himself. However, this lesson should take place *when he is clean*.

Organize the necessary equipment (washcloths, sponge, liquid soap, towels, clean underwear and so on) in one specific, accessible area of the bathroom, and put him through the paces of cleaning himself. Practice the sequence several times, in an encouraging and positive manner.

When he tells you he feels the pressure of a b.m., tell him to go to the bathroom and sit on the potty, "just as everyone else does." If he wants you to take him (after all, he hasn't had to do the work up until now), tell him, "I will not help you have a b.m."

If he has an accident (count on it), send him to the bathroom to clean himself. If he comes out before either he or the room is clean, simply say, "You are not finished. Go back in and finish — then you may come out."

During the day, do *not* ask him if he needs to go or provide him with reminders. This age child no longer needs to be protected from the consequences of his own mistakes.

When he has success, keep your reactions low-key. After all, he's learning to accept this responsibility for *his* benefit, not yours. Furthermore, success is not a big deal — it's expected of him. "That's fine. No, I don't need to come see. You can do it all by yourself. You don't need Daddy to look."

Finally, give him plenty of time to adjust and expect some lapses along the way. If you can stay with the program, and roll with the initial ups and downs, he will eventually match the pace you set for him. Just as he has all along.

Bedwetting

If your child wets the bed almost every night, then you undoubtedly know that none of the "home remedies" are much help. Punishment, restriction of liquids, getting her up at intervals — none of these works. Some of these methods may provide temporary relief, but all of them together won't stop a child from wetting the bed.

Somewhere along the line, most of us have been taught that wetting the bed is a symptom of laziness or insecurity, and that it's a child's way of saying that things aren't going right at home. While it is true that many children who wet the bed do feel ashamed and are under a great deal of stress because of it, there is no reason to believe that bedwetting is an expression of a damaged emotional condition.

Actually, bedwetting happens, in most cases, because the child is an unusually deep sleeper. This deep sleep prevents her from waking when the bladder sends an "I'm full" signal to the brain. The signal is too weak, or the brain is too deeply asleep to "hear" it. In either case, the bladder does the natural thing, which is to empty itself. It's easy to see why the home remedies described above will be no more useful than beating one's head against a brick wall.

However, there is a way to approach bedwetting which requires nothing more than your patience and understanding. First, give the problem back to your child. Stop trying frantically to solve it for her. It's *her* body and *her* problem, and she can solve it only if *she* has possession of it.

Stop making "Did you wet the bed last night?" the first question of every day. Her bedwetting should not be a topic of family discussion.

Tell her that when she wets the bed she is to change her pajamas, lay a heavy towel across the wet spot and go back to bed without waking the family. In the morning, she is to strip her own bed and place the wet linens and wet pajamas in a pile just inside her bedroom door. After you have done the wash, put the folded linen back on her bed. At bedtime, have her help you make the bed, patiently teaching her how and letting her take over more and more of the chore until she is able to do it by herself.

Give her as much liquid as she wants all day. It's probably good to remind young children to use the bathroom just before bed, but do it casually.

Help your child understand her problem by providing some basic education. Tell her that there is a muscle just below her bladder (you can call it the "doughnut" muscle) which is normally closed. When she goes to the bathroom, she relaxes this muscle and it opens (open and close your fist to demonstrate). Suggest to her that she might want to make this muscle stronger by practicing tightening and holding it for several seconds off and on during the day. And when she goes to the bathroom, she can further strengthen it by turning off and on her flow of urine. Most children will cooperate willingly in this exercise.

A number of pediatricians now advise parents of children who wet the bed to eliminate all refined sugar from the children's diet. Substitute fruits, nuts, raw vegetables or peanut butter and crackers along with a glass of unsweetened juice for bedtime snacks instead of sugar-sweetened "goodies." (For further reading on this topic, see Dr. Lendon Smith's *Improving Your Child's Behavior Chemistry.*)

If, after doing these things for about six weeks, the bedwetting has not stopped, then I recommend that you purchase a bedwetting alarm. (One good one is the "Wee-Alarm-Alert," available from the Sears Roebuck and Co. catalogue for about $30.) A typical system consists of a set of pads which are arranged under the sheet and an alarm connected to the pads which sounds immediately when the child begins to wet. Through repetition, this device eventually teaches the child to wake to the feeling of a full bladder. Then use of the alarm can be discontinued.

This alarm operates on low voltage batteries, is completely safe, and when used properly, it usually works. The Wee-Alarm is *not*, however, to be used with children younger than four, many of whom are still developing night-time control. Nor is it to be used without the child's consent and a definite indication from her that she wants to stop wetting the bed.

Bedwetting kids are not "bad" kids. However, you can bet that the more of an issue you make of the problem, the more overwhelmed the child will feel, and the longer it will be before she can solve it for herself.

(Q) Our five year old, who has always been a bedwetter, has recently started wetting his pants during the day. He doesn't tell us about it, but waits until one of us points out that he's damp and suggests that he change his clothes. We haven't criticized or reprimanded him for these accidents, and the bedwetting is not a topic for discussion either. Do you think he could be wetting himself for attention? Do you have any suggestions?

(A) My first suggestion is that you break your vow of silence. Bedwetting can become an increasingly burdensome handicap for a child as he grows older, one which limits his social life and damages his self-concept.

Your decision not to discuss it, although motivated by good intentions, is actually preventing him from initiating any work toward a lasting solution. You seem to be giving tacit permission for the problem to linger indefinitely. This is not in anyone's best interest.

To begin with, I would wager that you *are* upset — about both the daytime accidents and the bedwetting. Your frustration at having to change and wash smelly sheets, pajamas and now clothes, nearly every day, needs to be acknowledged and accepted as legitimate. *How* you express that frustration, rather than *whether* you express it, is the central question.

You have probably succeeded admirably at suppressing your annoyance. But our children are more sensitive to us than we generally imagine. Although neither situation has been a topic for discussion, you probably cannot avoid sending subtle, non-verbal cues that tell of your displeasure—an expression, a gesture, an exchanged look. Your silence itself is perhaps the most blatant message.

The topic needs clarification, but because no one has permission to talk about it, your son can't ask, "Are you mad, or aren't you?" So, in an attempt to resolve this ambiguity, he begins wetting his pants during the day, when you can't fail to notice. Will you say anything *now*? How much will it take to bring you out of hiding?

It is probably wrong to say that he's doing this for attention. The fact that he waits for you to mention it strongly suggests he is trying to draw you out. It's time to show your hand.

Begin with a discussion of his bedwetting. Define it as a problem for you. Tell him you don't enjoy changing and washing sheets and pajamas every day. Bring it out in the open, so you can begin helping him solve this difficulty.

Be careful, however, that you *don't* take responsibility for it. The responsibility must be *his*. He needs a clear, straightforward message from you regarding your feelings and a commitment of understanding and support.

"Junior, we want to talk with you about wetting the bed. You are wetting your bed almost every night, and we both think it's time you began staying dry at night. We want to know how you feel about this. Do you want to continue wetting the bed, or do you want to stop?"

Some indication from him that *he* wants to stop wetting the bed is essential, but you cannot force this point of view upon him. However, it will be much easier for him to make that statement once he knows where you stand.

He also needs to hear a clear message concerning the daytime accidents: "We also want you to stop wetting during the day."

Once you have squarely faced the issue and settled your ambivalence, he will no longer need to wet his pants. The chances are also good that he will stop wetting the bed. If he doesn't, and he begins to express some frustration at not having the success he wants, I would recommend that you purchase a bedwetting alarm (see page 148).

I have heard these alarms criticized as artificial, impersonal means of conditioning a child to stop bedwetting. This is completely off the mark.

My son began wetting his bed shortly after we moved to North Carolina when he was four and a half. Nine months later, a friend and colleague told us about the bedwetting alarm. We bought one and asked Eric if he would like to try it out. The first night, he wet the bed before he went to sleep just to hear the alarm go off.

Over the next three weeks, he *alone* triumphed over what all of us struggling together had managed to make worse. At the end of that three weeks, he proudly informed us that he did not need the unit any more. I'm certain he had never felt so proud of himself. If that smacks of something impersonal, then I must have missed something.

The manufacturer does not guarantee success, and it would be foolish of me to imply that it's foolproof. However, your child's self-esteem is worth the relatively few dollars it will cost you to give it a try.

A Tantrum Place

Children usually begin having tantrums around the age of two. Tantrums happen for a variety of reasons. First of all, they are an inevitable by-product of even the most normal, healthy childhoods. Children become frustrated and angry just as we do, but they can't see that there is "more than one way to skin a cat." They also have difficulty expressing their frustrations and knowing what questions to ask. If at first they don't succeed, they just might have a tantrum.

A cardinal rule is don't respond to tantrums by taking over the problem for the child. If parents rescue a child often enough, she learns that tantrums solve problems. If a child has a "this-dumb-toy-won't-obey-me" tantrum, take the dumb-toy and tell the out-of-control child that it will be returned when she is calm.

A second rule-of-thumb is don't give in to demands because of tantrums. It's true that giving in turns off the screams, but it also guarantees their eventual return.

Spankings don't cure the tantrum habit. In fact, they *increase* the likelihood that tantrums will occur. You can't fight fire with fire.

The occasional tantrum can be handled best by letting it run its course and then being there when it subsides to help the child cope with whatever is making her upset.

Frequent tantrums are often an indication that the parents are not enforcing rules consistently. One day, Miranda wants a cookie before supper and gets it because Mom is too tired to be firm. The next day, she is refused a cookie before supper because Mom took an afternoon nap. She throws a tantrum. Mom may (A) spank her, (B) give her a cookie, (C) put her in her room, (D) throw a tantrum, (E) all of the above. This kind of inconsistency places stress on a child. Stress provokes tension, fatigue and tantrums.

Remember what Grandma did when you told her you were running away from home? She probably said, "That's a wonderful idea. You should have left home to see the world long before now. After all, you're six years old and time's a-wastin'. So, I'll help you pack and fix you a sandwich. . . ." And there you were back at Grandma's door 20 minutes later, having seen quite enough for six years old.

Grandma had some fine ideas. She could tell the big people from the little people without a program, and she never needed a score card. So let's lift a page from Grandma's memoirs and see if tantrums can be handled with some homemade "reverse psychology."

Pick a calm time when everyone in the family is feeling relaxed. Sit down with your young one and say something like, "Miranda, we want to talk with you about tantrums. A tantrum is when you are very angry and scream and throw things and foam at the mouth.

"You make about 10 tantrums every day, so we have decided to give you a special place to have tantrums in. We call it your Tantrum Place. Your Tantrum Place is the downstairs bathroom" (or any relatively private place in the house).

"From now on, when you want to make a tantrum, go (or we will take you) to your Tantrum Place, close the door and make it. You may make all the tantrums you want in there. No one will bother you while you make tantrums."

Whichever place you choose, make it seem it's the best location in the whole house to make tantrums in. No where else is quite good enough for the fine tantrums that Miranda makes.

"We decided to give you the bathroom, because it seems just right for making tantrums. It's small, so the tantrum will be louder. It has a toilet you can use if you have to go potty. There is a light switch for you to turn off and on to make tantrums bigger. You can lie down on the comfy rug and kick and scream. When the tantrum is done, you have tissues to dry your tears and water to wash your face. We hope you like it. In fact, it would be all right if you want to go in there *right now* and make a tantrum, just to see how well it works."

Chances are that she will make a few trial runs the first day, and then, finding that the thrill is gone, will begin having shorter tantrums less often. As she begins having fewer tantrums, point this out to her, and thank her for helping keep the house quiet.

Should she forget about her special place and begin making tantrums in the living room, say something like, "Oh-oh, remember the Tantrum Place. You had better get in there quickly before it's all gone." If necessary, take her there while she is screaming, firmly but without anger.

If she continues to have an occasional tantrum outside while you aren't around, or in her room by herself, let these run their course without notice.

Is it a trick? No. The parents are not one-uping the child with an elaborate practical joke. It's actually a game in which everyone learns something valuable about dealing with stressful situations.

I've seen this technique work with children between the ages of two and a half and five, the ages at which tantrums occur most frequently. Children older than five probably will not cooperate in the game so readily and may simply have to be told, "I do not like tantrums. From now on, when you have a tantrum, I am going to put you in the downstairs bathroom. When you go in there, the door will be closed. You are not to open it and come out until the tantrum is completely over. If you come out before it's over, I will put you back in again."

If Grandma's game doesn't appear to be working, then you may need to be more firm. If nothing you try appears to be having any positive effect, consider seeking professional help. Whatever you decide, if at first you don't succeed, don't throw a tantrum.

Headbanging

(Q) We have a three year old who is a headbanger. At six months, she began banging on the bars of her crib, hard enough to cause bruises. When she was nearly two, the banging shifted from bedtime to almost constant banging on the floor, a chair and so on. There are two types of banging: one to soothe or put her to sleep; the other to express anger or frustration. She knows this gets to us, and we have been known to give in to her just to get her to stop. I know this is not a solution, but nothing else we do seems to have any effect. Our pediatrician insists she cannot hurt herself. He does, however, feel that she has a psychological problem. Friends and relatives are beginning to ask what's wrong with her. What can we do to stop her?

(**A**) To begin with, your pediatrician is correct: She is not likely to hurt herself. That certainly isn't her aim.

But I don't think she has a psychological problem. While it *is* true that many emotionally disturbed and autistic children headbang, it is also a fact that many normal children do the same thing.

Headbanging is fairly common among infants and toddlers. Generally speaking, it begins around the sixth month, shortly after the infant is first able to raise herself to a crawling position. At this stage, infants test their balance by rocking back and forth on their hands and knees, looking as though they're trying to build up enough momentum to take off. If a solid object, such as a wall or headboard is immediately in front of them, they are likely to discover the untold pleasures of headbanging.

The monotonous combination of rhythm and self-stimulation is hypnotic, lulling the child into a blissful, self-absorbed trance. In this respect, headbanging is no different from thumbsucking or nuzzling a favorite blanket. All of these behaviors are soothing, and the child who discovers their benefits has found an ingenious way of providing for herself some of the comfort she might otherwise be demanding of her parents. By sucking her thumb or banging her head, she is able to put herself to sleep, separate from her mother, occupy idle time and even postpone the need to be held or fed. In one sense, then, it's a fortunate parent who has a headbanger.

But that's *not* the way most parents look at it. In the first place, good parents don't allow their children to hurt themselves. Furthermore, rocking and headbanging have been erroneously associated with severe emotional problems. The idea that we might be raising a child who is so disturbed that she actually enjoys pain is too much to deal with.

So, we try to stop her. First, we give her something else to do. The distraction works—temporarily. A short while later, we hear a thud-thud sound coming from the den. We rush in to find that she has crawled over to the wall and is steadily ramming her head into the baseboard. We pick her up, carry her into the kitchen and offer her a cookie.

This goes on throughout the day, and eventually she puts things together—banging her head not only feels good, but is a form of communication. When you want Mommy, just bang your head on something—it's like Morse code.

The more she bangs her forehead, the greater her threshold for pain in that area becomes, and the harder she must bang to feel anything at all. Bruises become discolored bumps, and people begin eyeing us suspiciously, their imaginations in high gear.

But the harder we work at getting her to stop, the more she bangs. When she reaches her "Terrible Twos," the headbanging is absorbed into her tantrums, and, since she is already out of control, the banging becomes more violent. By this time, we will go to almost any length to stop her, and she learns that headbanging can get her just about anything she wants. What started as an irrelevant, self-indulgence has become a focus of tension in the family. The entire family is obviously edging closer to the brink. You must gain control of this situation.

What should you do? Do very little. The more fuel you funnel into this issue, the higher the flames will leap.

Find a time when the house is calm and running in tune, for both parents to talk with her about the headbanging: "We have decided that you need a place to bang your head. Banging your head is O.K. with us, but we don't want to watch or listen. If you want to bang, go to your room. You can bang on anything you want in there. Mommy and I will help you remember the rule."

Keep it short and to the point. Don't expect her to remember. Every time she bangs, whether it's to soothe or express rage, say, "You forgot the rule. You may bang your head in your room. I'll help you get there."

Whether she resists or not, take her there and leave her, saying, "When you finish banging, you may come out."

You may not see any results for several weeks. In fact, an upsurge may occur as she pits her will against yours. The more violent form should subside within six weeks, but she may continue to bang her head as a means of relaxing for several years to come.

After all, it still feels good.

Zeke and the Tar Baby

In one of Joel Chandler Harris' Uncle Remus stories, Brer Fox and Brer Bear make a tar baby, hoping to catch Brer Rabbit once and for all. Sure enough, pretty soon Brer Rabbit meets up with the tar baby and makes some remark about the weather, but the tar baby says nothing. After failing several more times to strike up a conversation, Brer Rabbit becomes angry and hits the tar baby smack in the piece of coal Fox and Bear had used for its nose. Naturally, Brer Rabbit's fist sticks in the tar baby's face, which makes him even madder. So he hits the tar baby again with his other hand, which also becomes stuck. Furious, Brer Rabbit begins kicking the tar baby. In no time, he is covered in tar and unable to move. Enter Fox and Bear.

Sometimes parents get bogged down in problems with their children the same way Brer Rabbit did with the tar baby. First, they make the mistake of attributing more significance to something than it deserves. Then, instead of learning from their mistakes, they become frustrated and begin flailing away at the problem. The more they flail, the more stuck they get. Eventually, the issue begins to infect nearly every aspect of their lives together, and as Brer Rabbit would surely testify, once the tar baby gots you, you ain't goin' no place.

Several years ago, a young couple asked my advice concerning their three-and-a-half-year-old son, whom I shall call Zeke. Zeke was not unlike many other three and a half year olds in that he refused to take "no" for an answer and was determined to run as much of the show as his parents would allow.

And how Zeke's parents had allowed! At three and a half, Zeke did pretty much as he pleased. His parents claimed to have run out of ways to control him. "Nothing works!" they chorused. Guess who was in control?

They had tried spanking him. Small spankings made him laugh, and big spankings made him furious and frenzied. To make matters worse, Zeke's parents spanked too late and always felt guilty afterwards, which Zeke was sensitive to and made the most of.

Taking privileges away didn't work either. And no wonder. After all, what's a mere privilege to a child who is calling most of the shots as it is?

His parents had tried talking to Zeke. Oh, and how they talked to him. Like a lawyer in his closing argument they talked to him. When they were finished, Zeke would say, "I'll be good," and proceed to do whatever it was they had asked him not to do. With a smile on his face, no less!

Putting him in his room didn't work. Oh, Zeke would go in all right, but then he would go berserk, turning over bookcases, emptying drawers, and throwing toys and clothes everywhere, all the while giving forth a shrill, lunatic scream. If his parents told him to clean up his mess, he would get worse (if you can imagine that), continuing to scream and thrash about until one of them came in and picked up for him. Maid service in the booby hatch!

After describing all this, they asked me what I thought they should do when Zeke misbehaved.

"Putting him in his room sounds fine to me," I told them.

"Well," they countered, "what are we supposed to do when he goes on one of his rampages?"

"Is he capable of cleaning up afterward?' I asked.

"Oh, yes," they said. "The problem is not that he can't, it's that he won't."

"Well, then," I ventured, "since he's capable of cleaning up after himself, make him stay in his room until he does."

They thought that was funny. "He'd be in there for days," they chortled.

"So? What's a few days?" I replied.

After convincing them that I wasn't kidding, and that what I was suggesting wasn't too extreme (just a minor, and rather fitting inconvenience), we made a list of Zeke's most frequent transgressions. Zeke would go to his room whenever he did any of the things on the list.

And a new rule was created: if Zeke went on a rampage, he had to remain there until he had completely cleaned up his damage, regardless of how long it took. Meanwhile, he could come out to go to the bathroom, attend his preschool program (three mornings a week), eat meals with the family (with no discussion of his room) and accompany his parents whenever they both left the house. Otherwise, it was full quarantine for Zeke.

Here's what happened:

Day 1, at 3:45 p.m.: Zeke hit his mother and was sent to his room where, just as expected, he went bananas. Refusing to undo any of the destruction, he spent the rest of the day in seclusion (except for supper), screaming insults at his parents (example: "Doo-doo heads!").

Day 2: Except for morning at the preschool and a brief trip to the store with his mother, Zeke stayed in his room.

Day 3: Zeke remained in his room, refusing to budge.

Day 4: Still in his room, Zeke showed signs of weakening. At one point, Zeke offered to clean up some of his room if his mother would do the rest. Wisely, she refused the deal. He called her a "doo-doo" (dropping the reference to her head was a definite sign of progress).

Day 5: That afternoon, a friend dropped by, bringing her son, who was also three and a half. In less than 15 minutes, Zeke had his room in order.

Zeke tore up his room several times in the following weeks. Each time, he straightened it up before the end of the day. To my knowledge, he hasn't torn up his room since, and that's where his parents send him when he misbehaves. Because it works.

Another tar baby bites the dust.

Bedtime

A Very Hoppy Bedtime Story

A long, long time ago, in a bedroom far, far away, there lay a three-year-old boy named Grumph Nadly, who would not sleep.

Every night at 8:30 his mother would say, "Grumph Nadly, it's time for bed."

He would yell, "I don't want to!" and his mother would ask, "Why not?" Grumph would reply, "Cuz."

He would scream, "I'm scared!", and his father would inquire, "Of what?" Grumph would earnestly answer, "Things."

His mother would say, "Let's go Grumph, it's time for munchkins to be asleep," and Grumph would collapse in a heap on the floor. The heap that was Grumph Nadly would not move, but it would sob and moan piteously.

At last, Grumph's father would pick him up and carry him, shrieking, off to bed. Then, when Grumph was finally quiet and looking the other way, his parents would scurry off and hide. But it was no use. The sound would always find them.

It began softly, ". . . Mommy?"

But if the sound got no answer it grew louder and louder until it fairly shook the rafters: "MOMMEEEEE!"

Then the sound would get an answer. "Yes, Grumph, what is it?"

Sometimes Grumph would say he was hungry or had to go to the "bafoom" or wanted to tell somebody "sumpun." Whatever it was, he would make all the noise he could until the whatever was seen to properly.

Grumph usually went to sleep around midnight and woke up with the sun. His parents had dark circles under their eyes and shuffled when they walked.

One day, Grumph Nadly's mother set out from home and shuffled deep into the woods, seeking peace and quiet. She had shuffled for several hours and was passing a small pond alive with water lilies and butterflies, when she heard a small baritone voice ask, "Are you lost, or what?"

"Who's there?" she asked, startled and looking around.

"Me. Look down here, lady."

And sure enough, when she looked, there he was, a rather unremarkable frog. Unremarkable, that is, except for the fact that he talked, which is *quite* remarkable for frogs.

Before the startled woman could say anything, the frog

spoke again, asking, "What brings you to my front yard?"

And Grumph's mother felt suddenly moved to tell the frog everything about how Grumph would not sleep and the heap and the sound and the rest until the frog, having heard quite enough, said, "Hold it!" You wanna know how to get this Grumph-child into bed and off to sleep?" With hardly a pause, he went right on, "I'll tell you. But first you have to promise *not* to kiss me when I'm done."

"But why on earth should I want to kiss you in the first place?" asked Grumph's mother.

"Mark my words, you'll want to, and if you manage to grab me and do it, I'll turn into the most handsome and charming prince you ever saw, which is the worst thing that could *ever* happen to a frog who wants to just spend the rest of his life sitting on water lilies, eating bugs."

"All right, I won't kiss you," promised the woman, who had never kissed a frog anyway. "Tell! Tell!"

"Well," the frog began, "you make a book, see, called 'Grumph Nadly's Bedtime Book.' All you need is some sturdy paper, paste, a hole-punch and yarn.

"First, make a list of what's done to prepare the heap for bed.

"Then, gather up several magazines and find pictures to go with each of the things in your list. Make sure you find one of a kid sleeping—draw one if you have to.

"Paste each picture on a separate sheet of paper, put them in order, with the picture of the kid sleeping last. Punch holes in the left-hand side, and tie a loose loop of yarn through each hole.

"Then, write a story to go with the pictures, and every night, read the story to Grumph right before bed.

"For example, the book might begin, 'It's 8 o'clock, and time for Grumph Nadly to begin getting ready for bed. The first thing he does is . . . ,' and you show him the picture of a child taking a bath. Together, you and the Grumph say, 'Take a bath.' The next page reads, 'After his bath, the Grumph dries himself and puts on his pajamas.' And Grumph sees a picture of a kid in pajamas. Keep going until the last page, which says something like, 'And when everything is done, Grumph's Mommy and Daddy tuck him in, kiss him goodnight and Grumph Nadly goes to sleep like a good little tadpole."

When the frog finished his description, he looked at Grumph's mother, adding, "By the time you get to the end, the Grumph should be so involved in his story that he'll take the cue and go right off to sleep."

Grumph's mother thanked the frog profusely, being careful

not to kiss him, and hurried home with nary a shuffle in her step. She did exactly as the frog had told her and, lo and behold, that night Grumph Nadly was asleep by 8:45.

Every night thereafter, Grumph and his mother would read the "Bedtime Book" together, and he would go quickly and quietly off to sleep—which is where our story should end, but it doesn't, because . . .

Several years later, Grumph's mother was skipping through the woods when she happened across the same pond.

"Well?" a familiar baritone voice intoned. "Did it work?"

Grumph's mother stopped short and, looking down, saw the very same frog, looking not a year older.

"Yes! Oh, yes! It worked, just like you said!" she replied. Then, remembering what the frog had said about being a handsome prince, she grabbed him and planted a big kiss in the middle of his face. Nothing happened.

She kissed him again, longer this time (with her eyes closed). Still nothing happened.

"Hey! What's wrong?" complained Grumph's mother. "Turn into a prince, already."

The frog just laughed as he hopped back onto his lily pad.

"Sorry, lady, but I'm just a talking frog who likes to be kissed." And without even a goodbye, he jumped off his pad, landing in the center of the pond with a great splash and was never seen again.

The moral, good reader, is simply this: don't ever kiss a frog, no matter what he may have . . . toad you.

More Than Meets the Eye

(Q) Our first child is 13 months old. For 13 months, I have been rocking him to sleep at night and also for his naps. I don't mind doing this—I'd rather rock him than listen to him cry, which he does if I put him in his crib before he's completely asleep. Although I'd like for him to be in bed by 8:30 p.m., the actual time varies because there are nights when he just doesn't seem tired until nine or ten o'clock. But regardless of when I put him in bed, he always sleeps the night. Recently, my pediatrician told me to stop rocking him, put him in bed at the same time every night and let him go off to sleep on his own, even if it means some crying. The doctor says Robbie is learning that if he cries at bedtime, I'll pick him up. Do you agree with this?

(A) Almost. I definitely agree with your pediatrician that you need to stop rocking young Robbie off to sleep, establish a definite bedtime (with allowances built in for occasional times when it isn't possible to keep him on schedule) and let him go to sleep on his own.

There's far more at stake here, however, than a relatively simple matter of learning to connect crying with being picked up. In fact, it's what Robbie *isn't* learning that warrants the lion's share of attention and concern.

For instance, Robbie *isn't* learning how to go to sleep by himself. Instead, he is becoming increasingly reliant on you. There's a strong possibility that he may eventually think that being next to you is essential to falling asleep. Having a 13 month old cry for a while at bedtime is one thing; having a three year old *fight* you at bedtime is quite another.

Robbie *isn't* learning how to predict when bedtime is at hand. It is important that there be some certainty about this, because a child's feelings of security rest, in large measure, on being able to "read" the environment for cues that certain events are about to happen.

In a child's world, *time* needs to be as well organized as the furniture and other things. Confusion over where-things-are or when-things-happen encumbers a child's attempts to make sense of his surroundings.

Routines help a child develop a clear sense of cause and effect (logical thinking), and they contribute to his feelings of competence and confidence.

Robbie *isn't* learning that you control when things occur. Instead of deciding when Robbie's bedtime is, you seem to be looking to *him* for a signal, a vague sign of some sort that he is ready. This puts him in the driver's seat before he has even learned to be a good passenger.

But the biggest "isn't" of all is that Robbie *isn't* learning how to let go of you when the day is done. You aren't learning how to comfortably let go of him either.

The importance of bedtime has little to do with *when* children get tired or how much sleep they need. It has, on the other hand, *everything* to do with parents who need time together and, most of all, with teaching children that letting go is O.K. Bedtime is really nothing more than a ritual of separation.

Virtually every important issue that comes up between parent and child involves, to some degree, questions of attachment versus non-attachment. To the extent that these questions are successfully resolved, a child can be less dependent upon his parents. In other words, learning how to let go of parents (mother in particular) is learning how to grow up.

Bedtime problems often bring up this larger issue for the

first time. How they are handled will set a precedent for dealing with future separations of many kinds: staying with baby-sitters, going to school and so on.

It's up to you, as Robbie's parents, to take the lead and set a good precedent. If you are indecisive about letting go at bedtime, he may interpret your hesitation or reluctance as a signal that something is wrong with separating. And, believe me, few things are more stressful to a family than a clinging child.

If you want Robbie in bed at 8:30 p.m., first establish a routine that begins at eight o'clock and lets him know that bedtime is coming. Cap the routine with a tucking-in ceremony; then leave the room.

If he cries (as he almost surely will), you and your husband should take turns going back into his room every five or ten minutes to calm him and reassure him that you are still there, taking care of him. Don't pick him up, and don't hang around.

Bedtime Is for Parents

(Q) We have a three-year-old son who is afraid of the dark and will not go to bed unless one of us stays with him until he is asleep. This started about one year ago, but he was O.K. at bedtime as long as the hall light was on. Now that's not enough. When we put him to bed (at 8:30 every night), he screams about being afraid of the dark until one of us goes back in to stay with him. If we do that, he usually stays up until eleven and sometimes twelve o'clock; then he sleeps until 6:30 a.m. and is rarin' to go. I don't see how he could be getting enough sleep. We have tried spanking him and keeping him up later to make him sleepy, to no avail. My doctor said to let him scream, but the first night we tried that, he went on for three hours. We are all about to go crazy. Can you offer any suggestions or hope for the future?

(A) I'll take a stab at both.

To begin with, let's get this whole *reason for bedtime* business straightened out. Once we do that, I believe everything else will fall right into place.

It is my sworn professional obligation to inform you that bedtimes do *not* exist because children need to sleep. Yep, you've been hoodwinked.

Rumor has it that three year olds need 10 to 12 hours of sleep each night. Hogwash. Except in the most unusual of circumstances, children get all the sleep they need, *regardless* of when they fall asleep or how long they stay that way.

Generally speaking, a child will let you know when he's tired, and if he needs 12 hours of sleep, he'll get it. On the other hand, there are some three year olds who need only eight hours of sleep (and some even less) a night.

In other words, every child's need for sleep is different. That makes sense, doesn't it? Why should we expect that two children who have different appetites, dispositions and activity levels will both need ten hours of sleep each night?

You may not understand how he can get up at the crack of dawn all bright-eyed and bushy-tailed while you feel like leftovers, but that's the way it is. I assure you, he is getting all the sleep he needs.

But that has nothing to do with bedtime, because (I repeat) bedtimes are not necessary because of children's need for sleep. A bedtime is for the *parents'* benefit, *not* the children's.

Only after the children are in bed can parents renew their acquaintance with one another without being interrupted for "feed me's" or "hold me's" or whatever the latest "me's" may "be's."

What difference does it make if the children aren't asleep? Who cares if they want the lights on? Not I.

When Amy, my daughter, was three and a half, she absolutely refused to go quietly off to sleep at her appointed time (also 8:30 p.m.). She pulled the old cry-a-while-and-then-come-downstairs-for-one-last-look routine.

"Yes, Amy, what is it?"

"Uhhhhhh . . . I wanna as' you sump'in."

"Well, what is it?"

"Uhhhhhhhhhmmmmmmmmmmmmm . . ."

"We're waiting."

"Come on, Amy, let's hear it!"

"When's my birfday?"

And so it went, night after night until we realized that sleep wasn't what she needed and wasn't necessarily why we were putting her to bed in the first place. We put her to bed because of *lust!*

At that point, we simply told her she had to go to her room at 8:30 p.m. And stay there. But she didn't have to sleep if she didn't want to. She could, after we tucked her in and kissed her "nigh-night," turn on her light, close her door and play to her heart's content while we relaxed our bodies and renewed our relationship.

By the time we were ready for bed, she was usually asleep on the floor, surrounded by her playthings.

Amy is now nine. She *still* goes off to bed at 8:30 p.m., is asleep by nine o'clock (usually), and I couldn't care less.

Monsters in the Closet

(Q) Our five-year-old daughter, who just started kindergarten, is afraid to go upstairs by herself. She will not climb the stairs, day or night, without one of us in front of her, and she demands that we check her bedroom and the closet in particular, for monsters. If we balk or insist she go by herself, she becomes hysterical. I'm afraid this may be the beginning of a serious emotional problem that, handled wrong, could have a permanent effect on her. What should we do? We have another child, who is fourteen months old.

(A) There's a monster in your closet, too. It's the Something-Horrible-Will-Happen-To-My-Child's-Mind-If-I-Do-The-Wrong-Thing Monster.

This foul creature lives in closets wherever there are parents who believe that children are little Humpty Dumptys in life's biggest egg-toss game: one wrong move and they'll be broken forever.

This monster in *our* closet haunts our relationships with our children, jumping out at us when we least expect it, zapping our common sense and paralyzing our spontaneity.

He lurches through our waking nightmares, hissing, "Your children have emotional problems, and it's all because of you."

Well, I'm afraid I bring you bad news. *All* children grow up with emotional problems. Emotions *are* a problem, especially for children. Emotions are powerful, unpredictable, violent, stormy, confusing and often painful. Most of a person's growing years are spent learning how to tame these beasts within.

For the first 20 years of her life, a human being stumbles through one emotional upheaval after another—birth (the all-time champ), separation, being two, learning to share, going off to school, puberty, sexuality and leaving home.

Just as one crisis begins to subside, another comes along to knock her over, turn her upside down and shake all the change out of her pockets. That's enough to put monsters in anybody's closet.

Being a parent, however, can be just as frustrating and confusing and emotionally painful as being a child. The important difference is that, while children have little control over how rough their lives are, parenthood is only as rough as *we* make it. One way of making it rough is to feed the monster that waits in *our* closets.

Most children have monsters of one sort or another lurking about. But the only ones that hang around for long live in homes where the parents have a pet monster too.

By himself, a child's monster is impotent. But put him in

league with a parent-monster and pandemonium is guaranteed to break loose.

Banish your monster first. Children aren't fragile little eggs who can't be put together again. If they were, they'd never survive past their third birthdays.

Children are tough, resilient, flexible little people who rebound extremely well from hardship, frustration, trauma and all the other slings and arrows of their truly outrageous fortunes. With a little support from us, they also do quite well at chasing monsters out of their *own* closets.

Sure, your daughter's fear of monsters is probably an indication that her world is suddenly a bit more scary than it ever was before. She has to go to school all alone and watch all that attention go to baby sister, who is home with mommy all day long just as big sister used to be. Ah, well, that's life, right?

So get in there and do what you already know you have to do. Refuse to scout the way to her room. Tuck her in as usual at bedtime, and if she screams for you to stay, say, "I'm sorry. I won't stay. *You* put the monster in your *own* closet by pretending him there. Now you must pretend him gone." (For a discussion of fears as they occur with younger children, see Fears, page 98).

Once you chase *your* monster off, hers will waste away in no time. After all, it's lonely being the only monster in the house.

Food Fights

(Q) We have one child, a two-and-a-half-year-old daughter. She was breast-fed until she was ten months old. When she was five months old, our pediatrician told me to begin giving her solid foods. I was reluctant to do that since she seemed to be getting enough nourishment from me, but he told me bluntly that my attitude was irresponsible. She refused to cooperate with her new diet, spitting out food, turning her head, screaming and so on. At the pediatrician's insistence, I began virtually force-feeding her. To make a long story short, the same situation exists today. My daughter will not eat anything resembling a meal. She eats cereal and toast in the morning and cheese, potato chips, popcorn, peanut butter and crackers and celery slices for snacks. Lunch is a sandwich, maybe. Supper always turns into a scene. We have **made** her sit at the table, spanked her, bribed her and literally forced food into her mouth to make her eat. But if we make her eat something she doesn't like, she throws it up later. As a result, every aspect of our relationship is strained. What can we do?

(A) Food has the potential of acquiring tremendous

significance within a family, involving issues completely unrelated to its nutritional value.

The transfer of food from parent to child during the first year of life entails lots of physical closeness and stimulation, so that while the infant is receiving nourishment, she is also being nurtured.

As the child strides into her second year of life, the parents' role of keepers of the cupboard can easily become a central issue in the almost inevitable power struggles that develop as the second birthday approaches.

As the almost-two year old grows increasingly verbal, she is likely to begin asserting definite likes and dislikes for particular foods and demand to be fed on a schedule that runs counter to family custom.

In addition, the toddler is no longer wholly dependent on her parents to give her food, and she further flexes her independence by experimenting with ways of obtaining it for herself. She discovers how to climb on the counter, open the refrigerator and take the lid off the pickle jar.

In short, the giving of food from parent to child can, under certain stressful circumstances, become confused with the quality or quantity of affection in the relationship, the question of who is in control of the family and how much autonomy the child is permitted.

When food assumes this significance, it begins to "mediate" the relationship. In other words, it becomes the substance through which (or over which) parent and child attempt to resolve certain issues.

Everyone can easily forget that the reason for sitting down to a meal is *not* to consume food. Eating is secondary to the social and ritual aspects of mealtime.

Meals, and the evening meal in particular, bring the family together. They are a setting in which the values of sharing and unity are reaffirmed. It matters little *what* people eat or *how much*; good conversation and the feeling that "we are all of one family" are what count.

So the idea is *not* to persuade your daughter to eat. She is eating enough and her diet is adequately balanced. The goal is to involve her in the ritual of unification at the dinner table.

During the day, you can cater to her preference to a reasonable extent, but retain control over *when* food is served (remember that two year olds usually need a mid-morning and mid-afternoon snack).

At the evening meal, prepare your daughter's plate with small portions of the same food that the rest of the family are eating. If she mentions her distaste for any of the items on her plate, ignore the content of her statement, but take the opportunity to involve her in conversation by responding with something like, "Tell Daddy what we did today." Encourage her participation in conversation, although there should be times when the talk between adults does not involve her except as a listener.

Any comments that adults make about the meal should be brief and complimentary. Require her to remain at the table until everyone is excused, but do *not* at any time ask her to eat even a single bite.

Don't serve dessert as an extension of the meal. If something special is on the menu, serve it one or two hours later, before her bedtime perhaps. Don't use dessert as an enticement for eating. Nor should her right to share in late-evening treats be made conditional on how much she eats for supper.

One last word: for your next child, find a pediatrician who is supportive of breast feeding and more knowledgeable about infant nutritional needs.

Keeper of the Cupboard

(Q) This may sound trivial, but my daughter, who is four, asks for food almost constantly throughout the day. The rule is that she may have one small snack midway through the afternoon, but she can't seem to understand and won't accept that limit. I'm tired of her demands and whining and am counting on you for an idea.

(A) Have I got an idea for you! But first, let's clear up one thing. This is not a trivial question. Any question involving food is important. After all, what's more essential than food?

For that reason, food can acquire potent symbolic character within a family, and disputes regarding *what* people eat, when and *how much* can generate lots of conflict among family members. Food takes on even more significance in the relationship between parent and child.

Certainly one of the strongest and most enduring associations formed during the child's first year is that of food and parent (usually mother). As the child grows, parents retain the role of food givers. From this perspective, it's easy to comprehend why food so often becomes the issue-of-choice in power struggles between parents and children. The conflict can take many forms, but the basic issue remains "who controls the food?" And, in a broader sense, the over-riding issue is, "who controls the family?"

Therefore, it is as essential as food itself that parents exercise absolute, unquestionable control of the distribution of food in the family. This is not to say that the system cannot be flexible enough to allow children some freedom to serve themselves, but the final authority must rest with parents.

If parents cannot demonstrate their authority in this area, then how can they claim to be authorities at all?

It is a legitimate and necessary exercise of their responsibility and authority for parents to restrict the "when?" of eating to certain set times of the day. Most children require a mid-morning and mid-afternoon snack, so plan for one or both, depending on the age of the child and the mealtime schedule.

There is a hassle-free, field-tested way of announcing snacktime, while at the same time communicating your authority as keeper of the pantry. I assume there is a relatively large clock face somewhere in your house, probably in the kitchen. Take a piece of paper and make an identical clock face, minus the hands. Now, decide when snacktime will take place. Then, draw the hands on your paper clock to indicate snacktime. Tape the paper clock next to the real clock, call your youngster in and tell her, "When the hands on the real clock look like the hands on the paper clock, I will give you a snack. Now you can tell when snacktime is!"

It is unlikely that any preschooler will grasp the connection immediately, so expect her requests to be off the mark for several days. When they are, simply show her the two clocks, point out that they are not "the same" and reassure her that when they are, she will get her snack as promised. Be sure you remember to show her what you mean by "the same" when the magic time arrives.

Techniques such as this are especially effective when you want to establish routines with a young child. Children often need some visible reminder of rules, times and other boundaries that are otherwise invisible.

Security Blankets

Big people really don't know much about children. We like to think we know it all, but nothing belies that more quickly than the things we get ourselves upset about.

Take little Sammy, for instance. He's going to be five years old next week and he still carries a blanket with him wherever he goes. At least, that torn, ragged piece of cloth used to be a blanket. Once upon a time, it was the blanket that kept him warm in his bassinet. Then it moved with him to his crib, and then to his bed and then . . . As Sammy goes, so goes the used-to-be-a-blanket.

"What's the matter with Sammy?" ask his parents. Something must be wrong because children aren't supposed to carry blankets around for five years. Sure, Linus carries a blanket, but that's just in the funny pages, and so you think Linus is cute. When it's your own little Sammy it's not so funny.

Maybe Sammy is insecure. That means nervous, doesn't it? "Oh my gosh," exclaim his nervous parents, "we must have done something terrible-awful to Sammy to make him so nervous!"

Maybe they took his bottle away too quickly. Or perhaps they toilet trained him too early. The separation . . . yes, that must be it . . . when they had that big argument and separated for three months when Sammy was only 20 months old. . . . He missed his daddy so much. "What have we done? Maybe we should take him to a psychologist!"

Something must be done to make Sammy more secure so that he will give up the blanket. He goes to kindergarten next fall, and his teacher will know what fiends his parents are if he walks in waving that blanket around for the whole world to see.

"C'mon, Sammy, give us the blanket. You're a big boy now. You don't need that smelly old blanket anymore. If you give us the blanket, we will buy you a new bicycle. . . . Why not, Sammy?"

Take the blanket while he's sleeping? Say that Santa Claus took it? How about having the blanket-fairy come and leave him some money for it?

No, we musn't force it away; that might make him *more* insecure. Then he might start sucking his thumb. On and on go Sammy's parents.

But the problem with Sammy is not Sammy at all. The issue is with his *parents*.

Big people must have answers for everything. The more complicated the answer, the more blind faith we invest in it. In the process of becoming big, many of us forget how simple life can be.

Big people become upset, and even frightened, by things that they do not understand, such as children.

When big people do not understand something, they weave security blankets out of words and call them explanations. Sometimes these explanations get ponderous and cumbersome. When they get sufficiently complicated, they become fantasies.

This is what happened to Sammy's big people. They do not

comprehend the insignificance of the blanket, because they no longer see the world in simple terms. They have learned too many words.

They do not understand why Sammy wants his blanket with him wherever he goes, and this is upsetting. The four year old down the street doesn't carry a blanket around. Sammy is different. Sammy's parents think that something is wrong, so they invent a fantasy filled with dragons and demons and, in no time, the blanket becomes the most important thing in the house. The issue of the blanket grows to such proportions that is suffocates everyone's common sense.

"Hey, Sammy! Just between you and me, tell me about your blanket."

"I jus' like it."

That sounds simple enough. On the other hand, maybe Sammy *is* a bit insecure. After all, everyone's trying to take his blanket.

Sumbthucking

Until recently, my daughter, Amy, would park her thumb in her mouth when she was bored, tired, cranky or just plain laid back. And that was fine with me. She began perfecting her technique the day she was born.

Not everyone feels the way I do. Quite a few people believe that something is wrong with the Amy's of the world.

Thumbsucking defies convention, and this makes adults uncomfortable. As long as adults have "reasons" for things, they feel O.K. So, they have invented some to explain why an occasional thumb is where it shouldn't be. Take your pick:

The "Bad Nerves Theory" says that sumbthucking is a thign of inthecurity. To parents who buy this idea, a thumbsucking child is a constant reminder of what monsters they are. They become especially distraught when their child sucks in public, thus broadcasting her miserable condition to the world.

Another theory, attributed by some to a certain Sigmund Fraud, says that children suck their thumbs because during infancy they experienced some trauma associated with breast or bottle feeding. These poor kids grow up sucking on one substitute nipple after another—cigarettes, straws, siphon tubes, Life Savers, anything. As adults, they are the perverts who prefer to drink their beer straight from the bottle.

Sometimes it's easier for little girls to get away with sucking their thumbs than it is for little boys. There are even people who think a girl who sucks her thumb is "cute" (until she goes to school). A thumbsucking boy is in mortal danger of growing up to be effeminate, or so the story goes. The solution? Paint the offending digit with colorless yuk. That'll make a man out of him.

Then there are the horror stories — Bedtime Tales for Thumbsuckers: "There once was a frog-prince who sucked his thumb. When he grew up, his teeth were crooked, his eyes were crossed, his ears stuck out and flapped in the wind, he caught a dread disease, his cheeks dimpled, and the Princess would not marry him." The part about the dimples gets 'em every time.

I have my own theory. Because of thumbs, people can build the things they dream of, like rocket ships and time machines. A child who sucks her thumb is saying, "I love my thumb. I love being human." Now isn't that nicer than bad nerves and a face like Alfred E. Newman?

As far as I can tell, children suck their thumbs simply because it feels good. Thumbsucking is calming and relaxing to a child. It is a portable source of pleasure, always right on hand! The answer to why some children suck their thumbs and others don't is simply, "Because." It's no more significant than liking or not liking spinach.

So, the big fuss is over something rather insignificant. A child is not going to stop sucking her thumb because of ridicule, threat, criticism, demands or punishment. These "persuasive" measures can, in fact, create a problem where there was none to begin with.

A child cannot separate the feelings we communicate to her about thumbsucking from the feelings she has about herself as a little person. If she is harassed about sucking her thumb, it is a good bet she will begin to feel bad about herself. She may withdraw and spend more time alone so she can suck in private or seek relief from her growng insecurity by sucking more and more. Where there was once a healthy child who sucked her thumb for pleasure, there is now a child who sucks to relieve the anxiety and discomfort of feeling that there's something wrong with her.

If your child sucks her thumb, leave her alone. If you must mention it, say something like, "Hey there! I see your thumb in your mouth. I'll bet that feels pretty good. You know something? I love you."

One of these days, when she feels like it, and she has developed other interests, she will stop — but it will be in *her own* time, *not* yours.

Discipline in Public Places

Mommy took me to the store
To shop and spend the day,
But I had other things in mind,
Like, for instance, play!

While she was looking for a dress
I ran away and hid;
I went under a table
And found another kid.

Mom found me in the make-up
Playing with this other child.
Together we were having fun;
Mom said that I was *wild*.

I cried for her to carry me,
I said I hurt my feet.
I cried cause I was hungry
And then I wouldn't eat.

I asked for toys but she said, "No!"
And so I threw a fit.
I screamed and kicked and pulled my hair;
When she bought the toy, I quit.

I took my shoes off in the store,
But can't remember where.
Mommy got all red and shook
And bought another pair.

We're home now; Mommy's resting.
I'm playing with her fountain pen.
When she wakes up I'll ask her,
"When can we go again?"

Controlling children in public places is a sticky problem, to be sure. If you scream at them or spank them, everybody looks at you, and you feel lower than a rattlesnake. If you look the other way, children play "Hide and Seek" (quess who does the seeking?), or they break something, or they help themselves to some candy or something horrible like that. If you hold their hands, they fight you. If you don't, they run wild. Shopping can be loads of fun.

Try this. First make a list of rules for public places. It could read something like this:

1. You walk with me and stay with me. I will not hold your hand unless you want me to.

2. You are quiet in the stores. You do not scream, yell or have a tantrum.

3. You walk. You do not run.

Those three are enough to cover most of the child's favorite public pastimes. Besides, three is probably all the child can remember.

Next, cut some "tickets" out of stiff, colored cardboard. When that's done, you are prepared to meet with your youngster. You are the chairperson (chairparent?) at this conference. Begin by saying, "Moe, you are probably wondering why we are having this little talk, and so I'm going to tell you. We are going to talk about going to the store, Moe, and after we talk about it, we are going to get in the car and go there. When we go to the store, I get mad because you run in the store, and you scream, and you yell, and you throw tantrums when you want toys, and you run away from me. I'm not laughing, Moe.

"I'm going to tell you what the rules are before we go to the store. The first rule is: You will walk with me and stay with me while I am shopping. I am not going to hold your hand unless you want me to. The second rule . . ." and so on.

When you finish going over the rules, pull out the "tickets" and say, "Before we go to the store, I am going to give you these tickets. The tickets are yours, so don't lose them. Everytime you break a rule I'm going to take away a ticket. If you lose all of your tickets in the store today, then I will not let you go outside to play after supper (or some such desirable activity). You must have at least one ticket in order to play outside tonight. Do you understand? Good. Then let's go practice the rules at the store."

When you get to the store, review the rules in the parking lot, give Moe the tickets, remind her what the deal is, and proceed. If Moe breaks a rule, say, "you were running. The rule says you will walk. Give me a ticket for breaking the rule." If you must take the last ticket, do so without any big fuss, but gently remind Moe what the consequences are, in case she "forgot."

The number of tickets should vary according to the time you expect to be shopping. Start by estimating how many hours you are going to be gone, add one to this number, and give that many tickets. In other words, if you think it's going to be a two-hour trip, give three tickets.

Try to remember when you were small and what torture shopping was. When children are bored or tired, they are more likely to misbehave. So don't expect a preschool child to tag along with you cheerfully for more than an hour. Bring a stroller, or take the time to hunt one when you get to the store (many stores provide them).

The deal made with the tickets should involve some privilege that the child would normally look forward to doing at home that same day. Do not offer bribes such as ice cream or mini-bikes for good behavior.

Credit for this idea goes to Won Sung Lo, of Won Sung Lo's Irish Laundry, who coined the phrase, "No tickee, no washee."

How to Survive a Trip

A friend of mine has a recurring nightmare in which he is handcuffed to the steering wheel of a car traveling down a deserted stretch of four-lane highway. There are two young children in the back seat, both gorging on junk food. In his dream, the highway has no exits. The children are bouncing up and down in the back seat, screaming about needing to use the bathroom, fighting over toys, crying and constantly asking, "When are we going to get there?"

My friend should be thankful this is just a nightmare. I know a lot of parents for whom this nightmare is all too real. Back seats were not designed with children in mind. They are confining and boring, and it's asking much of a child (or any human being) to sit peacefully in one for any extended time.

The mood of an entire vacation is set during the trip, but there is no reason the tone of the ride must be one of anger and frustration. Parents can spare themselves and their children a lot of misery by planning thoughtfully for everyone's needs during the journey.

To begin with, pack a small cooler chock-full of a variety of healthy, sugar-free snacks. These can include raisins, carrot and celery sticks, dry roasted peanuts, crackers, peanut butter sandwiches, fruit and such good, old-fashioned drinks as apple and orange juice.

Let the children eat freely: just the act of eating will help them stay calm. Keep junk food off the menu. The refined sugar (and often caffeine) in it doses children with an over supply of quick energy, turning a car into a pressure cooker. When you eliminate all sugar-sweetened foods and drinks from the trip menu, the children probably won't have to use the bathroom as often. How about that? Two birds with one stone.

Pack a cloth bag or box with books, coloring books, colored pencils (crayons melt on the back shelf) and other "trip toys" to hold the children's attention and interest. Keep this inventory in the front seat, with an adult acting as "toy librarian." When you sense that a child is losing interest in one toy, take it away and provide another in its place.

It also helps to vary the seating arrangement during the trip. For instance, the adults can switch back and forth between driving and sitting in the back with one of the children. Keeping the children separated in this way, at least part of the time, may be a good idea. An older child can ride in the front with whoever is driving, while another adult keeps younger children occupied in the back by reading stories or carrying on quiet conversation.

Word games are fun, and even the driver can play. Rhyming games (what rhymes with *cat?*), guessing games (I see something that is green. What is it?) and name games (I am an animal with a long neck who eats leaves from trees and . . . Who am I?) are just some ideas for keeping everyone in a positive frame of mind.

Plan regular stops so people can stretch and empty their bladders. Trying to travel more than six or eight hours in a day with children can easily backfire. By leaving in the middle of the night, however, my family has managed to drive a straight 12 hours without turning into a bunch of blithering idiots. Blithering maybe, but not yet to the idiot stage.

There is even a creative answer to the question, "What do we do when they misbehave in the car?" It's a game I call "Tickets." All you need to play are pocket-sized rectangles of colored cardboard.

Before anyone gets into the car, explain to the children the rules governing behavior during the ride. Keep the list brief. Some suggestions might be: (1) seatbelts must be buckled, (2) no fighting or arguing, (3) no yelling or screaming, (4) no throwing, and (5) each child is allowed to ask, "When are we gonna be there?" just once.

Remind the children that they have a special event waiting for them at the end of the trip (swimming, exploring, playing with cousins, for example). Now comes the clincher: "I am giving five tickets to each of you. Each time you break a car rule, I will take a ticket away from you. If you fight, I will take a ticket from each of you, regardless of who started it. When we get to the beach, you must have at least one ticket left to go swimming. If you don't have a ticket, you must sit on the beach with me for 30 minutes."

It works, believe me. Take careful note of the punishment — it is quite enough that you promise to withhold the special event for a brief time. Vacations are not for suffering. Besides, if one suffers, all will suffer. The number of "tickets" can vary with the anticipated length of the trip — one ticket per hour, perhaps, up to a maximum of five or six.

Have an enjoyable vacation. Plan ahead, drive carefully and don't forget the sunscreen.

Preschool Follies

(Q) My son is four years old. He has never been a perfect child and I don't want him to be, but he has always been easy to raise. He misbehaves sometimes, but my husband and I enforce the rules and nothing ever gets out of hand.

But he gives his teachers at the day-care center a hard time. I don't work, but I put him in a center so he can be with other children. He goes there only in the mornings. Every time I pick him up, his teacher has another story of what he has done. It all seems like such little stuff to us, but she gets upset because it happens so often. For instance, the other day he pulled down his pants on the playground. Last week, he stuck his tongue out at the teacher and then laughed while she chased him around the room.

What I don't understand is why he isn't like this at home. Is he rebelling so he can spend more time with me? Is he not getting enough attention at home? Please tell me what you think I should do.

(A) To begin with, children always manage to get enough attention, wherever they are. Some of the attention is positive (praise, interest, enthusiasm and encouragement) and some is negative (criticism, punishment, reprimands). Children need more positive strokes than negative, but they will work for whatever kind they can get.

It sounds as though you are sensitive to your child's needs. You put him in day care so he can be with other children, you enforce rules and so on. I would guess he gets many more positive than negative strokes from you and your husband.

Sometimes, however, it's more *fun* to work for negative strokes. For instance, wouldn't it be fun to drop your pants and listen to everyone howl and scream? And wouldn't it be fun to have the teacher chase you around the room? This doesn't work out well with every grown-up, but some will go for the bait every time. Your son is not doing anything malicious, he isn't hurting anyone and he's having loads of fun doing what all the other children (and most adults as well) wish they had the nerve to do.

Call it the class clown syndrome. Once the bug strikes, it's almost impossible to cure. In fact, I doubt this is something that we even *want* to cure. The class clown is blessed with an irrepressible sense of humor, a flair for the absurd and an imagination that defies convention.

What this all adds up to is a happy and extremely creative child. Happy, creative children, if not given enough opportunity to use their talents constructively, will use them any way they can. What is more exciting and creative than to entice a grown-up into your game and then beat her at it? The problem is that some grown-ups can't stand being outdone by a child.

Your son's behavior may be an indication that he is with the wrong age group at the center. Perhaps he would fare better with five year olds. Or the program at the center may be too structured for him. Generally speaking, creative children need less structure and more open-ended opportunities to explore, discover and experiment with the environment. Perhaps a different program is the answer. Shop around and see what other centers have to offer.

Perhaps a day-care program is not the answer to his needs. Look into other possibilities, such as swimming, dancing, gymnastics (tumbling) or art classes.

There is one small point to consider: dropping your trousers and sticking your tongue out at grown-ups are fun and get everyone's attention; nonetheless, this is not desirable public behavior.

The teacher could ignore the behavior. Unfortunately, ignoring behavior such as this simply doesn't work. There is no way that a classroom of four year olds isn't going to laugh and squeal when someone's pants come down. Forget about ignoring.

The teacher could put your son in isolation for five minutes whenever this kind of behavior occurs. In this case, however, I doubt whether this alone will work. If your son is bored, then he needs more stimulation, and the teacher needs to provide it before he provides it for himself by dropping his pants again. If the teacher cannot give him more opportunity to earn positive strokes, then my earlier suggestions about another age group or program should be considered.

If you feel that the program is what you want for him and wish to leave him there, then ask his teacher to give you a brief daily summary of his misbehavior. Take privileges away at home based on the number of incidents which occur at school. For instance, one incident at school and he can't ride his bike that day. Two incidents, and he can't go outside in the afternoon. Three incidents, and he can't play his records in the evening. But whatever you do, don't offer him any special rewards for being "good."

Just hug and kiss him and tell him you're pleased that he's found other ways to have fun. Talk about what those other ways are. After all, what's more special than a parent's love and attention?

Kindergarten Kapers

Rodney's kindergarten teachers said he was "uncontrollable." Rodney's doctor said he was "hyperactive." His parents called him "wild."

When I first saw Rodney, he was running from one end of his classroom to the other, making demented, mechanical noises as he ran. Not only running and making noises, mind you, but also pushing and hitting other children who got in his way.

Trouble was, no one knew quite where Rodney's way was going to be next, so you took your chances just being in the same room with him. One thing's for sure: his teachers deserved combat pay.

"See what I mean?" said the teacher who had asked me to observe Rodney.

I saw what she meant. Seconds later, I also felt what she meant as Rodney ran his way into my way, bounced off and kept running. That did it! Rodney's hyperactive ways were definitely numbered.

First, his teachers made a list of all the "bad" things Rodney did in school. This consisted of specific, concrete descriptions that Rodney could easily understand. When it was finished, the list read something like this: (1) Rodney runs in the classroom, (2) Rodney hits other children, (3) Rodney picks up the gerbils by their tails, (4) Rodney says "Make me!" when a teacher tells him to do something, and so on. There were 37 misbehaviors on the list.

Next, his teachers numbered ten index cards from one to ten, punched a small hole at the top center of each card and hung the stack on a nail in the wall so that the number "ten" faced out. They put a second nail into the wall next to the first one.

Then, Rodney's teachers and I met with his mother. She, too, was at wits end over Rodney. "I'll do anything," she said.

"Will you come to the school and take him home on really bad days?" I asked (Rodney's mother was at home with a younger child during the day).

"If it'll help, I certainly will," she said.

The preliminaries taken care of, we proceeded to lay the plan on Rodney, beginning with a careful review of his list of "bads." We told Rodney that every time he did something on the list, two things would happen: first, he would go to a chair in the corner and sit for five whole, big minutes. A teacher would set a timer so he would know when five minutes were up. Second, a teacher would take the top card off the stack and hang it face down on the second nail. As each card was turned over, Rodney would see how many were left.

If he refused to go to the chair or argued about being sent there, another card would be turned over.

If he got up before the bell rang, another card would be turned over.

If he made noises or caused any disturbance in the chair, another card would be turned over.

When and if card number one was turned over, a teacher would call Rodney's mother. She would come take him home and confine him to his room for the remainder of the day, except for supper with the family.

The entire plan was based on a hunch that Rodney would rather be in school, where everything was happening, than in his room, where not much was happening at all.

First day (Monday): Rodney lost all 10 cards by 9:45. Second day: they were gone—and so was he—before lunch.

Third day: Rodney stretched it out to 1:30 in the afternoon. Thursday and Friday, he managed to hold on to at least one card until school let out. Our hunch was working. Rodney was playing the game.

So, when he came to school the following Monday, he saw the number eight on top of the stack.

"How come?" he asked.

"You only *need* eight cards, Rodney. Your behavior is much better already. Besides, the whole idea is to get so good at this game that you don't need any cards at all.

Rodney's mother had to come get him only twice that week.

On Monday of the third week, there were only *six* cards in the stack.

"It's not fair!" said Rodney.

"We like you, Rodney," said his teachers.

Rodney went home once that week.

The stack kept shrinking and Rodney kept getting better and better at playing the game. Two months after all this got started, we did away with the cards entirely, with the understanding that we would go "back into business" if Rodney reverted to his old tricks. But Rodney never had to go home again.

Uncontrollable? Hyperactive? Not any longer.

Fancy that.

School Daze

Several years ago, a second-grade teacher asked my advice about one of her students, a seven-year-old girl who, within six weeks after the beginning of school, had managed to walk away with the "Outstanding Nuisance Of The Second Grade" Award by—believe it or not—asking questions.

Indeed, blue-eyed Julie asked, according to the teacher's first estimates, close to a hundred questions a day. This usually patient veteran of 13 second-grade campaigns was showing unmistakable signs of going "blotto" as we stood talking in the hall. She apologized profusely for taking my time with such trivia ("You must think this is silly"), grinding her teeth, her hands fluttering in and out of the pockets of her smock like a pair of lunatic hummingbirds—showing all the classic symptoms of a sudden mid-year retirement.

Just then the classroom door opened and out walked (as I quickly learned) the infamous, blue-eyed Julie herself.

"Mrs. Boulderdam?"

Immediately, hands fluttering madly, Mrs. Boulderdam's eyes darted down the hall, measuring, I'm now sure, the distance between where we stood and the front door. For several moments her eyes jumped back and forth between Julie and freedom, finally coming to rest on the child's upturned face.

"Why, yes, Julie, what do you want?" Her lips were stretched into a tight smile over clenched teeth.

"Is this the way to write my name?"

Mrs. Boulderdam tensed, and I thought I saw her hands flutter toward the child and then quickly back into the smock, but it happened too fast to be sure.

"Yes, Julie," she stammered, "That's the spell you write—make you name," and then, with great effort, "the way you write your name now go back into the room I'll be there in a minute."

As Julie disappeared through the door, Mrs. Boulderdam looked at me with one of the most pitiful expressions I've ever seen on a grown-up.

"Help," was all she said.

A rough count through the remainder of the day showed Julie was asking between six and ten questions an hour, and her pace never slacked. The really amazing thing was that Mrs. Boulderdam had lasted even six days, much less six weeks.

Almost all of Julie's questions were unnecessary, in that she probably knew the answer or could have figured it out. Intelligence, or the lack of it, was definitely *not* the problem.

Actually, Julie's only question, asked in various ways throughout the day, was, "Will you reassure me that I'm an important person around here?"

The trick was going to involve getting her to ask fewer questions and feel better about herself.

To begin with, I advised Mrs. Boulderdam to draw a large question-mark on each of 12 index cards.

Sometime later, she took Julie aside and told her how much she liked her (she really did, too) but that Julie needed to begin thinking through answers to her own questions. Mrs. Boulderdam offered to help Julie practice "thinking without help" by giving her the cards as "reminders."

Every time Julie came to Mrs. Boulderdam with a question, she had to give up one of her cards in exchange for an answer. When Julie's 12 cards were gone, Mrs. Boulderdam would refuse to answer any more of her questions for that day.

Julie started each new day with the 12 cards in her possession. When Julie had a question, Mrs. Boulderdam would ask her, "have you thought about it, Julie?" and then, "Do you want to give me a card for the answer?"

Julie caught on very quickly. After a week, she was asking fewer than ten questions a day, most of them "necessary."

Julie felt important because Mrs. Boulderdam had done something special—just for her. She also learned something valuable about independence.

Mrs. Boulderdam's hands stopped fluttering, and she finished out the year in fine form.

Madness in the Morning

(Q) I am writing to you out of sheer desperation. My problem may seem trivial, but it is driving me absolutely up a wall. Both my husband and I work and it is necessary that we leave the house by 7:45 every morning. On the way to work, I drop our Jamie, who is four and a half, at his day-care center. The problem is that every morning Jamie plays and stalls and everything else you can think of—except getting dressed.

I lay out his clothes when we all get up at 6:30 and the fight begins. I start by calmly telling him to get dressed, but always end up yelling at him and oftentimes putting the last few pieces on him myself. The only thing he can't do by himself is tie his shoes. We all end up angry and everybody's day begins on this miserable note. The problem is not that Jamie is tired. He goes to bed (no problems here) at 8:30 (after a bedtime story—his favorite thing) and is alert in the mornings. He just finds all kinds of reasons for not putting his clothes on. Can you help us?

(A) Come down off the wall. Your problems are almost over. It's quite clear that Jamie is a clever little fellow. Clever enough to figure out that when mom and dad are busy and in a hurry, one surefire way of getting everybody's attention is to *not* cooperate. After all, what's the rush? Who wants to hurry up and be without mom and dad all day long?

You made two very important statements. First, Jamie *can* dress himself. Second, Jamie likes being read to in the evening. If you will purchase a kitchen timer (see page 49), we will have all the ingredients for our recipe.

Now, with the timer in hand, mom and dad sit down with Jamie and say, "Hey, big guy, we aren't going to yell at you about getting dressed in the morning any more. Instead, we are going to play a game called Put Your Clothes On. Here's how the game is played. When we wake you up, we will put your clothes on the chair in your room. Then we will set the timer for 15 minutes and put in on your dresser.

"When we set the timer, it will begin ticking like a clock, and in 15 minutes, a bell will ring like this (demonstrate the bell ringing). If you have all of your clothes on before the bell rings, then you win the game. The prize for winning is that you get to pick a bedtime story that night. Isn't that exciting?

"If the bell rings and you don't have your clothes on, then mom and dad will put them on. But you don't win the game, so you cannot have a bedtime story."

Then, do exactly that. If he wins, make a big deal about it, letting him know how nicely he dresses himself and so on. Read him a short story before school. If he doesn't win the game, dress him yourself. If you have to do this and he protests, simply tell him that those are the rules, and you want him to win tomorrow. He *will* start to win, believe me.

You can gradually shorten the time until he can put his clothes on at a comfortable pace. A "star-chart" taped to the refrigerator is an additional way to reward him when he wins. It's called the no-more-footprints-on-the-wall method of child-rearing.

A Cure for the "Sloppies"

(Q) My seven year old is the sloppiest child you ever saw. He never puts anything were it belongs. His coat is never hung up, his bike is always parked dead center in the driveway, his dirty clothes are piled where he took them off, his books land on the sofa when he comes home from school . . . need I go on? It seems as though I yell at him all the time, but nothing changes. Help save my hair!

(A) Yelling is a trap fraught with paradox. The more you yell, the less you accomplish. A yell is threatening, and the sheer volume may prompt a child to follow instructions, but once the shock wave passes, it's generally back to business as usual.

Yelling is also a waste of energy. You invest a tremendous amount of your self and get nothing of lasting value in return. The more you yell, the more of yourself you exhaust, until finally you're bankrupt. And your seven year old is ready to cash in all the chips.

A yell is aggressive, but not assertive. It is an expression of frustration and an admission of powerlessness. In fact, the yell transfers control of the issue to the child, who is all too willing to be the center of the storm, in control of the family.

It is essential that you do something more constructive than yelling, before the entire family gets hooked into behaving as though a seven year old sits in the driver's seat!

Take a piece of paper and, down the left-hand side, make a list of all the things your son "misplaces"—bicycle, coat, school books, dirty clothes, shoes and so on. Be very specific, so there is no room for misunderstandings ("It only says *coat*; I didn't know you meant my *raincoat* too!"

Then, to the right of your first list, make a second which tells *exactly* where each item belongs. Coat . . . on a hanger in the hall closet. Bicycle . . . parked against the side wall of the car-port. Dirty clothes . . . in the hamper in the upstairs bathroom.

Find a quiet time to sit down with your son and go over the list of things and places: "You and I have not been working together very well. I have made this list to help both of us know what the rules are for putting things away."

After your discussion, post the list on the refrigerator door or some other equally visible place. Beside it, post a "scorecard"—a sheet with seven boxes in a row, representing seven days.

"For the next seven days, we are going to keep score on how well you are learning the rules. If you leave something out of place, I will call it to your attention. You must mark a check in the box for that day and then put the item where it belongs. In return, I promise *not* to yell."

During the week, monitor his compliance, but don't crowd him. If he refuses to put his own check in the box, make it for him. Be sure to call his attention not only to things *out* of place, but to things that are *in* place as well, letting him know you appreciate his help. As the days go by, discuss his progress, or lack of it, in optimistic, matter-of-fact terms.

Don't offer him any goodies for a certain level of performance, but if you are so moved, you might reward several days of improvement (or a "perfect" day) with some spontaneous show of affection and gratitude: "You have done so well, how would you like to go with me to MacArnold's for a Crabapple Swizzle?"

On the other hand, the week may not produce any measurable change in his willingness to abide by the rules. He may not be quite ready to stop fighting with you. In that case, at the end of the week, be prepared to make him a "deal."

Put up another scorecard. Write a large number "four" at the top. Arrange a second summit conference. Inform him that he will be confined to his room for 30 minutes when he receives his fourth check of the day, and that any additional checks will immediately earn him another 30 minutes apiece.

Then you simply enforce the rules. In the end, it's largely a matter of trust. You trust him to abide by the rules, and he learns to trust that you will enforce them.

By following this plan, or a variation of it, you will make significant changes in the way you handle the situation. You will define the nature of the problem in clear, precise terms. You will give accurate, non-judgemental feedback on his compliance with the rules. Finally, you will take an authoritative position on the issue, letting your son see you stand firmly, but gently, in one place.

He can be expected to test the system for weaknesses. That is his right! If you hold firm, he will eventually accept that you are no longer willing to participate in a struggle over "where things belong."

Pet Peeves

(Q) Our eighteen-month-old son is forever pulling our cat's tail or picking it up by the neck. Punishing him and talking to him have not worked. How can we teach him not to do this?

(A) At this age, your son is driven to touch, feel and squeeze everything in sight. Every squeeze, every poke, is a way of asking the question, "What are you, and what do you do?"

Parents should child proof the toddler's environment, so he can interact freely and safely with his surroundings. Child proofing also improves the mental health of the parents, who might otherwise struggle constantly to keep the child out of places where he shouldn't be.

When a pet is part of the child's world, decide how to deal with the child's curiosity about the animal. One way to prevent frustration or harm is to keep the child and the pet completely separated, but this may be incompatible with the place the pet occupies in the family.

Another option is to hold the child's hand and patiently teach him how to stroke and handle the pet. Don't, however, bank on seeing any immediate results. Teaching a toddler restraint, tenderness and sensitivity requires lots of patience.

Another way of handling the child's interest in the pet is to let them interact freely (which usually means as often as the pet will allow). Personal experience tells me that when the pet is familiar with the child, and the child means no harm, no harm is likely to come to either.

When my son was this age, we had a cat named Roy that Eric would maul every time their paths crossed. At first we were concerned that perhaps Eric was hurting Roy or that Roy might scratch him. Whenever Eric had Roy in his grip, we talked to him about being gentle or became mildly excited and pried them apart. Eventually we noticed that whenever Eric grabbed him, Roy went limp and endured the assault looking like last year's dish rag. After seeing how well Roy handled it, we stopped paying attention to the situation. Roy was obviously surviving the attacks and seemed to "know" that Eric meant no harm.

Lo and behold! After we stopped making it an issue, Eric stopped chasing Roy around the house.

To satisfy my own curiosity, I asked the opinion of several veterinarians. They all said they thought separation was the best solution if the parents were concerned about the child's handling of the pet. However, they knew of few pets injured by toddlers. The smaller the pet (kittens and puppies), the more vulnerable it is to innocent abuse. These veterinarians also thought that a family pet was not likely to retaliate against a child and that the pet could, in most cases, take care of itself.

A supervising emergency room nurse told me that although emergency room personnel see many children who have been hurt by animals, almost all of the injuries involve older children or animals that are either strays or that belong to another family. It is very rare, she said, to see an injury inflicted on a toddler by a family pet. In fact, she was unable to recall any incident of that nature in her many years of experience.

Young children require supervision, pet or no pet. For the sake of the animal, it is probably unwise to raise toddlers and kittens or puppies at the same time. For the child's safety, keep toddlers away from pets with a history of belligerence, strays and other families' pets, that may not be tolerant of strange, probing hands.

All these approaches have drawbacks. If parents choose to take the path of least resistance and let Mother Nature take care of the situation, however, harm is unlikely to come to either child or pet. That the child will ever become intentionally cruel and abusive to animals is even more unlikely. Most important in determining a child's permanent attitude toward animals is the example *we* set.

BB Guns

(Q) My father wants to give my eight year old, his grandson, a BB gun for Christmas. I don't like the idea, but Grandpa says Billy is old enough to learn to use a gun and develop respect for it. What's your opinion?

(A) My opinion is that guns are dangerous machines and have no place in the life of a child. A BB shot can seriously injure a human and kill a small animal. This potential disqualifies a BB gun as a toy.

I question the value of teaching a child "respect" for a gun. Respect implies an attitude of reverence and esteem. I don't see how a gun could possibly take on such significance in a child's world. In fact, I think it is impossible to teach respect for *anything* with a gun, unless you are confusing respect with fear.

It doesn't matter what you *intend* to teach a child by giving him lessons with a gun. The actual outcome will be determined as much, if not more, by methods and materials as by intent. The medium is the message and the message is quite dangerous.

Children are impressionable, easily excited and impulsive, and they demonstrate an unremarkable lack of self-control and foresight. God gives every child a parent so that someone can hold the reins.

And because we hold the reins, children have relatively little control over their own lives. Growth is a product of the dynamic tension generated as a child pulls against the restraints we impose upon him, and this inevitable conflict is also inevitably frustrating.

Children translate this conflict and frustration into play and daydream, both of which are often saturated with themes of power and control. In fantasy, a child can safely pretend that his strength and authority have expanded to fantastic proportions. He *becomes* his favorite super hero, and his need for power finds harmless expression on the magic carpet of imagination.

Put a weapon into that context, and you've added an ingredient that can ignite the whole mixture. The danger is that the child will soon absorb the weapon into his play as a tangible symbol of power. Go one step further, and you've got one child holding a BB gun and another child who just lost an eye.

I have an idea: if you want to give your child something that will help him develop a sharp eye and allow him to shoot animals and even people without any risk . . . buy him a camera.

How to Divide Your Attention

(**Q**) Being a first time mother, I have difficulty knowing how much one-to-one attention my three-year-old daughter needs. It seems the more we give, the more she demands. What are some general guidelines? I interact with her all day long during housework and shopping as I answer questions, tie bibs on dolls and so on. We try to have a story at bedtime and some time during the morning to play as she directs, but it's never enough. Any suggestions?

(**A**) With the first child, parents are prone to confuse what is actually *needed* with what is simply *wanted*. It's an easy trap to stumble into for several reasons, not the least of which is our anxiety about dealing with a relatively unfamiliar set of demands and responsibilities. Hand in hand goes a desire to do everything just right, which further blurs the already faint line between what is necessary for the child's well-being and those things that are simply whimsy.

Don't count on children to help clarify matters. They are just as likely to scream for a toy firetruck as they are for something to eat when they are hungry.

Children *need* nutritious food and water and warmth and room to explore and stimulation and people who talk softly and loving relationships and routines that organize their lives and cuddles and kisses and praise. They need parents who set limits and enforce rules and give lots of warm, accepting strokes.

On the other hand, children *want* parents who will be at their beck and call and solve all their problems and carry them everywhere and make them the center of attention and let them do and have whatever they demand and give lots of warm, accepting strokes.

It's not difficult to see why many children come to believe that parents are for anything and everything. From the moment a child arrives in the world, parents bathe and feed and carry and hold and rock and wait on her hand and foot. From a young child's point of view, parents are servants. Mom is a lady in waiting and dad is a valet.

Ah, but good domestic help isn't easy to find these days. Sometimes the servants get uppity and refuse to follow instructions. That's usually no problem for a child with a healthy set of lungs. Servants are easily intimidated by tantrums.

Many parents interpret tantrums as screams of genuine pain, a symptom of needs that have gone abused and neglected. So they perform whatever peculiar act the scream demands, and by-and-by, the child learns that tantrums push all the right buttons. In the long run, then, the child gets the lesser part of what she needs and the greater part of what she wants, some of which she doesn't need at all. How confusing!

The solution? The same one that solves most other problems of raising children: establish predictable guidelines, set firm limits and enforce them consistently. Set aside several times during the day – say, once in the morning, afternoon and evening – when you will devote 30 minutes to nothing but your child. Give each period a name, such as "playtime," "doll-time" and "story-time." A child of three and a half has no concept of what 30 minutes means, so use a timer. At the beginning of each period, set the timer for 30 minutes and say, "Mommy will read stories until the bell rings, and then I am going to do my own work (be specific)." When the bell rings, you then excuse yourself, saying how much fun you had and leave the little one with a suggestion for occupying her time.

If you stay with the routine and let her know how determined you are, then things will settle into place quickly.

Children may *want* servants, but they *need* parents.

Hitting: Two Views

(Q) My three year old has recently started hitting me when he's mad, usually because I won't let him have his way. I have tried talking with him about why he shouldn't hit and even suggested other ways of expressing his frustration, but he doesn't listen. I know it's wrong to spank a child if he hits you, so what can I do?

(A) As you already have discovered, a rational discourse on the "why nots" of hitting won't produce any constructive change in his behavior. In the first place, he is simply too young to understand all the ins and outs of what you're trying to tell him. In the second, you're overstating the issue, making it bigger than it really is. The more you talk, the more he will hit.

What does he need to know? That he isn't allowed to hit you. How can you get this across to him? Easy. Don't let him.

Surely you know his behavior well enough to predict when he is about to hit. When the attack comes, protect yourself and demonstrate your control of the situation by intercepting the blow. Take his wrists firmly in your hands and tell him that you will not, under any circumstances, allow him to hit you.

In most cases, spanking is probably *not* the most effective response, but I wouldn't rule it out altogether. Instead, take him immediately to his room and tell him to stay there until he calms down. If he needs more structure than this, set a timer for three to five minutes.

Your authority is on the line. Retain it.

(Q) What is your opinion of teaching small children to hit back? Our son is four years old. We live in a neighborhood in which there are lots of other small children, and a certain amount of hitting goes on. Our son isn't one of the more aggressive ones, so he's usually getting the hit rather than giving it. We aren't sure what to tell him to do.

(A) Children need to know that retaliation is one of several possible ways of dealing with a physical attack, including: refusing to fight, running away, asking for help from an adult, finding someone else to play with and coming home.

I've told my own children, for instance, that they are allowed to hit only when another child has hit them first. I have also gone over the advantages and disadvantages of other options, making it clear that the choice must be based on the specifics of the actual situation. I have stressed that while hitting back is the *least* desirable alternative, there will be times when it is unavoidable.

"Betcha!"

(Q) My son is almost four years old, and he is driving me crazy. He will hardly do anything I ask until I become upset enough to spank him. And this is the child I promised myself I would **never** spank. When I ask him to do something, he gives me this "You gotta be kidding!" look and turns away. It's maddening! Sometimes he just says "No" as cooly as you please. If he knows he is going to get a spanking (and he almost always does) then why does he do these things?

(A) Your almost-four year old is only doing what every young child must eventually do — he is challenging your authority. He demands to know, "By what right do *you* tell *me* what to do?"

As long as the question is unanswered, he is free to engage in a power struggle with you.

After all, no one told him the rules before he got here. It is *your* responsibility to describe the rules to him, not *his* to figure them out. If you aren't clear on what they are, then he is free to make up his own game and his own rules. And he has. It's called "Betcha!"

In Betcha! the parent starts the play by asking the child to perform some task, however small. The child counters by refusing to cooperate. Parent then responds, "Oh yes you will!" The child says, Betcha!, and the game is on!

Betcha! isn't much fun, however, because no one ever wins. In fact, both people always end up losers. How monotonous! But when it's the only game in town, well . . .

"But he almost always gets a spanking," you say. So what? Who pays *that* price. You do.

The game repeats itself because it has never been resolved. And it will not be resolved until you stop expecting *him* to change. He's not gong to stop inviting you to play Betcha! until you stop accepting the invitation. In fact, he doesn't even know *how* to stop.

To begin the end of Betcha! stop *asking* your son for his cooperation and start *telling* him exactly what you want him to do. Begin every "request" with the phrase, "I want you to . . ." and then fill in the blank with a clear, concise description of the task. Stop apologizing for having brought him into a less-than-perfect world.

Here are two of many possible approaches you can take to bringing Betcha! to a close. Choose the one that suits you better, or use them as models for devising a solution of your own.

Plan A: Instead of spanking as a *last* resort, spank as a *first* resort. I have no problems with spankings per se, as long as they are used effectively, to accomplish something. Up until now, your spankings have been an expression of frustration and defeat. Use your hand to emphasize your authority and to stop the game before it has a chance to get started.

Tell him what you want from him. If he signals his refusal, immediately reach around and clap him firmly on the rear (*do not* announce what is coming with warnings or threats). Then, face him and repeat what you want. Remember in the movie, *The Godfather*, when Marlon Brando made someone an offer he couldn't refuse? Use that tone of voice. If he still refuses (he probably will the first few times), take him to a chair and have him sit until he's ready to comply. Meanwhile, you go some other place and busy yourself.

If that sounds too mean, then try Plan B: buy a kitchen timer if you don't have one. Sit down with almost-four and say, "Yesterday (all things in the past happened "yesterday" to an almost-four), when I told you to do something (use an example), you said "No!" I got mad and yelled and spanked. I don't like that. Today, if you say, "No," I'm going to put you in your room for five minutes. When I put you in the room, I'll set this timer and when five minutes is over, it will ring, like this. Then you can come out and do what I told you to do. Understand?"

He will nod his head, which means that he doesn't understand, but knows when to nod his head.

You are letting him know that you are changing the game. You must then show him what kind of change you're talking about.

Now, it is *your* move.

"Look at Me!"

(Q) We have a four-and-a-half-year-old daughter, and an eighteen-month-old son. Our problem is other people—neighbors, friends, even grandparents—who pay lots of attention to the baby and very little to the older child, to the point of virtually ignoring her. When other people come over, my daughter begins "performing," interrupting conversations and misbehaving in other ways to get attention. How can I get other people to understand that she needs attention too?

(A) I'm sorry, but your daughter's plight fails to evoke my sympathy. It seems obvious that the *real* problem is her misbehavior when you have guests in your home.

This problem involves other people only to the extent that they have become *her* audience and *your* excuse for failing to control her. You have unintentionally given her permission to misbehave when there is company, and she has seized the opportunity to command as much attention as possible.

I suspect that she would get *more* attention if her behavior was appropriate to her age and the situation. She is probably being ignored *because* of her "performance," not because your guests are insensitive.

One disappointment in being an eldest child occurs when the spotlight takes its turn on the second born. Babies attract lots of attention. That's a fact of life your daughter is capable of living with. But she won't make a comfortable adjustment to her slightly diminished status unless you stop trying to protect her from the hardship of having a younger sibling.

Take a quiet moment to sit and talk with her. Tell her you understand how difficult it is to share things, including attention from other people. Point out that she must nonetheless learn to share and promise to help her.

Make a list of the inappropriate things she does in front of guests — cartwheels, Ed Sullivan impressions and so on. Make it clear that you will no longer accept this behavior, and let her know how you *do* expect her to act.

When she entertains company with one of the items on the list, put her in Time-Out (see A Matter of Timing, page 51) for five minutes. Make sure you give her a hug and a kiss when she manages to control her enthusiasm in front of visitors.

The world may be a stage, but your daughter is a bit young for a leading role.

Tattle Tales

"Mrs. Brickyard! Elmo just said a bad word to Angela, and she didn't do anything to him. He's *mean!* Are you gonna paddle him? Are you, huh?"

When children fight, the easiest solution is often to appeal to the nearest adult to come bail them out. Because it is the easiest thing to do, it also takes the least amount of thought and effort on the part of the child or children. Therefore, when we respond to a tattle tale, we encourage children not to think.

Webster's Dictionary defines "tattling" as "making idle talk; to chatter or to gossip." It defines "idle" as "something worthless" and "chatter" as "nonsense."

Tattling is senseless and destructive. Not only does it often prove unfair to the child who is tattled on, but it is harmful as well to the child who does the tattling. The "tattle tale" is usually the child least liked by siblings, shunned by peers and held in disfavor by adults.

We adults inadvertently create the problem. The unfortunate victim of our actions is the "tattle tale," because the child who tattles will have trouble being trusted and accepted by peers.

Tattling should be discouraged. When a child comes to you with a tale of woe or wanting to play "informer," do her a favor by saying, "I'm sorry that happened, Ashley, but I will not be able to come and help. This sounds like something you and Johnny can work out peacefully on your own."

If tattling is a habit with the child, be more definite about your feelings: "You are tattling again. You and I have talked about tattling before, and you know that I will not settle your problems for you. You must solve this one for yourself."

Don't make the mistake of saying, "I don't like tattling," and then rushing to the scene anyway. Children learn more by what we *do* than what we say.

If the problem occurs frequently in a certain group of children, take the time to talk to everyone in the group or class about tattling and proper ways of solving problems. Help children make the distinction between what you *want* to know about (cuts, falls and so on) and what you don't want to hear.

Tattling is the beginning of a long string of yarn that, unless cut early, grows larger and larger, becoming a burden for the child who must carry it around.

Bad Words

"Bad Words." We all know what they are. Worse than that, we know what they *mean!* Horrible, unmentionable things, all of them. We don't use them . . . much. Or we at least use them "properly," for pardonable reasons such as, "I was drunk," or "I lost my temper."

In the life of a child, there are three stages in the development of bad words. The first stage occurs when the child first hears the words. Bad words are more likely to attract a child's attention than "good" words. Bad words stand out because of the emphasis we give them in tone and volume.

Take the phrase, "That worthless blankety-blank." Say it out loud, substituting your favorite bad word for "blankety-blank." See what I mean? Any young child, hearing that for the first time, will remember "blankety-blank." The child may also notice, if the "blankety-blank" is a person who is present, how she turns red and begins to act strange. The thing most apparent to the child witnessing such a scene is the power of the words and the attention they command. End Stage One.

Stage Two. The child runs outside where his friends are playing and says, "Hey Timmy, you know what you are? You're a blankety-blank."

Timmy runs to his mother and says, "Matthew called me a blankety-blank."

Timmy's mother calls Matthew's mother, Matthew's mother calls Matthew's father, who beats the blankety-blank out of Matthew. Poor Matthew doesn't even know what blankety-blank means.

That's just one possible scenario. Matthew might wait to let go with blankety-blank at kindergarten. Then the whole world knows.

In any case, when Matthew shows off his new words, people almost always show him, in return, how tremendously significant they are.

Stage Three finds Matthew testing the shock value of his new vocabulary on an assortment of people and finding out what a wide range of reaction they provoke. Grandma faints, Sally runs away, Jeffrey cries, Billy fights, Billy's older brother laughs and the teacher talks herself blue in the face. What a great time Matthew has — making magical, meaningless sounds.

Actually, a fourth stage will emerge several years later, when Matthew discovers that blankety-blank has a definition, of sorts. At that point, Matthew may begin to use it "properly" — only when he's drunk or angry, for instance. Ain't life amazin'?

There is nothing to be accomplished by trying to prevent Stages One and Two from occurring. All children hear the words from somebody, sometime. And all children use them on somebody, sometime.

Trying to prevent this makes a problem where there was none before. I call it the Magnifying Glass principle. Matthew says a bad word and the adults around him teeter on the verge of hysteria. The exaggerated reactions have the same effect on Matthew's behavior as a magnifying glass seems to have on a butterfly wing.

Matthew's bad language gets a great deal of attention. Isolating his bad word and acting as though it is the most significant aspect of his behavior confirms Matthew's hunch that these are powerful words indeed. Never mind what else Matthew might have learned and accomplished during the day — he said a bad word. That's more important than anything else, isn't it?

When we isolate and over-react to any particular behavior, we hold an invisible magnifying glass up to it, causing that behavior to get bigger and more noticeable.

If you don't want Matthew to use "bad" words, then obviously you shouldn't use them yourself, not even "properly." What you *do* will have more influence on Matthew than what you *say*, especially if the "say" and the "do" don't jive.

When Matthew says a bad word — and he will — be cool. Say something like, "Listen, Matthew, I know that some people use words like "blankety-blank" when they talk, but no one in our family uses them and neither will you." That's clear and will make a more positive impression than, say, beating the blankety-blank out of him.

By allowing ourselves to get upset by the small things that children do, we set the stage for repeat performances. Once we set the stage, children play the parts we assign them.

Lying

Why do parents ask their children questions when they already know the answers?

For example: one day, mom discovers that $20 is missing from her purse. Later she notices a new and expensive-looking pocketknife on top of her twelve year old's chest of drawers. Looking through his pants pockets, she finds three $1 bills and a receipt for $14.68 from a sporting goods store. She finds her son and asks, "Where did you get the money for this knife?"

"I found it," he replies.

Situations of this sort raise an interesting question: who is hiding the truth? The son, for not admitting that he took $20 from his mother? Or the mother, for not admitting that she knew where her son got the money?

In either case, the game is the same. First, the child breaks a rule. The parent finds several clues lying about, which, when put together, reveal that the child did it.

The parent then confronts the child and gives him an opportunity to lie by asking a variation on the basic theme of "Did you do it?" The child cooperates by denying any knowledge of the dastardly deed. The chase is on, and the parent is "It."

There is an old saying, attributed to a wise man who called himself "Anon." It goes, "Ask me no questions and I'll tell you no lies." Anon must have had children.

The "did you?" question invites the lie, and the lie serves the child in two ways.

First, it is a diversion. You begin with a relatively clear-cut issue (the child broke a rule), which requires but one simple consideration (what shall be done about it?). But by asking questions, you allow the child to create a second issue: where is the truth? Now you are juggling two issues and two considerations. Which do you respond to first—the broken rule or the hunt for the truth? Most parents react more immediately to the lie. So, the *real* issue (the broken rule) fades into the background where it may disappear completely.

Second, the question sets up a game of "hide-and-seek" in which the child controls the thing being hidden—the truth. A parent cannot play this game without yielding authority to the child, because the child defines how and how long the game is played.

Another incentive for lying is that the odds are good. If you are asked 20 questions and respond with 20 lies, the chances are excellent that at least one of the lies will work. Because the thrill of escape is addicting, the child keeps on lying. With practice, he grows skillful at lying and begins to improve his percentage.

So, by asking a child a question to which you know the answer, you are not giving him a chance to tell the truth. You are teaching him to lie. That's an unsettling thought, isn't it?

Children who become liars generally lack a sense of accomplishment. Lying fills this void and develops into a game at which they can excel, something they can be proud of.

Parents should have no trouble dealing with an occasional untruth. However, with a child who lies continually, you must approach each situation as though the child is guilty until he proves his innocence. *Never* give him the benefit of the doubt, but, at the same time, steer his need to achieve in more constructive directions.

The way to prevent lying, whether the child is hooked or not, is to tell the truth about what you already know. Take Anon's advice and make statements of fact instead of fishing for fiction.

The mother in our example could have told her son, "Twenty dollars is missing from my purse. You have a new pocketknife on your dresser and $3 in your pants pocket. The pocketknife belongs to me, the $3 belongs to me, and all your free time for the next week belongs to me."

A child who lies is hiding more than the truth. He is hiding himself. If he is allowed to play this game over a long period, he runs the risk of one day forgetting where he put the real "him."

It Takes Two

The storm gathered upstairs while I sat reading the paper. It began as a rumbling confusion of voices, suddenly punctuated by a gruff, insistent, "GET OUTA HERE!" Then came a piercing screech. Another who-done-it was unfolding at the Rosemond's.

"Daddy!" It was Eric, my 12 year old, calling from the top of the stairs. I kept reading.

"DADDY!"

"Eric?" The sound of his name brings him thundering down

the stairs, an avalanche of indignation.

"Dad, Wayne and I want to play in my room and Amy won't leave us alone."

"Oh really? I'm reading the paper here on the sofa."

"DAD! She's messing everything up and we can't play!"

"Sounds complicated."

"Will you tell her to leave so Wayne and I can play?"

"No, I won't."

"Why not?"

"You know why not, but if you want to hear it again," (deep breath) "I am not a referee. The two of you can work these things out without my help."

"All right then, can I drag her out and lock the door?"

"You know the rule for fighting in our house — nobody gets hurt. And keep Wayne out of it."

"I won't hurt her, but can I lock her out?"

"I'm not going to tell you what to do."

"O.K. I'm gonna ask her one more time, and then I'm throwing her out and locking the door."

"Remember the rule."

Dramatic about face and exit, stage left. A few moments later, I hear the unmistakable racket of a body being dragged, kicking, across the floor and dumped in the hall. *Slam!* Little fists pummel the door . . . "LET ME IN! I HATE YOU! YOU'RE THE WORST BROTHER IN THE WORLD!" Then, down the stairs she flies, the one-and-only, Amy the Screech. "Daddy!"

"Yes, Amos?"

"Eric pushed me out of his room," (here come the crocodile tears) "and LOCKED THE DOOR!"

"Oh really? *I'm* reading the paper."

It's the same message I've been giving them for years — Daddy will not referee their fights or judge who was "right" and who was "wrong." Despite my refusal to intervene, they still occasionally ask, and I expect the invitation.

I never appreciated the meaning of "it takes two to tango" until Eric and Amy began "dancing" with each other. In fact, this particular tango is probably an inevitable consequence of having more than one child in a family.

It takes the better part of childhood for children to learn the art of getting along. While they may need a coach occasionally, it is generally best for adults to maintain a respectable distance from the dance. It takes two to tango and a third to get tangled.

Children have a talent for turning what could have been a simple exercise in learning how to live together into a melodrama, peopled with cardboard characters straight out of "The Perils of Pauline."

Someone is the villain, heir to the throne of Snideley Whiplash. Someone else is the victim — oppressed, downtrodden and certain to evoke lots of sympathy. We adults are generally typecast as a cross between the Pope and Henry Kissinger. It's a generous offer, which I always refuse. But they keep offering, because as often as they tangle, the trivial becomes the grandiose, and another melodrama begins. It's the alchemy of childhood.

I suppose that transforming real people into two-dimensional stereotypes makes their conflicts seem less threatening, less personal and therefore less enduring. That may have something to do with the way children are able to forgive and forget so easily.

Ah-ha! The trick of growing up involves learning to keep conflict personal, and *still* being able to forgive and *learn* rather than forget.

I stay out of their conflicts because I trust them to work things out for themselves. I stay out because any solution *they* devise will be more valuable and enduring than one *I* impose on them. I stay out because I don't want them growing up to believe in melodrama. I stay out because I want them growing *out* of their stereotypes, not *into* them.

Meanwhile, I keep waiting for the last tango.

Twins

If you've been blessed with twins, here are some recommendations — more "don'ts" than "do's."

First of all, don't hang rhyming names on them. It may be cute and all the relatives may expect you to, but it may contribute to problems later.

Identical twins have as much right to separate identities as any other two children. Names like "Fred" and "Ted" obscure the fact that, although they may share identical physical characteristics, they are fundamentally different people.

Rhyming names can also create confusion. Young children have difficulty discriminating between similar sounds. When you ask a two year old to "Get the hat," he may walk over and pet the cat! That may be funny, but one problem twins don't need is never being sure what their names are or whose name you called.

Don't *ever* dress them in identical clothes, even for a family portrait. You get more for your money buying two interchangeable outfits rather than two matching outfits. When the outfits are interchangeable, each child shares two, and maybe even four, different groupings. When the outfits match, each child has one outfit.

Not only is matching clothing impractical; it's confusing to twins and to other people. Matching clothing encourages the false idea that they are the same person in two bodies.

Don't buy them identical gifts for special occasions. Identical toys may seem fair and impartial, but they will create several problems and solve none. Identical toys, like identical clothes and rhyming names, create turmoil and conflicts. You may know "whose is whose," but young children won't. Besides, it's an extension of the unhealthy "you-are-one-person" idea.

Buying identical toys will not prevent fights, either. Children will fight over toys no matter what you do, until they are old enough to see the value of sharing. This won't happen until they are at least four years old. They will learn the art of sharing much sooner if each has her own unique set of possessions. What's to share if everything is alike?

Several years ago, I talked with the parents of twin girls who were then nine years old. They had rhyming names, wore identical clothing and had identical possessions. At the time, Sherry had developed an outgoing personality, while Cherry had become quiet, shy and dependent on her sister to do things for her. I persuaded the parents to refer to Cherry by her middle name, to see that the girls never wore matching outfits, and to purchase no identical things for them. Several weeks later, the parents told me thay had seen a great transformation in Cherry, who was now called "Lynn." She had become as independent and outgoing as her sister. When the girls had attended a family reunion, Lynn had run up to a favorite aunt and exclaimed, "Look at me, Aunt Lydia, I'm a brand new person!"

If you have twins, encourage each to develop an individual identity. Appreciate and nurture their separateness. Making them carbon copies of each other will plant the seeds of competition, resentment or dependence.

Broken Homes

(Q) My husband and I separated three months ago under bitter circumstances. Ever since then, our five-year-old daughter has been extremely clinging and whiny. She wants to sit on my lap if there are strangers present and wants to be in the same room with me all the time. If I tell her to sit in her own chair or stop following me around, she cries. This is not the outgoing, happy little girl I once knew. She has also started overeating and gaining unnecessary weight. Her questions pose another dilemma. Almost every day, for instance, she wants to know whether her daddy is coming back. My mother thinks I should say, "Maybe," or "I don't know," as a way of, in her words, "Giving Angie something to look forward to." Wild horses couldn't drag me back to him, but I'm afraid the blunt truth would make matters worse. Please help!

(A) Following an abrupt separation, it is not uncommon for young children to cling almost desperately to the remaining parent.

Preschoolers are often closer to, and more dependent upon, their mothers. Nevertheless, they depend on their fathers too.

Your husband's predictable presence within the family was essential to your daughter's security — to her "picture" of the family as a constant, unchanging unit. Her father's sudden, incomprehensible departure altered this picture and exposed her to a threatening, and sometimes intolerable, level of instability. To reduce her anxiety, she clings to you, the remaining parent.

As it happens, this is an extremely vulnerable time for you as well. Your sense of stability and adequacy is threatened, and your emotional resources are stretched to their limits. It may be difficult for you to respond to your daughter's intense, often overpowering need for reassurance.

The more anxious a child in this situation becomes, the more unsure the remaining parent becomes, provoking even more anxiety in the child.

If you are caught up in this cycle, you would do best to see an experienced child and family counselor (psychologist or clinical social worker). A competent professional can provide invaluable assistance to a single parent by helping restabilize the modified family.

Under the circumstances, it isn't unusual for a child to exhibit several forms of regression — returning to some object or behavior more appropriate to an earlier stage of growth. Your daughter's clinging is an example of this, and so is her overeating.

During the first two years of life, food becomes closely linked to satisfaction of both physical and emotional needs. Under stress, children (and many adults) overeat in an unsuccessful attempt to recapture the security of those early years.

You must not allow your daughter to believe that food is a way of managing uneasiness. To the extent that she comes to rely on food as a way of handling crises, her growth toward autonomy and self-sufficiency will be impaired.

However, simply preventing her from overeating is not

enough. Your daughter must also see that you *alone* are capable of meeting her needs. And, of course, you *are*.

Let her know that there are times for closeness and times when both of you need to be in different places, doing different things. If you don't want her sitting on your lap or following you, be clear and firm about that. If she cries, it is because she doesn't know what else to do with her anxiety. Give her a place of her own to cry in.

Answer her questions clearly and honestly. If daddy isn't ever coming back, tell her so, and explain what role daddy *will* continue to play in her life.

Absentee Fathers

(Q) I am divorced and the mother of a five-year-old girl. My ex-husband sees our daughter every other weekend. He has the money to do things for her that I simply can't afford, so her time with daddy is generally very exciting, which, in turn, means that I have problems settling her down after every visit. For a day or two, she is moody, irritable, very active and wants to talk constantly about what "she and daddy did," which is the last thing I want to hear. She has recently started screaming things like, "I like my daddy better'n you!" and "I wanta live with my daddy!" when she's upset with me. This tears me up, and I don't know how to handle her at these times. I've tried talking calmly, but she can probably tell I'm upset. What can you suggest?

(A) The problems and frustrations you describe are all part of what I call "single-mother syndrome."

You resent the freedom and the range of options your ex-husband enjoys in his relationship with your daughter. You resent the fact that he can afford to fill their time together with goodies, but doesn't have to invest any of his time toward the day-to-day responsibilities required of a full-time parent. The arrangement seems to guarantee that you get all the work while he gets most of the rewards.

So, naturally, the last thing you want to hear from your daughter is what a funtastic time she has with daddy. But you will hear it anyway, because she comes back with her batteries fully charged, already looking forward to next time. You may feel like somebody who just fills the gaps between one "holiday" and the next.

It would help if you developed more understanding of your daughter's point of view. It is, for instance, common for a child whose parents are divorced to put the absent parent (usually the father) on a pedestal. In the child's eyes, daddy becomes a heroic figure without fault or blemish. The ideal quickly becomes a substitute for the real. The child appoints herself Keeper of the Image, which she polishes and keeps spotless from one visit to the next.

This hero-worship is quite enough to push any single mother's tolerance over the line. After all, you probably remember daddy as a genuine unmentionable.

Unfortunately, the more irritated you are with the talk about daddy and the marvelous things he does, the more defensive and protective your daughter will become about her relationship with him. Furthermore, she will sense the power which daddy's name commands in her behalf. When things don't go her way, she will let fly with, "I like my daddy better'n you!"

The best thing you could do for yourself is *listen* when your daughter wants to describe her adventures in pater-dise. In fact, don't just listen—ask questions and probe for details. Take control of the conversation so you will be in a position to say, after an appropriate length of time, "Well, that's all very exciting to talk about, and I'm glad you have fun with your daddy. Mommy is going to stop talking now and go finish my magazine, and I want you to go play in your room." In this way, you begin to redefine the terms of your relationship as soon as she comes home.

Accept that she has a glorious time with daddy. That's the way it *should* be. You wouldn't wish her a rotten time every two weeks, would you? Furthermore, dad has a right to take her higher than a kite every time he sees her. Her joy and enthusiasm make being a once-every-two-weeks daddy *almost* meaningful for him.

The trouble you have managing her after she comes home is not dad's fault. Your resentment is your own undoing. It incapacitates your authority, drives a wedge between the two of you and sets up confrontations.

Everything rests on your willingness to lay down the sword and listen. By listening (and talking), you invite her to become reinvolved with you and make it less likely that she will carry daddy's banner around the house.

The more interest you show in her, the easier it will be to reestablish control and the more she will appreciate and look forward to the low-key, secure predictability of home. After all, there really is no place like home, and she knows it.

Adoption

(Q) Seven years ago, I became pregnant out-of-wedlock and gave birth to a son. When he was 15 months old, I married a wonderful man who adopted my son and has a fantastic relationship with him. We now have another son who is three years old. We have not yet told the oldest boy the facts of his birth, but feel that he ought to know. However, several people (friends and relatives) have advised us against telling him, saying it will hurt him or he's still too young. We want to be honest with him, but we're confused. What is your opinion?

(A) He needs to know, he has a right to know, he needs to hear it from you before he figures it out or hears it from someone else, and now is an excellent time to tell him.

A seven year old will be able to grasp the subtle complexities of the situation. A child of this age can think more flexibly than a child even two years younger; therefore, he stands less of a chance of becoming confused.

A seven year old's emotional character is more clearly established and less vulnerable than a younger child's. He is more capable of dealing successfully with emotional conflicts that might temporarily surface when the circumstances of his background are presented to him.

An excellent case can be made for not waiting any longer. Unless old power struggles are still begging for resolution, the early elementary years are relatively calm. There is, however, an upsurge in rebelliousness beginning at nine or ten and building to a peak sometime during early adolescence.

A child's reaction to finding out that he was adopted by one (or both) of his parents is likely to be more extreme if the parents wait until the rebellious period to tell him. He could interpret their delay as an indication of a lack of trust in the relationship. That might be all the excuse he would need to escalate his rebelliousness to an inappropriate, and perhaps even deviant, extent.

So, having established this as an opportune time to give him the information, I have a few suggestions which might help prevent everyone's going into a tailspin:

• Make sure your son understands the basic facts of conception, pregnancy and birth and that he knows what "adoption" means. If he isn't clear on these concepts, you need to give him a mini-course in sex education, with an explanation of the different kinds of families (natural, single-parent, blended) and the difference between natural, step- and adoptive parents. Give him examples of people he knows to bring all this into sharper focus and allow several weeks for it to sink in.

• Anticipate that he may react by becoming temporarily sullen and withdrawn. There's also a chance that he will exhibit mood swings in which he becomes suddenly angry, accusatory and more easily frustrated.

It's a good bet that he will throw a few curves into the system to test how well it holds up under any stress he might apply to it.

To him it may seem that a lot has changed, including his definition of who he is and how he "fits" into the family. The news may create some temporary disruptions. If so, you must, acting through the strength and solidarity of your marriage, demonstrate to him that nothing has changed. He is the *same* person, in the *same* family, living by the *same* rules, sharing the *same* love as before.

• Schedule a family vacation to begin several days after you explain things to him. Use this time together to re-affirm your bonds. The vacation will make it possible for both parents to be available to each other at nearly all times, thus preventing the child from "cornering" either of you. And clarifying, disciplining, comforting and so on which needs to be done can be handled immediately by both of you.

• He may have questions about his biological father, including "When can I meet him?" Answer everything in a straightforward and honest way. It is not wise to allow the child to meet the third party immediately. Explain that his biological father has a life, and perhaps even a family, of his own, and that uninvited contacts would invade his privacy.

If the child persists, assure him that you will share the identity of the biological parent later, perhaps after he graduates from high school. By then, he will be old enough to make a reasonably well-thought-out decision about using that information.

Above all else, let him know that *you* are his real parents, *both* of you. And remember, almost anyone can be a mother or a father, but only very special people can be mommies and daddies.

PART FOUR

Sounding Off

Television

The average American preschool child spends more time watching television than in any other waking activity. Between her second and sixth birthdays, she watches 32 hours a week, or 6,656 hours during four of the most important years of her life. By the time she enters first grade, she will have spent close to one-third of her waking hours in front of a television set.

Since the late 1960s, groups like Boston-based Action for Children's Television (ACT) have fought to improve the quality of children's programs. ACT has succeeded in eliminating vitamin ads aimed at children and commercial pitches by children's program hosts, and in reducing by 40 percent the commercial time on Saturday morning television.

But better television viewing may *not* be what our children need. A growing body of evidence strongly suggests that television's harm to children—to preschoolers in particular—has little, if anything, to do with *what* they watch.

It doesn't matter what's on the screen. The harm is in the very *watching* itself.

When a child watches television, she is inert, physically and mentally. She is passive, disengaged, uninvolved (or involved only momentarily and superficially). She can choose from a small set of programs (often similar in nature), but she cannot determine what she sees, or from what perspective, or in what sequence.

As she watches, her pupils are fixed on one stationary point in the visual field. Instead of scanning, she stares. Most of the time, her hands rest limply in her lap. She is a spectator, a bystander, along for the ride down a one-way street.

In short, watching television is akin to doing nothing. It is perhaps the most democratic technology ever invented. Anyone can watch, and almost everyone does. No prerequisites are necessary—no talent, no prior experience. One working eyeball is all you need.

Even the claims made for such so-called educational programs as "Sesame Street" and "Electric Company" are suspect. A study done by the Russell Sage Foundation and summarized in "Sesame Street Revisited" (Russell Sage Foundation, 1975) determined that regular "Sesame Street" watchers actually made fewer gains in reasoning and problem-solving skills than children who watched only occasionally.

The preschool years are the most critical formative period of a human being's life. In this brief time, a child develops an enduring personal style of relating to the world — socially, emotionally, perceptually and intellectually. Research has clearly demonstrated the importance of exploration, play and fantasy to the growing child.

But instead of being a stimulant to intellectual and physical activity, television acts as a narcotic. Dr. T. Berry Brazelton, a Cambridge, Mass., pediatrician and author of "Infants and Mothers," says television induces a trance-like state in young children. "(It) assaults and overwhelms a child," Brazelton has said. "He can respond to it only by (becoming) more passive."

Children's television advocates disagree. Dr. Edward Palmer, head of research for the Children's Television Workshop (producers of "Sesame Street" and "Electric Company"), asserts that watching television is a "remarkable intellectual act."

"All the while kids are watching," Palmer says, "they are making hypotheses, anticipating, generalizing, remembering and actively relating what they are seeing to their own lives."

But one look at the glazed, vacuous expression on the face of a young child immersed in a program convinces me that watching television is hardly remarkable, barely intellectual and in no way an act.

Contrary to what children's television proponents would have us believe, television is not, and can never be, a child's best friend. It is, instead, one of his worst enemies. A child's time is better spent doing just about anything other than watching television.

Since 1955, the number of hours preschool children spend watching television has more than tripled. During these same years, academic achievement scores have declined steadily, the national literacy level has deteriorated, and public schools have been beset by an epidemic of young children who have painful difficulty learning to read.

A recent study of a half-million California school children concluded that the more television children watched on school nights, the lower their achievement test scores. Wilson Riles, California superintendent of public instruction, said the results show a link between television watching and poor achievement that, up till now, educators have only "suspected . . . and talked about."

Watching television is not in any way comparable to reading. You don't *learn* to watch television — you just do it. Reading requires involvement — a quality noticeably absent from the television experience. Reading is an active, problem-solving exercise — a two-way street. You cannot "watch" a book.

We have evolved a brain ideally suited to this challenge. But the brain of a six year old who comes to school with 6,000 hours of television under her eyelids is potentially in big trouble. Unless some drastic changes are made, she may not be willing or able to alter the habit of being a passive "watcher."

Researchers at the National Institute of Mental Health have found evidence that brain cells grow in response to intellectual exercise and stimulation (much as muscle cells respond to physical stimulation) and atrophy, or weaken, for the lack of it.

That research raises the possibility that many "learning disabled" children are just average video kids whose brains, weakened from too many hours of watching television, cannot rise to the challenge of learning to read.

Recent research on children who can't read also indicates that watching television trains their eyes to stare instead of scan. Dr. Edgar Gording, a remedial reading expert, says many of the nonreaders he works with have never learned to move their eyes from left to right. That basic visual skill would presumably have developed had these children spent less time during their preschool years staring at a television screen and more in play and other active pursuits.

Equally frightening is the addictive quality of television. The more children watch, the more they want to watch. If they are prevented from watching, they often go through a period of emotional withdrawal that's stressful not only to them, but to their parents as well. They become sullen, moody and irritable. They become obsessed with the television and make repeated attempts to "connect" with it. They become aggressive, unruly and anxious. Their frustration and anxiety build, choking off their ability to engage in constructive behavior.

When addicted children aren't plugged into the television set, they will probably plug themselves into one or both of their parents, hassling and whining, "Do for me! Do for me!"

After reaching the limits of tolerance, parents are likely to put them back in front of the tube, hoping to buy a moment's peace. They don't realize that their children's inability to occupy themselves is partly a result of the time they spend glued to the tube. Television drains children of initiative, motivation and autonomy and weakens their tolerance for stress.

But why is television addictive while radio, for instance, is not? It's a matter of different technologies. Typically, live or filmed television productions are shot using several cameras, each watching the action from a different angle.

The networks have found that viewers will watch the screen longer when the scene shifts from one camera to the next. So shift it does, at four-second intervals, on the average.

This is why small children will sit for long periods, transfixed by programs they cannot possibly comprehend. The incessant shifting of reference point overrides the need for understanding. It does not interest the child—it mesmerizes her.

Paradoxically, a child who sits staring at a television screen for several hours is learning how *not* to pay attention. She is adapting to an attention span of a few seconds.

After 6,000 hours of this insidious training, the child arrives in a public school classroom where her teacher discovers that she cannot concentrate long enough to finish her work. The teacher also notices that she is in almost constant motion. Eventually, her teacher refers her to the school psychologist, who calls her "hyperactive."

But such labels mask more than they reveal. Television watching has rendered this child unable to tolerate a stable visual field. In the relative boredom of a classroom, she tries to re-establish the level of stimulation she is used to when sitting. Her eyes bounce from one thing to another and, in many cases, her body follows.

Since watching television has never required anything of her, she doesn't finish anything she starts. She doesn't know why she can't sit still, can't pay attention or can't finish her work—she just knows she *can't*. And so, "I can't" becomes more and more a part of her self-image.

Veteran teachers have remarked to me that, as a group, children today are far less imaginative and resourceful than children were a generation ago, when childhood television viewing was less than half what it is today. This observation is hardly surprising. The explicit nature of the television experience leaves little to a child's imagination. In fact, it subtly discourages children from exercising their creative resources.

Over the past 30 years, we have allowed the television networks to create their own myths; among them are the terms "children's program," "family program" and "educational program."

Presumably, programs like "Captain Kangaroo" and "Sesame Street" are "children's programs." But television watching is not an appropriate pastime for children, preschoolers in particular. Television is a handicap to childhood, not a help. There really are no children's programs. The so-called children's program exists and thrives because of *parents*, not children.

These shows keep children "occupied," but, contrary to what their producers would have parents believe, they offer nothing of value. There are no programs for families either. The terms *family* and *program* are incompatible, because the moment a group of people calling themselves a family sits down to watch television, the family process stops.

The terms *watch* and *together* are also incompatible. You don't watch television together. You watch alone. Regardless of how many people are in the same room watching the same television, each has retired into a solitary audio-visual tunnel.

Television may not actually be spawning communication problems, but it certainly becomes an excuse for maintaining them. The more people in a family drift apart, the more watching television becomes a convenient means of dutifully enduring each other's presence while simultaneously avoiding acknowledgement of it—all under the pretense that watching television is a "family affair."

"All television is educational," said Nicholas Johnson, former member of the Federal Communications Commission. "The question is—'What's being learned?'"

On the surface, a child watching a Saturday morning cartoon and a child watching "Wild Kingdom" are viewing entirely different kinds of programs—one pure entertainment, the other supposedly educational. But there are no programs that earn, more than any others, rights to the term "educational." A child watching a cartoon and a child watching "Wild Kingdom" are both exposed to the same educational message: *You can get something for nothing.*

Children are impressionable little people. They have no way of evaluating, and therefore resisting, television's insidious message.

They accept. They absorb. They adapt. And they become whatever they are massaged into becoming by whatever influences prevail in their environments.

Toys

I've been trying to remember what toys I played with when I was four or five years old, but the only one that comes to mind is an electric train Uncle Ned gave me for Christmas in 1952.

I must be getting senile. Surely I had more toys than that! After all, I was a child, and children have lots of toys. Therefore, I had lots of toys!

What were they?

This is driving me crazy. I'm going to call my mother.

"Listen, Ma, I was sittin' here tryin' to remember my toys. You know, the stuff I played with when we lived in Charleston, and . . .

"Toys? We didn't buy toys for you."

"No toys? None?"

"Well, let's see. Come to think of it, Ned gave you an electric train one Christmas and you had some lead cavalry and a set of Lincoln Logs. But those were rainy day things for you."

"So what did I do when it wasn't raining?"

"You played outside. Lizard hunts and other great adventures. You were never at a loss for things to do. I could hardly ever find you. I remember one day . . ."

Lizard hunts. Great adventures. Gone all afternoon. What a life! I remember now. My toys were things of the earth. Stones and puddles and sticks and stuff. I was never bored. I didn't know *how* to get bored.

Is it my imagination, or do lots of children today have trouble getting un-bored?

How many times have you heard a child say, "I've got nothin' to do!"

Today's children expect, and even demand, to be entertained, because they've been entertained. Every day, in every conceivably irrelevant way. They are, by and large, a stubbornly inert generation.

Parents who give their children too much of their time, too much television and a roomful of toys: these are the environmental afflictions of today's children. These are the things that stand in the way of their learning to occupy themselves creatively. They are barriers to the free outpouring of intelligence.

Paradoxically, children quickly become dependent on these obstructions — unwitting participants in their own undoing.

Take toys, for instance. Today's child is, generally speaking, a toy addict. He's gotta have 'em. New ones. All the time.

He lives in a clutter of toys. They're everywhere. Bits and pieces of broken toys sift to the bottom of an oversized toybox. His shelves are stacked with them, his closet and cabinets are packed with them, his floor is strewn with them. Everytime his grandparents come for a visit, they bring him more obligatory toys. Everytime his parents go shopping, he gets a toy.

Yet he says, "I've got nothin' to do!"

He is almost right! The choices are too overwhelmingly many. The clutter fogs his imagination, obstructs his vision and frustrates his growing. He avoids the frustration by avoiding the clutter. The only thing he knows to do is to compulsively add to it. Translated, "I've got nothin' to do" means, "I forget how to do for myself."

The more toys he has, the more he depends on them and the more he wants. Ultimately, the toys themselves have no value whatsoever. He ignores them. He doesn't take care of them. That's what happens when supply outstrips need. The ritual trip to the toystore becomes an end in itself: his fix.

The more toys he has, the more he expects of *things* and the less he expects of himself. He acts helpless, and we continue to feed his helplessness, slowly but surely strengthening an overall "I can't" attitude toward the challenges of living.

Here are a few of my thoughts on toys:

• The best toy is one the child creates. Take your child outside and show him how to build forts out of sticks, to dig moats with an old soup spoon, to make boats out of folded paper, to build walls out of stones, to fashion trees out of pinecones—the possibilities are infinite!

• The best commercial toys are flexible (they can be combined in lots of different ways) and encourage imaginative play. Small, doll-like figures and other true-to-life miniatures are fine. So are simple building sets, clay, crayons, water colors, finger paints and so on.

• For the most part, steer clear of so-called educational toys. Generally they have little, if anything, in common with a child's developmental needs. Their "problems" are largely irrelevant and tend to inhibit, rather than encourage, creative thinking.

• Instead of buying toys that "do"—toys that perform—give children a few, basic things they can manipulate. Let the children's imaginations do the "doing."

• Don't limit children to toys traditionally considered appropriate to only one sex. If a boy wants to play with dolls, buy him dolls. If a girl wants to play baseball, buy her a bat and ball. The freer they are to explore the possibilities of living, the better choice-makers they will become.

In the final analysis, *less is more.*

Learning Disabilities

If there were a recipe for "learning disability," it would probably read something like this: take equal parts Myth, Fad, Confusion and Impatience. Mix ingredients vigorously until thick. Take one child who is not doing well in school. Thoroughly coat the child with the mixture. Serve up one "learning disabled" child.

Now, let's examine how these ingredients work.

Myth: No one has yet discovered just what a learning disability is. The term has been manufactured to explain why some children have more difficulty in school than they presumably "should." The prevailing thought is that these troublesome children have some minor malfunction in their brains which interferes with their ability to read, write or work with numbers. But there is no proof that such a kink in the brain actually exists. It is, therefore, a myth (otherwise known as a "theory," if you prefer the aura of scientific respectability).

Fad: In the past two decades, we have seen several "progressive" approaches in education come and go. Each one was heralded as the ultimate improvement. Dr. Allan Cohen, an educator and author of elementary reading texts, calls this the bandwagon era — full of fads and gimmicks, but short on real know-how. He asserts that many of the books and methods used to teach reading are confusing and inconsistent with what is known about how children learn to read. In other words, we create bewildering learning environments, and then say there is something wrong with children who act bewildered.

Confusion: When I was a schoolboy, there were no "learning disabled" or "dyslexic" children. There were some who did very well in school, those who did well enough and those who did not-so-well. The not-so-wells stayed after school to work with the teacher, were given easier assignments, simpler textbooks and so on. Quite often, they were retained an extra year in one grade or another. Lots of my buddies were retained. Almost all of them finished high school, and some went on to college. They *all* learned to read.

Now we have a national epidemic of learning disabled (L.D.) and dyslexic children. But the experts cannot agree among themselves on how to define these terms, how to identify the children or how to correct the problem. The definitions are so vague that almost any child who has ever misspelled a word, stumbled over a pronunciation or multiplied when he should have added, can be included. In a recent screening project in Indiana, every child in one school district was found to have a learning disability. The hunt is on for L.D. children. Educators and psychologists are convinced they are out there by the score, and so they hang the tag on scores of them.

Impatience: Everything is geared to "quick," "fast," "do-it-now." Some contemporary historians say that we are no longer capable of making a comfortable adjustment to the rapid acceleration of progress. Our enthusiasm for constant change and improvement has begun to influence our thinking about children.

We often act as though children are products subject to the same principles and expectations that apply in the field of product engineering. We can go from New York to Paris in half the time it took 20 years ago, but is it reasonable to expect that our children can be taught the three Rs in much shorter time as well?

Basic reading, writing and math skills are being pushed at three and four year olds. Never mind that this doesn't fit what we know about what children are capable of learning or how they learn—this is the Twentieth Century.

It is fortunate that special programs offer individualized instruction for children who need that extra boost—the not-so-wells. Unfortunately, in order to qualify for these programs, the child usually must be labeled L.D. for the record.

The label implies that the child is handicapped, and it is potentially damaging to his self-esteem. There is also the very real danger that the label will become a crutch used to avoid responsibilities and excuse personal failures in later life.

The skills necessary for reading and writing mature earlier in some children and later in others. All children are different and learn at different speeds *and in different ways*. When the same yardstick is applied to measure the progress of every child, each child's individuality gets lost.

But the yardstick method has its conveniences. If a child doesn't "measure up," then one can assume there is something wrong with the child. That protects the image of our educational systems, and every American knows that the system is more important than the individual. Or is it the other way around?

The real difference between a child who reads well and a child who doesn't is involved parents, concerned teachers and lots of good books.

Hyperactivity

The term minimal brain damage, or minimal brain dysfunction (MBD), was coined in the 1950s by a group of researchers who compared the capabilities of brain-damaged children with those of normal children. They noticed that some normal children had difficulty performing certain tasks that were also difficult for the brain-damaged children. They resolved this paradox by deciding that the brains of some normal children must not function properly. The malfunction affects only cer-

tain specific skills, like reading or writing, and is not physically disabling. Therefore, it is minimal.

There are many possible symptoms of MBD, and no one
symptom appears across the board. Some MBD children have
difficulty with reading and other academic subjects. Some
have poor coordination. Others have problems understanding
what they are told or expressing themselves clearly. And some
children's difficulties are diagnosed as MBD because they are
"hyperactive."

Hyperactivity has its own set of symptoms. Hyperactive
children, as the term implies, are usually described as being
very active ("I can't keep up with him") restless ("He can't sit
still"), easily distracted ("The slightest noise or movement attracts his attention") and having short attention spans ("He
can't seem to finish anything.").

Hyperactivity, like MBD, is a medical term. It should be applied to a child only by a physician, preferably a pediatric
neurologist. The term has penetrated our everyday vocabulary
to such an extent, however, that most cases of so-called
hyperactivity have probably not been diagnosed through ex-
amination by a physician.

When a child has his teacher climbing the walls, the teacher
tells the child's mother the child might be hyperactive. A
mother who doesn't like the rowdy child next door tells a
friend that the child is hyperactive. When you visit Aunt
Maude's, her two year old throws one tantrum after another
for several hours. On the way home, you and your spouse
agree that the child is hyperactive.

I remember when children were "undisciplined" or "brats."
Those days are fading fast. Yesterday's undisciplined brat is today's hyperactive child.

We have thrown the term hyperactive around in ways that
belie its true significance. A label is, after all, an over-
simplification, a sort of verbal shorthand. It is a way of con-
densing a more complex explanation.

To suggest that a child is hyperactive simply because he is
bothersome doesn't explain anything. Applied in wholesale
fashion, as it has been, the term doesn't describe a child's
behavior so much as it reflects someone else's impatience,
frustration or lack of understanding.

As accustomed as we are to living in a world where
everything from bank loans to hot meals is available at the
push of a button, we somehow feel that children don't grow up
fast enough. But there is no way to accelerate the natural process of growth in a human being. You cannot push a river.

We desperately need to recognize that every child is a unique individual. We give lip service to the idea, but fail to practice what we preach. There is no other child like mine, and no other child like yours, and there are no two hyperactive children who are alike either. Nonetheless, we tend to react to the label rather than the child.

It's easy to see why the term has become so popular. It implies a neurological condition for which no one can be held responsible. There is no suggestion of neglect, emotional disturbance or implication that the parents have failed in their responsibilities. The hyperactive child is no longer "bad" (a brat). He is slightly damaged and deserving of our sympathies. Therefore, the term rests comfortably with all concerned.

I offered a cookie to one of Eric's playmates several years ago, only to have him refuse it with the comment, "I can't have cookies because I'm hyperactive." As I looked at his don't-you-feel-sorry-for-me? expression and thought about his generally rude, obnoxious manner, I did feel sorry for him — not because he *was* hyperactive and couldn't have cookies, but because someone had *told* him he was hyperactive, and it was becoming his excuse.

Interestingly enough, no one has yet found concrete evidence of the supposed neurological impairment. So, the idea that hyperactivity has anything to do with a problem in the child's gray matter is nothing more than an educated hunch.

Furthermore, definitions of hyperactivity are vague, and there is little agreement on what criteria to use in diagnosing the condition. Any boisterous, absent-minded, rebellious, persistently curious and energetic child could be called hyperactive.

In fact, descriptions of hyperactive children are similar to descriptions of normal, healthy preschoolers in general. This raises the possibility that hyperactive preschoolers are victims of someone's impatience, and that many older hyperactives are simply immature, undisciplined "brats."

There are probably a few children who have neurological problems that can be treated successfully with drugs or physical therapy. But it's in the best interest of both the child and his family to try other treatment approaches before using medication. Even with medication, the family should be in touch with a therapist.

Every child needs the best chance we can give him. If we fall short of that, then the labels we pin on him point at us.

Special Diets and Hyperactivity

In 1973, Dr. Benjamin Feingold, a California allergist, published a report linking diet and hyperactivity in children. He contended that the disruptive behavior characterizing hyperactivity is stimulated by artificial additives present in most processed foods. These include salicylates, a family of chemicals which, in addition to their manufactured forms, occur naturally in tomatoes, apples, oranges and elsewhere.

Feingold's original studies defined the battle lines of a controversy that continues to rage. Its cast of characters include pediatricians, educators, psychologists, nutritionists, and processed-food industry and the U.S. Food and Drug Administration. Mixed in the confusion are the testimonials of thousands of parents of hyperactive children who swear Feingold's diet was their salvation.

One thing is clear — thousands of hyperactive children have tried Feingold's restrictive diet and, if we accept the anecdotal evidence supplied by their parents, a surprisingly large number of them have improved dramatically. These parents would have nothing to gain by lying, so I believe them.

However, whether these improvements can be attributed to Feingold's additive- and salicylate-free diet is another question. There are other ways to interpret the evidence.

The problem is partly one of definition. Ask 15 experts to define hyperactivity and you are likely to receive 15 differing replies, all lacking measurable criteria. There is no single symptom which defines it, no blood test or other medical procedure with which to accurately diagnose it. Whether or not an active, disruptive child gets called hyperactive seems at times to be little more than a matter of his doing the wrong things in the wrong places at the wrong times with the wrong people watching (see Hyperactivity, page 215).

There is little agreement in the professional community concerning use of the label. Dr. Jon Rolf, director of the Vermont Child Development Project, recently said that, according to current descriptions, most preschool children could be called hyperactive. Hyperactivity, it seems, may exist solely in the eye of the beholder.

Hyperactive children may not have much in common, but the dominant issues in their families are generally similar. For instance, the question of "who is in control?" is usually undefined. Typically, the parents are not sufficiently united as the source of executive authority and have not found workable ways of handling the tremendous responsibility of raising a child. In many ways, the child's unstable behavior seems to mirror the instability of living in a family with no consistent center.

Although no one is in control, the *controlling issue* in the family is the child's chaotic behavior, and almost every aspect of the family's life — social, educational, occupational, financial, emotional — is affected. The tension is pervasive, and no one is comfortable.

Understandably, the parents of a hyperactive child are desperate for answers — desperate for a solution which will cool the child's behavior to tolerable and manageable levels. But in the parents' view, theirs is not a conventional child. If a conventional, common sense approach is offered, they often reject it, saying, "We've tried that — it didn't work," when, in fact, it might have worked if the parents had worked together at it.

What's needed is an approach which allows the parents to cooperate without requiring them to admit that they were ever unable to. The hyperactive diet fits this requirement. It lets the parents off the hook by implying that the child's behavior bears no relationship to their own. It cleans up the child's image as well — once a villain, now a victim.

Finally, and most importantly, the diet provides a non-threatening framework within which the parents can structure and stabilize their relationship with the child. The diet takes the spotlight off what the child *does* and focuses it on what he *eats*. Limits and rules, previously vague, are now clearly defined, and the problem of enforcement is considerably less complex and emotional. Within this framework, the parents are able to handle their executive responsibilities in an effective, straightforward way. In short, the diet becomes an exercise in sound child-rearing skills.

In nearly every case, we are told, the child cooperates with the plan and eventually learns to supervise himself. In other words, the child learns self-discipline, the anticipated outcome of any effective discipline program.

Having said all that, am I suggesting that these kids go back to additives and salicylates? Not at all. I'm suggesting that credit be given where credit is due.

Feingold has sounded the alarm on artificial additives and forced the scientific community to take a serious look at the damage they may be doing to our health and well being. That's all to the good.

Controlled studies, however, have failed to prove conclusively that Feingold's diet has any consistent positive effect on the behavior of hyperactive children. Perhaps, as I said before, the problem lies with how we define who is and who isn't hyperactive. That leaves a few thousand parents who have used Feingold's diet in a rigorously applied and conscientiously consistent manner — and learned, in the process, how to be better parents.

I think *they* deserve all the credit for the improvements they describe. I hope they don't mind my saying so.

Gifted and Talented

gift-ed (gif'tid), adj. having a natural ability or aptitude; talented. As in, "Is my child gifted?"

She sure is! Your child got gifts, my child got gifts, all God's chillun's gots gifts, gifts!

Every human being is born already gifted. This most special, although much underestimated, misunderstood, abused and neglected, quality equips each of us with the potential for being whomever and doing whatever we aspire and perspire to be and do.

Our gift is like a seed set to sprout at birth. If the sprout is nurtured it will thrive and become strong, and its branches will reach outward in many directions, to encompass many things.

Unfortunately, we seem hell bent upon doing all we can to ignore, supress and confine this honor God and Mother Nature have bestowed upon us. Even our efforts to enhance it often seem confused or misguided.

Take the existence of special public school programs for "gifted and talented" children. These programs were ostensibly created to meet the so-called special educational needs of students who possess outstanding academic abilities.

Actually, however, these programs reinforce the fundamentally destructive, widely held belief that "gifts" are in short supply.

Instead of recognizing ability, these programs often ignore it. Participants are selected on the basis of grades, IQ's, achievement test scores and teacher ratings of such things as motivation and leadership. Out of 20 students selected at random, *one* may fit the requirements, leaving the other 19 to — what? — just keep plodding along in their own untalented way?

To say that one child is gifted because she makes A's while another is not because he makes C's is a way of leading *both* of them to believe untruths about themselves.

Instead of offering *every* student the opportunity to discover her giftedness and find creative ways to expressing it, these programs create, in the most arbitrary manner possible, an artificial distinction between the supposed "haves" and the "have nots."

Thereafter, the have-nots must resign themselves to living with words like "regular" and "average," while the haves are elevated to special status within the system. In the long run, however, catering to the haves is insidiously harmful instead of helpful.

For starters, the "gifted and talented" label, because it narrows expectations of the child, subtracts from, rather than adds to, her options. Ultimately, instead of broadening the child's self-image, the label confines it.

These programs are fundamentally undemocratic and insular, rather than expansive, in practice. They restrict the free exchange of information and talent among children, and prematurely segregate the privileged minority from their less fortunate peers.

In short, these programs manipulate children, rather than enrich them. In the end, everybody suffers, and everyone's gifts are lessened.

What an irony! What shame!

(Q) At her teacher's suggestion, we recently had our daughter, who is six years old, tested in order to learn her IQ. The psychologist told us that she is "gifted." What would you suggest we do at home to nurture her abilities?

(A) To say that someone is "gifted" is like saying that someone is "nice." Both terms are fairly meaningless, and worse, they can be misleading and create false impressions.

For instance, if I tell you that So-and-So is nice, you will probably look forward to meeting him. Suppose that when you do, he is at the tail end of an argument with his wife and has just learned he made a bad business deal and is going to be audited by the IRS. Maybe under those circumstances he is not so nice after all. You may well come away from this encounter with So-and-So thinking of him as a gruff, sarcastic fellow. It's a shame that So-and-So won't get a second chance to make a first impression, but that's the way the tree falls. You could have been great friends, if only you had met *last* week.

And so it is with being "gifted." If Penelope is "gifted," she can do anything well; is creative, like Mozart; is obnoxiously self-centered, and will grow up to be famous. Right? Wrong! She may well be none of the above.

"Gifted" means only that someone did well on a series of

tests. The tests, which take about three hours, consist of questions and problems. Since a list of every possible problem would have no end, the ones included on the tests are nothing more than *representative*. The tests, therefore, *sample* a person's skills and general abilities.

A high score (a high IQ), by itself, means that the person scored well on the tests. Nothing more. The score is used, however, to *predict* some things about the person, such as how well she will perform on other problems, in other settings. But samples and the predictions based upon them, have built-in flaws.

The Gallup poll, for instance, is a sample. In 1976, it predicted that most Americans would vote for Jimmy Carter. And that's just what happened. But in 1948, a similar poll predicted that Dewey would beat Truman. Samples don't guarantee outcomes.

In the same way, a high score on an IQ test is no quarantee that the person will do well at everything or is creative. Just as "nice" guys have their off days, the "gifted" have their ups and downs. For instance, someone with a high score may do exceedingly well at math, but won't be able to write a good theme or play more than "Chopsticks" on the piano.

The problem is that people who think of her as "gifted" may expect her to write novels and play Beethoven. If she doesn't, they may feel "tricked" and then make the error of saying, "she's no different from anyone else," which isn't true either.

In other words, the term "gifted" can preclude a person's being seen for the unique individual, complete with strengths and weaknesses, that she is.

To answer the question of what you should do now that your daughter has done well on tests which sampled her ability to solve various sorts of problems — nothing. Let her live up to her own standards, not someone else's.

Open Schools

" 'How well his majesty looks in his new clothes,' cried all the people around. Nobody would let it appear that he could see nothing, for then he would not be fit for his post or else he was a fool." — From *The Emperor's New Clothes*, by Hans Christian Anderson.

"Anything for a change," she said, ruefully shaking her head. I was talking with a retired teacher who had dedicated 25 years of her life to the proposition that all children need to be proficient in the language of numbers.

She was allowing me to probe her opinions on the current state of public education. Her thoughts flew straight to the heart of every issue.

"I never taught in an open school," she said, "but I've observed in several, and the concept makes very little sense to me. In my mind, listening is fundamental to learning."

I needed no persuasion. Six years ago, my son started first grade in an open school. It was a brand-new building, chock full of the most up-to-date equipment—individual audio-visual centers, science kits, programmed learning workbooks, aquariums, mini-greenhouses, musical instruments—a carnival of things to do, all ready for some 270 children, in grades one through three, who coexisted under the domed roof of one warehouse-sized space.

Eric loved it. We never had a problem getting him up in the morning, and he never complained of frustration with either the work or his teachers.

I was pleased but skeptical. His classroom sounded like a playground. There was movement everywhere, all the time. Actually, the term "classroom" didn't apply, since only bookcases and chest-high pegboard partitions separated one group from the next.

During the seven months Eric was there, I made several visits to the school, but never once did I find his area without having to ask directions along the way. The environment itself was confusing. Perhaps that's as close to feeling "learning disabled" as I'll ever come.

Eric's teachers used phrases like "self-motivated," "readiness potential" and "ownership of responsibility." They glowed with enthusiasm and never looked afflicted with even a minor case of the "bad day."

Eric was very intelligent, they told me. He was mature, creative and a leader. They made me feel good. In return, I kept my skepticism to myself.

Then we moved. There were only five weeks left in the school year, but we had no choice except to pick up and go.

Eric transferred into a traditional school, much like the one I had gone to. Each class had its own room and each child his own desk. The school was quiet and orderly. I could find Eric's room without help. What a relief to be spontaneously cured of my former affliction!

Two days after he enrolled, his teacher requested a conference. She wasted neither time nor words.

"Eric can't read," she said. "I don't think he'll be ready for the second grade."

Progress strikes again. Eric's experience is not an isolated one. Thousands of other capable children have been sacrificed for an idea which has fallen far short of its original promise.

(Eric went into the second grade on schedule, thanks to a private summer reading program. It took him three years to completely recapture the ground lost in those first seven months. I might add that shortly before he left, his teachers at the open school told me he was reading as well as any other child in the class.)

I am convinced — from many conversations with teachers, administrators, school psychologists, parents and, naturally, my experience with Eric — that the open school is public education's white elephant.

Open schools have ripped-off many a child's precious talent and time, not to mention the taxpayer's precious money. The problem is not the teachers or principals but the concept itself.

There is, for instance, no healthy spirit of competition in an open classroom. The children "seek their own level of achievement" and are usually evaluated according to goals (contracts) which they themselves help establish. All of which sounds very good, but competition is the stuff of real life and frustration is often the catalyst of achievement. Without that sense of enterprise, mediocrity is the standard, and talk about "the child's potential" is as meaningful as an empty wallet.

The environment of an open school is, for many children, overstacked with stimulation and choice. It requires that children adapt to a relative lack of boundaries, both physical and behavioral, and a high level of visual and auditory distraction — almost constant "white noise." That's just what every child needs in order to develop a short attention span.

Nonetheless, children in open schools fare as well on standardized tests of achievement as children in more traditional settings. Those figures fail to show, however, that most of the studies in question are grossly contaminated by what statisticians call "sampling error."

In most cases, open schools are offered as *alternatives* within an otherwise conventional system. That means parents *choose* whether to seek admission for their children. Not only is the student population in alternative schools more select than usual, but it is reasonable to assume that parents who elect this option are generally more involved in their children's education than parents who do *not* make this extra effort.

The same can be said for teachers who apply to teach in open schools (again, the open school is usually an optional assignment). In all likelihood, they are more idealistic, more enthusiastic and more committed to their particular educational philosophy than teachers who are less selective about where they practice their profession.

The parents of a child who is not doing well in an open school can elect to move him to a more traditional school. By and large, children who *stay* in open schools for more than a year or two are those who do well there. This maintains the *illusion* of equivalence in student achievement levels. (Enrollment figures demonstrate that the movement in recent years has been back toward the conventional school.)

In short, open schools have all the cards stacked in their favor. When these hidden biases are considered, there is every reason to expect significantly *higher* achievement among open school students than those in conventional schools. The fact that they are *only equal* must mean that open schools have permitted, *and even rewarded* children for achieving less than they are capable of.

In 1975, Dr. Robert Wright carried out a meticulous study of open versus traditional education (with controls for sampling error). Writing in the American Education Research Journal, he reported significantly higher levels of achievement in the traditional setting.

Wright found *no* difference in verbal creativity or self-esteem between children in the two groups. This flies in the face of claims made by open school devotees that their "permissive, self-directed" approach is more conducive to creativity and building positive self-regard.

Few of the many cultural innovations spawned in the 1960s began with greater promise than alternative education, and few have been as disappointing.

Part of the problem, as many educators admit, is that open schools have tended to attract individuals more concerned with *escaping* what they regarded as an oppressive atmosphere in conventional education than with defining and achieving concrete educational objectives.

There is probably a place for the open school in American education, but it won't be found until its champions confront hard realities and discard the premise that they are capable of doing all things for all children.

After a child has learned the basics and developed a fairly reliable sense of self-discipline, it *might* make sense to gradually "open" his educational experience. In most open schools, though, children have been turned loose within an obscure framework before they are developmentally ready to handle such freedom. Most open schools encompass only the elementary grades – a blatant case of putting the cart before the horse.

Before giving parents the privilege of choosing among several educational alternatives, educators have a responsibility to determine, through rigorous research, the best match of option and child.

Public education is one arena where the consumer should *never* need to beware.

Teenage Parents

One in every ten seventeen-year-old girls in this country is a mother. Last year, more than 250,000 girls, age 17 or younger, gave birth – 15 percent of them for the second or third time. The only maternal age range in which the birth rate is currently increasing is among 12 to 17 year olds.

Teenage pregnancies present a significant health risk to both mothers and children. Babies born to teenage mothers are likely to be premature, underweight and have congenital birth defects. These mothers are highly vulnerable to complications arising during the pregnancy, labor and delivery.

Estimates of the maternal and infant mortality rates associated with these pregnancies run 30 percent higher than for mothers over 20. In addition, these children are more likely to encounter problems later in one or more developmental areas.

With few exceptions, adolescents are emotionally, educationally, socially and economically unsuited for parenthood.

Early childbearing frequently leads to early marriage, repeated (unplanned) pregnancies, an unstable family life, early divorce and welfare dependency. Whether wed or unwed, teenage parents are likely to cut short their schooling and acquire only marginal work skills.

Trying to raise a child amidst the emotional tangle of adolescence is more of a strain than most teenagers can handle. Because teenagers are – regardless of their protests to the contrary – still children themselves, they tend to think childishly about "having a baby."

Almost inevitably, reality gets lost in a whirl of drama, fantasy and wish-fulfillment. For some, having a baby (and getting married) becomes a way out of what may be perceived, for the moment at least, as an intolerable home situation.

For others, parenthood represents proof that one has "grown up" – a decidedly unsatisfactory way of trying to hurdle the last remaining years of one's own dependency.

And for some teenaged girls, having a baby becomes the fulfillment of a wish to be needed and wanted and loved and, most dangerously, *more powerful* than someone else.

Obviously, with that set of delusions, the fall is going to be quick and hard.

A recent study underlined the unrealistic expectations these young parents have of their children and concluded that children of adolescent marriages stand a much higher chance of becoming abused and neglected.

But, teenagers are by no means the only people who experience tremendous difficulty raising children. Many, if not most, new parents find themselves inadequately prepared to deal with their changing roles and responsibilities.

Unfortunately, we humans don't get as much help from Mother Nature as other animals when it comes to raising a child, and we haven't since our instincts took a back seat to the cerebral cortex several million years ago.

Furthermore, when the extended family went the way of the streetcar, so too did the natural family supports that were once available to nurse young marrieds through the first traumatic years of parenthood.

Nevertheless, the majority of today's children will grow up to be parents themselves, and our educational systems continue to neglect their needs in this area. While it is true that courses in child development, marriage and the family and so on have long been offered in public schools, most of them are dry, with no practical experience to spark and focus the classroom study. These courses usually are confined to home economics programs and attract few males.

The continued stability of the family is essential to the continued stability of our society. With that in mind, it seems obvious that public education for parenthood must become a national priority.

Our public schools, for all their current problems and failings, still provide the ideal setting for such an educational experience. Education for parenthood programs could begin at the junior high level to prepare our country's future parents – the guardians of our future.

Every high school in this country should have a four-year education-for-parenthood program built into its curriculum. This program should be required of every student from the ninth grade onward and should be given full academic status.

Every high school should also have a demonstration childcare center, where the students could get first-hand experience with real tots.

Sex education programs aren't going to stop youngsters from having children. (On the contrary, if the childbirth and venereal disease statistics are any indication, the overall value of school-based sex education programs is highly questionable). But a solid, national parent-education program could do a lot toward insuring the well-being of the children they *do* have, *whenever* they have them.

In 1974, former Vice-President Walter Mondale said, "The easiest people to ignore in American society are children. They usually accept being cheated with equanimity. They don't strike, they're just there." This year, millions of our tax dollars are being spent teaching high school students to be responsible drivers — a worthwhile expense. Virtually nothing was spent to prepare these same students for parenthood.

Is it, then, any wonder that so many teenage parents do a better job of taking care of their cars than they do their children?

Choosing a Preschool Program

A child who attends a day-care center full-time spends roughly 45 percent of her waking hours in the care of persons other than her parents. Anyone who shares this much time with a child has a considerable influence on her growth and development as a human being.

In light of this fact, choosing a day-care center is one of the most important decisions a parent can make. Unfortunately, the choice is rarely given this much significance. The decision is likely to be based on questions of location (convenience) and expense. In choosing day care, parents *should* keep in mind the following ideas:

A day care center should be stimulating as well as learning-oriented. In fact, if the environment stimulates the child's imagination and urge to experiment and discover, then it *is* learning-oriented.

Centers that boast about teaching the children their ABC's are *not* necessarily learning-oriented.

Preschools which offer reading and other academic-readiness programs have gone a long way toward solving one of the chronic problems in the business — namely, the trick of keeping costs down and revenue up.

By and large, the "Kentucky Fried Children's Kollege of Kiddie Kulture, Inc." is understaffed, under-stimulating (boring) and overly-regimented. The problems of breakage and loss are prevented by not having many small toys for the children to play with. Most of the playthings are "educational," which justifies their being kept in a closet or some other place accessible only to the teacher.

Programs that supposedly provide small children with an edge in the "Go To The Head Of The Class" game appeal to many anxious parents, who mistakenly equate "achievement" with such things as A's on a report card.

The building is modern, the rooms are big, the equipment is new, the environment is neat and orderly, and the atmosphere is dull. In short, this kind of day care center is designed more to impress prospective customers than to impress anything of real value on the minds of the children.

The teacher/pupil ratio is usually as high as the law allows (and violations of the law are not uncommon). Order is maintained by sitting the children at tables and teaching them things that are irrelevant to their ages and their needs, such as how to write letters and numbers correctly. Everything is carefully orchestrated to keep the noise and activity level as low as possible.

But by far the worst kind of center is what I term a "holding zone," where children are "kept" and "watched" with no real attention given to their developmental needs. Studies have shown that the baby-sitting center can actually *harm* children by causing them to become bored and depressed. They are then more likely to dislike and do poorly in school.

The materials available in a day care center should be so rewarding that it is unnecessary to "make" children do anything. All the learning opportunities should be compatible with the fact that young children learn through play. Each and every experience should be fun. A center should encourage children to explore, to experiment, to experience, to discover.

There should be enough of a variety of toys, games and creative materials to minimize hostile competition among the children. The diet should be balanced and contain very few sugar-sweetened foods.

There should be an ample outdoor play area with, again, a variety of equipment. The classroom should be uncluttered, uncrowded and well lighted. When the need for special disciplinary action arises, it should be carried out quickly, calmly and authoritatively.

There are day-care centers in which children are very active and loudly excited. But the level of activity and noise is no indication whatsoever of the quality of the experience. The most impressive day-care setting is one in which the children are busy and calm. They talk rather than scream, walk rather than run (unless, of course, they are outside).

Where is the teacher? She can be sitting and doing nothing more than observing. I am disturbed when a teacher moves around more than the children. She should always be available to the children, but should not become overly involved in what the children are doing. She should make sure that each child is engaged in some activity which exercises her will to discover and create, but the children should be playing fairly independently.

Children sometimes need to be organized into teacher-directed groups. However, this sort of activity should not make up the major portion of the day. The teacher should supervise, direct and conduct, but should do only what is necessary. A good teacher is not always bustling from one child to another, making sure that each of 15 children receives exactly one-fifteenth of her time.

In short, a day-care center should concern itself with no more and no less than giving each child the fullest opportunity to learn that learning is the most delightful and exciting of all human activities.

The Push for Preschool Literacy

Several months ago I came across a story about a Miami woman named Sally Goldberg who is developing and preparing to market a series of teaching toys for tots. She says that parents can use her toy designs to teach basic academic skills to preschoolers.

Her ideas evolved from work she did with her own child who, at the age of two, knew all the letters of the alphabet and had a reading vocabulary of 100 words. Goldberg was quick to point out that her daughter is not a prodigy and says every two year old has the same potential.

Goldberg is correct, and *that* is the problem.

Think of the world as a vast warehouse stocked with all the many things that make up the known universe. In one area are rocks, another is full of ferns, and so on.

When a child enters through the main gate, she is assigned a couple of guides whose job it is to provide whatever assistance she needs to become learned in the ways of the warehouse. When they do their job properly, the guides simply support the child's inborn desire to become competent.

Teaching a preschool child to read is equivalent to leading her into one area—the "Reading Section"—and saying, "This is the most important place in the warehouse. We want you to spend lots of time here."

Instead of enhancing a preschool child's relationship with the world, teaching her to read actually *restricts* the flow of information available to her, narrows her environmental experience, and is contrary to the most basic principles of human growth and development.

A child who is trained to pay disproportionate attention to any *one* aspect of her environment will pay insufficient attention to other, equally relevant, aspects. To say it is more important for a child of four to learn to read than to collect leaves, splash through puddles or play with the family dog is extremely prejudicial. To discriminate in this fashion against certain elements of the environment, or to arbitrarily and artificially enhance certain others, ultimately distorts the child's perception of the universe and, therefore, her sense of "place" within it.

Indeed, as Goldberg asserts, it *is* possible, using certain enticements, to teach very young children to read. The question is not "Can it be done?", but "Should it be done?"

A growing number of developmental theorists, including Hans G. Furth, who has written several books on intelligence in children, insist that teaching a preschool child to read seriously impairs her intellectual growth for at least several years thereafter.

Joseph C. Pearce, author of *Magical Child*, says that reading requires the preschool child to begin dealing with abstractions before she has finished building a coherent understanding of the tangible universe. Premature literacy, he says, disrupts the growth of intelligence in much the same way premature birth disrupts physical and neurological growth.

If the child does not benefit from this early training, who does? Quite obviously, her parents, who can take pride in having the "fastest child on the block"—almost as satisfying as sporting a new Mercedes.

An unfortunate, but not surprising finding is that, in most cases, the preschool reader's early lead completely evaporates by the second or third grade. The closer one looks at the push for early literacy, the more it takes on the character of a monstrous practical joke.

If a preschool child learns to read on her own (as many do), that is a creative expression of *her* initiative and takes its place as part of her overall inquiry into the world and its tickings.

That many children learn to read spontaneously, without ever being taught in any formal sense, is a testament to the amazing nature of human intelligence.

On the other hand, teaching a young child to read, before she is sufficiently prepared to take full advantage of the instruction, is nothing more than an abuse of her creative and intellectual potential.

(Q) We have an eighteen-month-old daughter. She is our first, and perhaps our only child. We are already looking ahead, as I suppose many parents do, to the time when she goes off to school. Several of our friends teach, and they tell us stories about children who have a very painful and frustrating time learning how to read. Are there things we should be doing between now and then to prevent reading problems later? When should we begin teaching her the alphabet and her numbers, and how far should we go with this?

(A) Don't go anywhere with it. If you want your daughter to be a successful reader, read to her. Nothing you can do will contribute more toward her desire to read and her life-long enjoyment of reading.

In fact, there may be nothing else so completely enriching as those tender and expressive moments. The time you spend reading to her is alive and flowing with love and trusting wonder.

Nestled safely in your arms, watching and listening as new worlds unfold, stretching the limits of her understanding and her imagination — she will learn that reading feels good. This is the most valuable gift you can give her.

The rest of my advice is all *don'ts*, beginning with television.

A growing body of evidence strongly and convincingly suggests that one big reason Johnny has trouble learning to read is because Johnny spent more time during his preschool years glued to the tube than in any other single activity.

Actually, watching the flicker of a television can hardly be called an "activity," and this is precisely why it constitutes a serious threat to a child's developmental vitality.

Sesame Street and other "new breed" children's programs, because they strive so hard and successfully to hook the preschool viewer are, in my estimation, the chief culprits.

So what if children learn their ABC's and other academic tidbits by watching "Sesame Street"? What's the rush?

"Oh, but John, if a child goes to school today without knowing at least her ABC's and her numbers, she'll be lost from day one," you may be thinking.

Bullfrogs! I am unimpressed by preschoolers who can perform the alphabet, count to one hundred, add one-digit numbers and so on. That's not readiness. That's trivia!

The developmental needs of a preschool child have *nothing whatsoever* to do with learning these nonsensical mnemonic games. These recitations benefit parents, *not* children.

Preschool children need to play, to explore, to imagine, to create, to do. They need to learn how to share and take turns. They need to learn that their independence is not threatened by obedience to authority. They *don't* need to learn the ABC's —unless they ask. If their *own* searching brings them to the questions, they need answers. But, by all means, keep the "lessons" informal and low-key.

Let the child initiate the games. Let the search belong to *her.*

(**Q**) Two years ago, my daughter, now four and a half, could recite her ABC's and numbers through ten. She has been printing her name since she was three and correctly identifies every letter of the alphabet. Now I am having a problem with her and don't know what to make of it. Every day, we sit down for at least 30 minutes and work on her letters, name and so on. For the past few months, however, she either refuses to work with me, complains that it's too hard or acts as though she has forgotten much of what I taught her. I am becoming quite frustrated. Could she really be forgetting? What do you think?

(**A**) I think she is trying to tell you something. The games she once enjoyed playing with you have ceased to be fun. Something about the way mom plays the game has changed. The rules are different.

As that first day of school inches steadily closer, you have become increasingly determined to insure that, when the dash to the head of the class begins, she will be in the pole position.

And she, in turn, has grown increasingly confused and uncomfortable with the expectations. This is no longer a game—this is serious business, the make-it-or-break-it stuff of real life. What began as a playful adventure two years ago has evolved into a repetitiously boring demand that shouldn't be made on a child of four and a half.

Where on earth did you get the idea that knowing letters and numbers is essential for a four and a half year old? Never mind, I know the answer. I've been there too.

Parenthood is an uncertain undertaking. No one comes around saying, "Good job, Mom!" The standards are vague and indefinite, making it virtually impossible to assess how well you are doing.

Somewhere along the line we begin measuring our own adequacy against how well, or quickly, our children "perform" the normal process of growth and development. Christy, who talked at 12 months, is "smarter" than 16-month-old Jody, who still says "goo-gaa." Therefore, Christy's parents must be creating a better environment than Jody's parents.

This absurd concern with who has the most advanced kid on the block is all too common. Whose lives are our children living? Theirs or ours?

Any developmentally healthy child can be taught to recite and even recognize the letters of the alphabet by the age of four. The same is true for numbers. But it doesn't mean a thing. Learning how to say, "Eff," when shown this shape—F—is no more outstanding an accomplishment than learning to say "Dog," when a furry, four-legged creature runs up and licks your face. The crucial difference, however, is that the meaning of "dog" can be experienced directly, while the meaning of "eff" is completely abstract. It doesn't mean a *thing* to a four year old.

Furthermore, the head start you hope to provide your daughter is unlikely to give her any enduring advantage. The child who enters school already armed with her ABC's (and so on) may enjoy a brief stint as valedictorian of her kindergarten or first grade, but within two years she will, in all likelihood, be performing at about the same level she would have been without the push.

Take the cue and stop working so hard. You aren't a teacher, you're her mother—remember? And she's just four and a half. If she has what it takes to excel, all she needs from you is the opportunity, and your support and confidence in her.

Instead of the daily "drill," take a walk together around the neighborhood. Go to a park. Feed the ducks. She's only four and a half once—for a very short time.

Afterword

Having begun this book by talking about my children, I think it appropriate to end that way, too.

As I write these final paragraphs, Eric, now twelve and a half, is in residence at Clemson University's Soccer Camp. I know he is having a swell time, because he hasn't called us for four days. He will return tanned and tired, with tales to tell of on-the-field heroics and off-the-field antics. Then comes a summer of swimming, golf, roller skating, dirt bikes and girls (not necessarily in that order) before he starts junior high school.

Amy is nine years full of giggles and wiggles and pure Hollywood. She constantly amazes me with the characters she can call up at will or whim or whatever lurks behind those dancing blue eyes—petulant pixie, dying swan, damsel in distress, chorus girl, scholar, ingenue.... Daddy's girl? Sometimes I almost think so, but she'll never tell.

At the risk of seeming to brag, I'm going to brag. Eric and Amy are Super-Deluxe-A-Number-One-Prime children. They are intelligent, polite, well-mannered, sensitive, outgoing, creative and inquisitive. But best of all, they are happy little people.

Nine years ago no one could possibly have predicted that things would turn out so well. When Willie and I learned that Amy was on her way, life with Eric was still unsettled (see Introduction). He was in the thirty-third month of the "Terrible Twos," which were virtually congenital with him. We lived in fear of his next tantrum, ready to do just about anything to prevent or extinguish it. He still did not sleep through the night, but he seemed immune to fatigue, a condition his parents had become accustomed to. So, what happened?

Willie and I made several fundamental changes in our thinking, that's what happened.

For starters, instead of racking and wrecking our brains trying to figure out how to keep Eric happy, we started asking ourselves, "What do *we* want?" and *making* it happen.

We stopped beating around the bush and began saying "No" when that was what our instincts (or inclinations) led us to say. We soon discovered that, after an initial protest, Eric seemed more comfortable with a firm "No" than with a prolonged bush beating from Mom and Dad.

We swallowed a few "I told you so"s and added "Because I say so" to our vocabularies. To those who say, "There's a reason for everything," my reply is, "Yep, and sometimes the reason is 'because I say so.' "

We decided it is all right for children to cry and for parents to let them. We identified two cries. One occurred when Eric was hurt or sad. In that case, we comforted him. The other occurred when the world did not turn according to Eric's whim. In that case, we let him cry, sometimes sending him to his room until he finished. Lo and behold! He began crying less and coping with minor slings and arrows a lot better.

We stopped using his unpredictable moods to determine the state of our well-being. We stopped worrying about him and started taking care of present business. We stopped flogging ourselves over mistakes, though we continued to make them (and still do).

We began paying more attention to one another than we paid to Eric. We restored the equilibrium of our family by planting our marriage at its center. We gave ourselves permission to be inconsistent, to spank in anger as a first resort and to be "unfair." And that has made all the difference.

I hope I've accomplished what I set out to do with *Parent Power!* — shaken up your thinking a tad, liberated it from the permissive labyrinth it may have been wandering in and helped make your family life more rewarding and enjoyable.

I have two final thoughts to pass along.

First, raise your children *your* way. Understand that people who write books, articles and newspaper columns about raising children have suggestions and ideas but *not* the Final Word. If you disagree with them, give *yourself* the benefit of the doubt.

Last, but by no means least, something we all tend to lose sight of when the milk is spilled and the children are urging us up the wall . . .

Enjoy!

Bibliography

Brazelton, T. Berry, M.D. *Infants and Mothers—Differences in Development*. New York: Delacorte Press/Seymour Lawrence. 1969.

————. *Toddlers and Parents—a Declaration of Independence*. New York: Delacorte Press/Seymour Lawrence. 1974.

The First Year of Life. *American Baby* magazine. Mid-October, 1980.

Furth, Hans G. *Piaget and Knowledge*. Englewood Cliffs, N.J.: Prentice-Hall. 1969.

————. *Piaget for Teachers*. Englewood Cliffs, N.J.: Prentice-Hall. 1970.

Keller, Martha A. The Myth of the Learning-Disabled Child. *Parents' Magazine*. February, 1976: 42.

La Leche League International. *The Womanly Art of Breast Feeding*. Franklin Park, Il. 1963.

Pearce, Joseph Chilton. *Magical Child*. New York: E.P. Dutton. 1977.

Pryor, Karen. *Nursing Your Baby*. New York: Pocket Books. 1973.

Smith, Lendon, M.D. *Improving Your Child's Behavior Chemistry*. Englewood Cliffs, N.J.: Prentice-Hall. 1976.

White, Burton L. *The First Three Years of Life*. Englewood Cliffs, N.J.: Prentice-Hall. 1975.

Williams, Jay. *The Cookie Tree*. Parents' Magazine Books. Out of print.

Winn, Marie. *The Plug-in Drug*. New York: Viking Press. 1977.

Wright, Robert. The Affective and Cognitive Consequences of an Open Education Elementary School. American Education Research Journal. 12:449-68.

Index

DATE DUE			
890709			
OCT 19 '92			
MAR 1 7 1996			
APR 2 1 1997			